**Learning Resources Center
Lower Columbia College
Longview, WA 98632**

TANK WARFARE

Shadow of Vimy Ridge
Armoured Crusader (Biography of Major-General Sir Percy Hobart)
Crucible of Power — The Fight for Tunisia
Tank — A History of the Armoured Fighting Vehicles (with John
    Batchelor)

KENNETH MACKSEY

Tank Warfare

A HISTORY OF TANKS
IN BATTLE

STEIN AND DAY/*Publishers*/New York

First published in the United States of America by
Stein and Day/*Publishers* 1972
Copyright © 1971 by Kenneth Macksey
Library of Congress Catalog Card No. 77-185954
All rights reserved
Printed in the United States of America
Stein and Day/*Publishers*/7 East 48 Street, New York, N.Y. 10017
ISBN 0-8128-1449-5

'Blighters' by Siegfried Sassoon is reprinted by
kind permission of G. T. Sassoon

DEFINITION

Strictly speaking, there has been only one tank ever, and that was the rhomboidal shaped, caterpillar-tracked machine which first went into action on 15 September 1916. Since then the shape has changed although the name has not. Caterpillar-tracked machines, whether with their guns encased in rotating turrets, buried in fixed mountings within the hull, or on open platforms above the hull, have all at some time come to be known as tanks though to be accurate they were, respectively, main combat vehicles, armoured guns or self-propelled artillery. Thus, even when the rabid proponents or critics of so-called 'all-tank armies' used that phrase they usually had in mind 'all-armoured mechanized armies' including in them, for good measure, the unarmed but armoured infantry carrier.

In this book, for the same reason of convenience that has served in the past, the noun 'tank' will sometimes be used in its looser sense but the reader is asked to remember the clear distinctions separating the various categories of armoured fighting vehicles.

CONTENTS

CONTENTS

ILLUSTRATIONS

Between pages 176 and 177

The photographs are reproduced by kind permission of the following: 4, the US Army; 6, 8, 13, 14, 19, 20, the Director, Imperial War Museum; 7, Sports and General Press Agency; 11, 12, Novosti Press Agency; 15, Central Press Photo Ltd; and 17, The Radio Times Hulton Picture Library.

LIST OF MAPS

PREFACE

From its inception the story of tank warfare has been dominated by emotion—emotion in evolution and in narration. Not only did tanks revolutionize the art of war in less than a decade and set the military pundits at loggerheads, but the very association with modern battle and immense destruction of these symbolically brutal machines became the pacifist's nightmare and the propagandist's dream. Such has been the fascination of the tank that, with the possible exception of the fighting aeroplane, it can claim to have generated more literary endeavour than any new weapon. For tank warfare is a microcosm of war and therefore of life—the reflection of man's struggle for survival incorporating the subtle, shifting nuances between defence and attack—aggression and regression.

It is hardly surprising, therefore, that accounts of the tank's progress have become enshrined in myth. A wholly objective view so close to events is impossible and the most reputable works on the subject are those written by men closely connected with tank development. Undeniably it was to the Tank Idea's advantage that its advocates were possessed of literary calibre and the propagandist's art—men such as Winston Churchill, Ernest Swinton, Albert Stern, G. le Q. Martel, J. F. C. Fuller, Basil Liddell Hart, Heinz Guderian and Charles de Gaulle, to name the most prominent, were the vital driving forces in pushing the tank into the forefront of military progress. But in telling their story it would have been surprising if, at times, they had not exhibited bias by emphasizing their successful contributions to the exclusion of their errors. Let us not be deluded into thinking that the literary outpourings of the tank pioneers are the products of absolute historic accuracy. For instance, there are contradictions between what Guderian wrote prior to 1939 and what he later recalled in his post-war and oft quoted book *Panzer Leader*. Similar discrepancies can be found among the successive works of Swinton, Fuller, Liddell Hart and all the others.

I have endeavoured to simplify a complex subject and reduce it as close to objectivity as possible without eliminating the drama. I take the view that tank warfare developed too quickly for mental digestion and that those who carped at the impediments to its meteoric career forgot how much slower had been the advancement of earlier revolutionary weapons. The machine-gun was 150 years from inception to production. I must also admit to a similar petulance myself on previous occasions while in no way rejecting the need for impatience in those who wish to inspire 'progress' of any kind. There is always something new to learn and one can always be wrong. Contemporary history remains a hotbed of distortions.

In writing this book it has been my good fortune to come into possession of new material and much good advice, not only from those who were involved in the tank struggle but from the band of enthusiasts who have carried out recent research into the documents of the case. I refer particularly to Tim Nenninger, who compiled a formidable thesis on the subject of US Armor, and General Walter Nehring, whose recent book helps clarify the evolution of the German Tank Force and with whom I have had a rewarding correspondence. I am heavily indebted to Lieu-tenant-General Sir Charles Broad and Major-General Robert Grow for their memories and diaries giving insight into the formative days of, respectively, the British and US armoured forces; to General-Major Heinz Guderian for a fresh interpretation of his father's writings, and to Herr Albert Speer for some shrewd judgments concerning Germany's struggle for tank survival in the Second World War.

To Colonel Peter Hordern, the Director of the Royal Armoured Corps Tank Museum, I am indebted not only for his help in guiding me through the archives of his incomparable establish-ment but also for reading and criticizing my first draft. And, as so often in the past, my deepest gratitude goes to the staff of the War Office Library—particularly Mr Potts and Mrs Davies —in making available so many important volumes for my study. The bibliography at the back of this book owes much to them.

Finally there are profound thanks to my Production Team—to Michael Haine who drew the maps and diagrams, Helga Ashworth who translated German documents, Margaret Dunn who typed and criticized the manuscript and my wife who, as so often in the past, read proofs and encouraged me in moments of depression.

TANK WARFARE

Chapter 1

OVERTURE IN THE MUD

Three preposterous shapes stand silhouetted against thin patches of snow, and in the rising dawn become more plainly recognizable. They are tanks ready for battle. Between the armoured walls crews shiver and anxiously wait the decision being taken by the group of officers gathered close to the leading machine. Huddled nearby in shallow scrapes, dredged laboriously out of the stiff Artois mud, crouch the infantry. Ahead, but not yet visible in the gloom, stands the silent village of Monchy-le-Preux, German held and crowning the crest which dominates the local scene. This morning it has to be taken if the two-day-old British offensive is to make worthwhile progress. Zero hour for the coming attack is set for 5 a.m. 11 April and it is nearly that already. But the tank commanders have heard, only this minute, that the artillery barrage which is intended to prepare the way has had to be postponed two hours; without it the infantry will not advance, for too frequently in the past they have been mown down in attacks put in without heavy gunfire. They have no reason to trust these tanks. Few in number and with barely six months' experience in battle they are no reliable substitute for artillery.

Tanks cannot hug the ground. Remain here until daylight and they will present themselves as bulls'-eyes to the German gunners and will be shot to pieces. The tank commanders know they must move, but they cannot retreat ignominiously and there is no cover nearby. They can only advance to their front on their own and tackle the Germans single-handed. Switches are on, engines cranked into life, machine-guns cocked and the breeches of six-pounder cannons clunked home behind the brass shell-cases. Three engines rev up with a splutter, tracks move, creak and rotate and the 30-ton creatures heave themselves up the slope towards Monchy. Here 200 German soldiers shelter in pill-boxes and in cellars, quaking in fear of tanks—weapons of inexorable power which, on first acquaintance, seems to them invulnerable. As the three tanks blunder down the village streets the Germans run and Monchy has fallen.

To one of the drivers, as they emerge on the other side, '... we could have gone a long way beyond ... and then we looked back and saw that Jerry had tumbled to the fact that we didn't have infantry with us.... The officer said, "Looks like we've got to capture it all over again." So we did.' This time it is not to be a walk-over, for the Germans recover their composure and fight back from side-streets, doorways, windows and roof-tops, firing a sheet of machine-gun fire at point-blank range to make the metal sides glow with a myriad of hits. Grenades explode all around as the three machines take their stand, Horatious-like in the central square.

One tank is soon ablaze but the others fight on, side by side, guns firing until the crews fall at their work from a shower of hot metal ricochetting around inside their poorly armoured cabins. A desperate situation arises when one German gun starts firing armour-piercing ammunition and this gun is not destroyed until a second tank has fallen silent. Miraculously the survivor keeps shooting and even seems to be gaining the upper hand in its duel against all comers, until at last, at 7 a.m., with a hiss and a roar, the barrage arrives, throwing houses into rubble, engulfing the village in flame, smoke and dust, cowering the Germans—and finally smashing the last tank.

Dazed, the handful of crewmen stagger out to meet the triumphant infantry entering to take possession. Behind, through fresh flurries of snow, a brigade of cavalry gallops the slope, dotting the fields with their carcasses as the German gunners find the range. Infantry has taken over what guns and tanks have captured, but horsemen have been swept aside just as they have been eliminated on practically every battlefield appearance since 1914.

Monchy has fallen to the tanks by default and in contravention of tactical doctrine. By chance, tanks, for the first time, have delivered a surprise, solo attack without giving warning from a single shot of artillery. Twenty-four men riding in comparatively cheap vehicles have achieved what several hundred on their feet dared not attempt. Again machines have demonstrated their efficiency as a substitute for flesh and blood. The seeds of far more ambitious ideas have been cast.

A paradoxical phenomenon of the nineteenth century had been man's failure to pursue ways and means to reduce losses of life in a plethora of wars when the weapons to take life had multiplied out of all recognition. Fatalistically the soldiers seemed to shrug their shoulders. As new instruments of mass destruction became increasingly available they appeared incapable of grasping the threat to the future. In their minds, perhaps, there prevailed the old rules of chivalry, when a man in combat was expected to strike personal, aimed blows at his opponent. But nerveless weapons which sprayed out death indiscriminately were likely to be superior to man's intelligence and skill, particularly when they could be fired most effectively from behind cover. Lightly-clad, unarmoured men could no longer evade fire, while the need for soldiers to pack close to produce intensive fire for themselves (as was essential in the days of single-shot weapons) passed. Quick-firing breech-loading weapons—above all quick-firing artillery—denied armed men the opportunity for hand-to-hand fighting and none but a few realists foresaw the battlefield constipation which would result—the relegation of tactics to a slogging match between unresponsive, conscript infantry armies herded to their doom in endless railway trains and kept up to strength by the scraping of every man from the bottom of each nation's manpower barrel.

Yet there had been warnings—the tactical truths of the American Civil War which had opened on the assumption of a quick and, therefore, cheap decision: that one had dragged on for four horribly expensive years, decided only by the total exhaustion of the Confederate side. But European military pundits viewed the American experience as being in the nature of a freak —and with some reason since their own most recent wars had all been short and decisive. Prussian arms had struck down Danes and Austrians in the 1860s by swift campaigns leading to wholly profitable political and economic advantages for the growing power of Germany. It could be argued that the skilful concentration of a mass of firepower and men at decisive points was a guarantee of success—a just reward for the triumph of matter guided by master minds. The new weapons could be made to apply their destruction more to the assistance of the attack than the defence—and rarely was this better demonstrated than during the lightning collapse of France following invasion by Germany in 1870. Yet moments of doubt were to come—for example when a few Boer irregulars upset the British regulars in

South Africa and when the larger-scale Russo-Japanese war in Manchuria became stalemated with a vast bill of casualties caused by artillery and machine-guns. Yet still the Europeans continued to base their plans on a lightning war such as would start in July 1914 and which, they believed, would bring economic and political chaos if it was not decided by Christmas. Pre-emptive wars were felt to be politically feasible and economically justifiable as a means of solving problems which could not be resolved by moral persuasion.

Every nation's military plan aimed at the instant success demanded by worried political masters. Each army, no matter its nationality, advanced in 1914 in the firm belief that the attack by mass must succeed. Each learnt, in turn and at terrible cost, the fallacy of its creed. Across the wide expanses of eastern Europe Russian armies groped in mutual slaughter with German and Austro-Hungarian armies without either side achieving an advantage. Shortly, in Belgium and France, German strategic brilliance, compounded by French myopia, allowed the Germans to overlap the French flank and gain a transient advantage. But a vast German horde, travelling and supported mainly by animal transport beyond the railhead, lost momentum out of sheer exhaustion. It was exhaustion which, rather than fighting, caused the reverse at the Marne in September—physical prostration allied to the doubts of dilettante German leaders.

When movement stopped from fatigue the real war began—the war of putrefaction held in deadlock by an endless trench system stretching from one end of the front to the other, from the North Sea to Switzerland. Shot down in droves whenever they moved above ground level, the fighting men instinctively burrowed for the only protection offered, below ground level. Contrary to their generals' theories of sacrifice by aggression, the fighting men scrambled to safety and enforced the stalemate by declining to offer themselves as targets until given additional aid and a chance of success. Political and economic systems held firm well beyond the Christmas deadline. Soon the infantry could attack again when more artillery was employed in the illusory belief that this was a solution to the problem. The war would continue.

Chapter 2

PRELUDE TO BATTLE

Field-Marshal Lord Kitchener, the British Minister for War, was one of those few in 1914 who foresaw a prolonged war. Contrary to the considered opinion of his Allies and many advisers, he had, in August, demanded a vast expansion of the British Army for use in 1915 and even later. Early in 1915 in gloomy but, perhaps, self-satisfied justification, he could write to the C-in-C of the British Expeditionary Force in France, Field-Marshal Sir John French: 'I suppose we must now recognize that the French Army cannot make a sufficient break through the German lines to bring about the retreat of the German forces from northern Belgium.' Again he was right, for try though they would again and again, with some British assistance, the French could not even dislodge the Germans from their own conquered territory, let alone advance into Belgium.

Throughout that frustrating year the Allies also attempted an alternative strategic ploy by outflanking the Central Powers by way of the Dardanelles and a subsequent reinforcement of the Russian Armies on the Eastern Front. It was in vain. The magnetic pole of decision remained fixed in France. But here there could be no outflanking except through Switzerland—and that was militarily unsound and politically immoral—or round the North Sea and Baltic coasts, until these were dismissed as technically impossible. It had to be faced that only by *breaking* the front could room for manoeuvre with all its practical and psychological advantages be made. Unfortunately each assault, preceded by longer and even more intense artillery batterings which infallibly announced the exact place and approximate time of attack, demonstrated with the piles of dead hung on the barbed wire the utter futility of persevering with an already bankrupt policy.

The means to solve a problem which, in essence, was the product of modern technology, could come only from an entirely new technological source. Ironically technical organizations in the armies were not held in high esteem and their activities tended to be emasculated or ignored by conventional General Staff

Officers who believed in the sanctity of personal combat. In most armies the ruling clique were cavalry or infantrymen while the technologists were drawn from the artillery, the engineers and the random handful who had become involved with mechanized transport vehicles. The former were out of their depth in technology and mistrusted the technologists, who, frequently in desperation, were impelled to cause friction with a 'hard sell' for their wares. Now the General Staffs had to bow with an embarrassed grace to the technologists when asking what instruments were needed to demolish the trench barrier. Nevertheless the advice they received from conventional technologists was usually to develop and multiply those weapons already in existence — guns and machine-guns, plus other weapons specially suitable for close-range, physical combat in the trenches. There were, however, just a few enlightened engineers and others searching for unconventional solutions.

Even before the trench barrier existed the basic tool to overcome it was already being employed in battle. Wheeled motor vehicles had been fitted with machine-guns and sent by the Belgians, British and French to harry the German cavalry screening the flank of their great wheel towards Paris and as the car crews became more hotly engaged they took to carrying steel plates to give an improved protection such as sheer speed and elusiveness could never give. There was nothing original in these developments. Armoured vehicles had frequently been employed in war in the past and once petrol-fuelled, internal-combustion engines had been put on the market they were adapted to propel fighting vehicles. Shortly before the war armoured cars had been in action both in the Balkans and in Italian Tripolitania, and in Belgium the Allied armoured cars raided much as they chose for several weeks. Indeed the slow-moving German horsed patrols had rings run round them by cars which rushed down roads from one threatened point to another, laid ambushes and inflicted losses at no great cost to themselves.

Paradoxically the bulk of British mobile forces operating in Belgium were of naval and not army origin because the First Lord of the Admiralty, Winston Churchill, took it upon himself to defend London against air attack. On 5 September his aggressive spirit had demanded 'a strong overseas force of aeroplanes to deny the French and Belgian coasts to the enemy aircraft and to attack all Zeppelins and air bases ... which are in reach'. In another letter he added: 'We require ... 200 or 300 men with 50 or 60 motor cars who can support and defend our advanced aerial bases.... They should be placed under the command of Commander Samson and should operate from Dunkirk.' These instructions led to the eventual formation of several motor-car squadrons which fanned out as 'Commander Samson's guerrilla' to dominate the country within a hundred miles of Dunkirk by speed, mobility and firepower. Armour protection came only later.

Enthused by the armoured cars' success and watching the advent of trench warfare (and with it the stymieing of the cars), Churchill directed, on 23 September, that the cars should be provided with 'an arrangement of planks capable of bridging a ten or twelve foot span quickly....' How these planks were to be laid under fire was not revealed, but the picture of a trench-crossing machine clearly occupied Churchill's mind, to be given greater clarity when, in October, he recalled a letter from Admiral Reginald Bacon saying that he had designed a 15-inch howitzer which could be transported by road. In fact, Bacon's gun-carriage turned out to be an unarmoured steam tractor based on agricultural models made by the firm of Fosters, but a modified version would lay and recover its own plank bridge. With the full concurrence of Kitchener an order for an experimental machine was placed.

Churchill, however, was but scampering round the periphery of the central problem of a genuine cross-country fighting vehicle. All the ingredients for such a machine, in fact, had been in existence for years: it merely needed somebody to mix them into a suitable compound. For instance, Mr Bramah Diplock had patented a footed wheel in 1899 and H. G. Wells had capitalized on the device as the suspension for 'The Land Ironclad' in an article published in the *Strand Magazine* in 1903. In 1906 the Holt Company of the USA had substituted a tracked suspension for the big-wheel they usually fitted to their steam tractors, and in 1907 the British firm of Hornsbys had built a petrol-driven tracked vehicle in response to a requirement by the War Office. Indeed so swept away was a Major Donoghue that, the following year, he proposed the War Office should use the Hornsby machine as a gun-carrier and protect it with armour, but

Donoghue was firmly discouraged and so, too, in due course, were Hornsbys, who sold their patents to Holts in 1912—the year when an Australian engineer called de Mole abortively submitted his own original design of a fully-armoured tracked vehicle to the War Office.

The atmosphere was no different elsewhere. An Austrian called Burstyn had produced drawings of a lozenge-shaped fighting vehicle and in that same country Holt's representative, Mr Steiner, received some slight encouragement from the General Staff with his tractors, though the German General Staff was frigidly cold, viewing vehicles such as these 'of no importance for military purposes'. There was more to it than that. In reality each arm of the service was competing for funds to buy proven weapons and there was little to spare for unlikely and expensive novelties.

A keen British historian, engineer and soldier was the first man to compound a practical formula with the various ingredients and to get his timing right. Lieutenant-Colonel Ernest Swinton was a regular Royal Engineer, with a reputation as an eloquent writer and, less well known, the official British historian of the Russo-Japanese war in Manchuria. In 1914 he was made the official British correspondent (Eyewitness) with the British Army in France because that army preferred not to be reported by civilian journalists. Permitted free access to the front and all the battle reports, Swinton was given a unique opportunity to sit back and study what was going on—and wrong. As a trained engineer he could analyse and make suggestions in the field of military science, and then could link them with his study of the first-ever trench stalemate in Manchuria.

Swinton recognized at once, but without surprise, that the Manchurian phenomenon was in course of repetition. On 20 October he wrote to both GHQ in France and his friend, Lieutenant-Colonel Maurice Hankey, the Secretary of the Committee of Imperial Defence in London, that a way through the trench barrier might be breached by armoured caterpillar tractors carried on a Holt track. GHQ executed a swift and crushing rebuff—for which they could hardly be blamed since, at that moment, they were straining every nerve to retain open warfare, though only just beginning to realize that the Germans at Ypres stood a chance of overwhelming the Channel ports. They were unlikely to have time for a device which should never be needed. But Hankey, from his higher and better-informed position, saw further and deeper, though when he broached the subject with Kitchener the reply was practical and dampening: 'The caterpillar tractor would be shot up by guns.' Yet Hankey persevered and returned to the charge on Christmas Day with a long paper appraising the now existing stalemate for the benefit of the Cabinet. Turning to the prospects of breaking the trench wall, Hankey wrote 'Can modern science do nothing more?' and suggested: 'A number of heavy rollers, themselves bullet-proof, propelled from behind by motor-engines, geared very low, the driving wheel fitted with "cater-pillar" driving gear to grip the ground, the driver's seat armoured, and with a Maxim gun fitted. The object of this device would be to roll down barbed wire by sheer weight, to give some cover to men creeping up behind, and to support the advance with machine-gun fire.'

Again it was Churchill, eager to gratify his own frantic drive and grasping at every possible stick to beat life into the war effort, who seized on the Hankey paper to give fresh impetus to his own schemes for armoured land warfare. To members of the Cabinet, on 5 January 1915, he wrote proposing the construction of 40 to 50 tracked, armoured shelters: 'The cost would be small. If the experiment did not answer, what harm would be done?' The Prime Minister, Asquith, supported him and so too did Kitchener—by bureaucratically referring the idea to a committee along with a request to evaluate Bacon's tractors. On 13 January this committee inspected two Holt Caterpillar Tractors, and a week later was considering a paper by a naval officer, Captain T. Tullock, which suggested 'a carriage which could move across country and to the passage of which neither barbed wire nor trenches nor embankments ... offer any hindrance: ... it would enable the attacker to place himself athwart and enfilade the enemy's trenches ... thus opening a road for the supporting infantry and even, eventually, for the cavalry.'

Let there be no suggestion that inertia held back these early pioneers—nor let there be a hint that they were prepared to be upset by the bureaucratic staffs who sometimes misinterpreted what their commanders intended. The bypassing of vested interests was frequently to be a well-trodden indirect approach towards tank progress. Thus from Prime Minister to designers there ran a strong thread of urgency linking their research. An

immediate trial by a Commander Sueter demonstrated the
impracticability of the 'roller' proposal, but the naval pack was
by now in full cry, discussing the need for 'land cruisers' and
'land destroyers', each armed and armoured in a manner appropriate to their nautical antecedents. In November 1914 a Lieutenant T. Hetherington had even proposed to Sueter a 'land
battleship' carried on three giant, 40-foot wheels, 'armed with
three turrets, each containing two 4-inch guns, propelled by an
800-hp Submarine Diesel set. . . .' Bombarded by a plethora of
ideas and advice, Churchill, like Kitchener, also took refuge in
bureaucratic method in mid-February, and formed his own
Admiralty Landships Committee. But he put a trained engineer,
the Chief Constructor of the Navy, Tennyson d'Eyncourt, in the
chair.

This committee, free from ingrained Army practice and preju-
dice, diverged from the current common line of thought and from
its terms of reference. Instead of recommending a combat vehicle
in its own right, it decided to investigate a 50-man troop carrier,
'a self-moving fort for the attack and destruction of enemy
trenches'. It was all for making experimental models on these
lines (in modern parlance, Armoured Personnel Carriers), carried
either on pedrail tracks or 15-foot wheels. This was grandiose and
Churchill, re-enthused, took personal responsibility on 20 March
to commit £70,000 of Admiralty funds to them. 'I did not inform
the War Office, for I knew they would raise objections to my
interference in this sphere. . . . Neither did I inform the Treasury.'

War Office interest had lapsed. The Army was engaged in
tackling vast problems beyond its experience or capability, building and equipping new armies with weapons that were *known*
to work and, in addition, struggling to give day-to-day support
to forces strung across many a battlefield where offensive operations were in progress. Swinton, told on 1 June that his appointment as Eyewitness was to be terminated, took a well-chosen
chance to influence GHQ just as it was becoming apparent that
the great French Spring Offensive was foundering. In a paper
entitled 'Armoured Machine-Gun Destroyers' he reflected that,
though it might be possible to blast a way with artillery through
the German trenches, 'this is not at present within our power'.
But he thought the enemy machine-guns could be engaged on
an equality by 'petrol tractors on the caterpillar principle . . .

armoured . . . and armed with—say—two Maxim and a Maxim two-pounder gun'. The paper then expounded a tactical doctrine for 50 destroyers, spaced 100 yards apart, to attack the enemy entanglements at dawn after a night bombardment. Travelling at three miles an hour they would be steered for the machine-gun nests, suppressing their fire and diverting the main enemy effort from the accompanying infantry who 'will be able to cross the fire-swept zone between the lines practically unscathed'. Swinton envisaged the destroyers crushing wire and obviating the need to bombard the enemy trenches: thus the artillery could concentrate on dousing the enemy guns. He also envisaged the destroyers moving ahead with the exploitation and, in defence, acting 'as mobile strong points which can be driven forward right amongst hostile infantry who have penetrated'.

This was a significant paper in every respect. It not only presented a realistic formula of technical and tactical ingredients for the first time but it interested GHQ (after one thoughtless rebuff by a staff officer) to the extent that the newly formed Inventions Committee under General DuCane took it up. By 9 June Swinton was writing a serious technical specification for his fighting vehicle, a document which forged a solid link between GHQ and London where, to the surprise of all concerned, it was discovered that the Landship Committee (wilting under a barrage of criticism as Churchill's influence waned) had made technical progress along similar lines to those adopted by Swinton.

The confluence of new forces and dynamic personalities revived the project. Coming to London at the beginning of July at the invitation of Hankey, and destined soon to take over the duties of acting Secretary to the Dardanelles Committee, Swinton found that d'Eyncourt's Landship Committee was weakened by internal dissent. It was just held together, however, by the vibrant energy and determination of a city banker-cum-wartime sailor called Lieutenant Albert Stern, but it was under severe scrutiny by Lloyd George's Ministry of Munitions, which dealt with questions of industrial rationalization.

Swinton found much to give hope. Trials had disposed of the more unpractical mechanical methods. It was conceded that caterpillar tracks of the Holt type provided the most likely solution to Swinton's specifications—specifications which the designers had been ordered to follow without knowing the identity of their author. Fosters' principal designers, William Tritton and Lieutenant W. G. Wilson, were at work on a pilot model called Little Willie. The supply of armour, engines, machine-guns and main armament (a 57mm naval gun) were all but agreed. Indeed, in early September, only the suspension and track, which persistently failed on rough ground, remained to be settled—and this was invented by Wilson on 22 September, in ample time to be adapted to what was to be the first fighting machine of rhomboidal shape.

Progress was, from then on, continuous and, compared with weapon development of the past (and indeed that of the present) electric. Voices in opposition were sustained by the justifiable worry that undue waste might occur at a time when British industrial resources were heavily over-taxed by the main war effort. Rightly the Ministry of Munitions had no desire to become committed to production until a practical field trial had proved feasibility and Kitchener minuted his agreement on 29 December: '... without such a test we may be wasting material and men uselessly'.

The project was now so recognizably a potent aggressive weapon that serious and desperate measures had to be taken to keep it secret. Before Christmas, as part of a new security cover, a less provocative name than 'landship' was sought, and since the completed vehicle looked not unlike a water container the choice fell on 'tank' rather than the less evocative words 'cistern' or 'reservoir'. Tank it was to remain—a title later used to cover a multitude of misrepresentations.

Meanwhile inaccurate news of progress had been sedulously carried to GHQ by Winston Churchill (no longer First Sea Lord). Now the newly appointed second in command of a Guards Regiment, and getting used to serving in the trenches, he was as eager as ever to chase progress at the highest levels. On Christmas Day General Sir Douglas Haig, the new C-in-C, read a paper by Churchill entitled 'Variants of the Offensive', in which the state of armoured vehicles was somewhat over-optimistically described. Instantly interested, Haig sent a Major Hugh Elles, Royal Engineers, to London to find out more, and on his return Elles reported favourably.

Soon Elles's optimism was to be echoed at the pinnacle of power for when the 30-ton rhomboidal tank called Big Willie was made to perform for, among others, Kitchener, Lloyd George and Chancellor of the Exchequer, McKenna, its ability in negotiating difficult obstacles and climbing steep slopes was enormously impressive. Big Willie looked as if it meant business, its slow, stately progress to the splutter of its 105-hp engine imparting a grimly menacing threat to the two guns protruding out of the sponsons projecting bulkily from either side of the eight-foot-high steel walls. Kitchener, in fact, may at first have been scared that these sailors and engineers were attempting a 'hard sell'; hence his demand for a private preview, his searching questions and scathing, provocative remark, '. . . a pretty mechanical toy'. Yet Kitchener's genuine interest was reserved for Stern immediately after the main trial on 2 February 1916, with an invitation to come to the War Office as Head of a Department to see to the production of tanks. But now Lloyd George stepped in to arrange production from the right source—the Ministry of Munitions—with a pilot production order for a hundred Big Willies, or Mark I as it was then to be known.*

Tanks were in. Rejoicing, Swinton sat down to expand his June 1915 paper into a formal tactical doctrine which could be understood by those who would have to order the tanks to war and those who would have to crew them in action. At that moment, of course, not one field commander had seen a tank and not a single crewman had been recruited. Swinton's tactical paper was a most comprehensive document and for that reason it did more than build the foundations of the first tank actions— it laid a cornerstone for hundreds of battles to follow, set the pattern for future technical development and was instrumental in grinding a doctrine—be it right or wrong when tried—into the minds of a generation of soldiers. Hence the parts which could not be closely defined from lack of knowledge or which turned out wrong in practice were to be the grit of future controversy.

Reasoning that to attack just before dawn would be best to ensure full co-operation with the infantry and to allow the crews to see their way and their targets, Swinton thought the tanks

---

* In *The Tanks* B. H. Liddell Hart omits to mention the invitation by Kitchener to Stern, preferring to give most credit to Lloyd George for putting the tank into production. Yet Stern, from whom Liddell Hart drew heavily for information in other respects, is perfectly clear in his reference to Kitchener's proposal.

'should move forward together ... sweeping the enemy's first line
parapet with machine-gun fire; and ... the assaulting infantry
should charge forward so as to reach the German defences soon
after the tanks have climbed the parapet. ... If the tanks ... are
successful, it is thought they will enable the assault to maintain
most of its starting momentum, and *break through the German
position quickly.*' But Swinton warned: 'Special stress is laid on
the vulnerability of the Tanks to artillery of different natures. ...
The risk might be reduced by indirect measures, such as counter-
battery fire ... to help the infantry by helping the tanks. ...'
Nevertheless he calculated that an average rate of progress in
the attack of a mere one mile per hour would 'take our troops
past the enemy's main artillery positions ... in one day'.

Weaknesses in Control and Command disturbed Swinton. He
asked for strong communications to the rear. 'One tank in ten'
should be equipped with small wireless sets, others to lay telephone cable as they advanced, while the rest made do with visual
signalling and smoke rockets to indicate progress. But Swinton
knew these could not be provided before the first action and that
tanks, *'at that moment* were ... an auxiliary to the infantry, that
... must be counted as infantry and in operation under the same
command'. The italics are mine: these words were later to be
forgotten in the heat of tactical debate.

As this paper was being published the French Army was coming
under fierce pressure from the German attritional offensive against
Verdun. Haig meanwhile was preparing to attack on the Somme
in June or July, and in April was systematically trying to lay
hands on every possible tactical aid for a battle which lacked a
strategic aim. Tanks were on his shopping list, but recruitment
of the crews had hardly begun and the tanks upon which they
would first train and then drive into action would not roll off the
factory floor until June. The earliest the original 50 could be in
France, manned by a few semi-trained men in a makeshift
organization, would be the end of August.

So the guns of the Somme offensive ploughed the ground and
yet left German machine-guns untouched to slaughter
unarmoured men advancing in frail open order. And of the first
50 tanks and their men who began their journey to the front to
take part in the last great convulsion of the offensive on 15

September in the Battle of Flers/Courcellette, one Tank Commander wrote:

> I and my crew did not have a tank of our own the whole time we were in England ... ours went wrong the day it arrived. We had no reconnaissance or map reading ... no practices or lectures on the compass ... we had no signalling ... and no practice in considering orders. We had no knowledge of where to look for information that would be necessary for us as Tank Commanders, nor did we know what information we should be likely to require.

Justly appreciating the capriciousness of the untried weapon, HQ Fourth Army Instructions for the battle, while reflecting the basic intention of Swinton's doctrine, laid it down that 'infantry must on no account wait for them', adding: 'If the tanks succeed and the infantry are checked the tanks must endeavour to help them.' The tanks were introduced only as a bonus since this was but a trial trip and not the overwhelming use of massed machines of which Swinton dreamed.

Very few tanks did succeed on the 15th. Of the 49 actually available only 36 reached the start line before dawn. The remainder, driven by men who, without exception, were unfamiliar with conditions at the front, either broke down or became ditched in churned ground when their drivers veered from the correct course in the dark. On the right of the main assault a single tank, D1 under the command of Captain H. W. Mortimore, sallied forth along the southern edge of Delville Wood. Mortimore recalled: 'I managed to get astride one of the German trenches ... and opened fire with the Hotchkiss machine-guns. There were some Germans in the dug-outs and I shall never forget the look on their faces when they emerged. ...' Though D1 soon received a hit on the starboard sponson which killed two of the crew and broke the track, she had made her mark in History.

Elsewhere, to a greater or lesser extent, D1's companions were making a fitful contribution. Only nine actually complied with their instructions and struggled into the forefront of the attack, though their unexpected arrival in the heart of the defences was quite unnerving to the Germans. Faced with something incomprehensible which, at first sight, looked indestructible, they panicked. Other tanks fell behind and thus, accidentally, created a second tank wave, superimposed on the leading infantry wave. These too made an important contribution. Tank D16 trundled through Flers village in company with infantry and paralysed the opposition; here three battalions of a German formation were eliminated and a prisoner, excusing what happened, said, 'somebody shouted "The devil is coming"'. It was at Flers that the tanks achieved most in a break-in enhanced by the relatively high concentration of machines engaged. Indeed, so astounded were the local British and New Zealand infantry that they fell into a confusion of delight, stood back and failed to press their advantage. Not so the tank D5 which, starting late from the northern edge of Delville Wood after mechanical trouble, cruised in isolated splendour right through the German lines to the outskirts of Gueudecourt where it became the sole tank to achieve Swinton's ideal by hitting the enemy field-gun line. There the first tank-versus-gun duel took place, won, in the first round, by the tank when its concentrated fire drove the German crews from their guns but lost in the second when, alone and without infantry, D5 could not complete the job. Its inevitable retreat gave the Germans the last word as, returning to their guns, they finally hit D5 and set her alight.

On the front of the Canadian Corps at Courcellette six tanks, working in close consort, had played their part. But if, in this sector, the tanks failed to impress the Germans with quite the same emphasis as at Flers, they undeniably encouraged their own infantry, who were given 'a feeling of superiority and security'— which was more than that felt by those crews who spent several abortive and perilous hours trying to dig out their machines after ditching. What was to be a recurrent theme had been established: once infantry recognized the advantages of tanks they were reluctant to advance again without them. To them even one tank would be better than none and so a taste for using tanks in driblets was whetted.

From a few survivors of the first action and those machines which had broken down and been repaired, small packets of tanks were made up and thrown into sporadic forays amid the battle which, six weeks on, seethed to an end. Nothing of great material advantage could be gained: the offensive had stalled as all such offensives were bound to stall so long as the pace of advance could not overtake the defence's rate of restoration. A crack in the German line on the 15th had been sealed by the 16th and thoroughly shored up on successive days. It was not recognized at the time that tanks alone possessed the stamina to maintain momentum in attack while, apart from their lack of personal protection, men and horses failed out of sheer exhaustion in the appalling going.

To the end of October, in scattered actions, all the tanks could do was exhibit their fatal unreliability and vulnerability when launched in solo attacks. Nevertheless one or two successful operations were enough to redeem their future. Haig, in fact, searching high and low for salvation, was more strongly convinced of the tank's virtues than many historians will admit. His views coincided with those of the fighting men who concurred in thinking that, for all their manifold deficiencies, the tanks had earned a second and bigger chance. The measure of Haig's confidence could be found in his request to the War Office to speed the construction of a thousand improved machines—with the emphasis on 'improved' since, realistically, Haig and his commanders aimed their main criticisms at the tanks' unreliability rather than their vulnerability.

This reliability factor was the decisive retort to those who stood up, later, to castigate the British for launching too few tanks prematurely into battle. The critics said that Haig should have waited until a mass had been assembled which could then make a wholesale breach in the German lines. Apart from the fact that, for political reasons, Haig could not hold back his offensive, the likelihood of the tanks achieving anything important by increasing their number at that point in development was small. Even if several hundred could have been assembled in secret (an almost impossible task since it would have to be concurrent with educating every senior commander and the mass of infantry to work with them) the roads and front line would have been choked by broken-down tanks. In principle it has almost invariably to be accepted that brand-new weapons, particularly those of revolutionary design, need a small battlefield trial; that to place reliance on sheer novelty to win battles is to despise the enemy since only if a novel weapon is really adequate in concept will it survive repetitive use in battle. A weapon's ultimate test of durability is its capacity for improvement by the intellectual evolution of its basic characteristics and the integration of each improved model into the changing strategic and tactical concepts of practical soldiers.

Haig and his colleagues recognized this (and the tank's prospects) when they established a central organization—a separate Tank Corps—on 8 October (before the Somme battle was over, be it noted). Thus they were quick to devise an agency to collect, synthesize and disseminate every scrap of information to be learnt about the new weapon, besides building an executive branch for policy making and technical support. Minor departmental hesitations and setbacks there would be—largely through misunderstandings due to poor communications and not to bigotry —in a military machine which had expanded too rapidly to be efficient. If, for example, the War Office should tell the Ministry of Munitions that the Army Council had prematurely cancelled the order for a thousand tanks, it was likely that the Council was ill-informed—for their slip was soon rectified.

But the Germans, quickly recovering from the minor tank shock at Flers when it was not immediately repeated, mainly took comfort in complacent exhortation. Soon, according to one German account, the troops 'learnt to know its vulnerable parts and attack it accordingly'. The tank was seen as 'a comparatively easy prey for the artillery who ... detailed special guns to engage it'. This sense of euphoria diverted the Germans from putting in hand their own energetic programme of tank construction. True they took a revived interest in Holt tractors and began investigations into building a tank of their own in November 1916. A wooden mock-up was ready by mid-January 1917, but the Germans dallied and did not organize thoroughly or come to grips with the formidable intricacies of design, development and production. As was customary, prisoners and others paid tanks the compliment of calling them 'barbarous'—but such titles are usually a compliment to a weapon's effect and have been bandied about from the introduction of boiling oil to the explosion of the atomic bomb.

Quite genuinely the Germans were not nearly so impressed as were the British. Unlike the British (who regarded the tank's attack as against material) the Germans saw it as a terror weapon which could be nullified by their army's superior techniques and morale. The French, on the other hand, were enthusiastic. They were already building tanks for themselves, though they were as ignorant of British activities as the British were of theirs. Colonel Jean Estiénne, an artillery officer of high repute, had thrice put forward the idea though his first two letters seem to have been lost among a mass of other suggestions to break the trench impasse. On 4 December 1915, however, the French C-in-C, Joffre, took a hand and by the 25th firm proposals had been made. Estiénne's engineering insight was not as sophisticated as the British. He more or less suggested putting an armoured box on a Holt chassis and arming it with a 75mm gun, building nothing less than a sort of armoured gun to be used in the forefront of the infantry attack. His first vehicles were, in fact, called *artillerie d'assault*. Neither on the military nor political level was there hesitation. By 31 January, Joffre had recommended large-scale production to the Under Secretary of State for War and on 26 February the firm of Schneider received an order to make 400—an order repeated to the firm of St Chamond in April.

If the French were quick in decision, however, they were nothing like as thorough in their investigations of the problem as were their Allies on the other side of the Channel. They were going to be content with an improvization and would commit it to action after only the minimum trial. Moreover they hit severe production difficulties, particularly with armour plate, and deliveries hung fire. But they were quite convinced of the need to use their tanks in mass and by surprise, and planned to conceal their existence until as many as possible could be used during their offensive on the Chemin des Dames in April 1917. So while the French Press waxed enthusiastically over the British tank exploits—'those gigantic infernal machines'—their General Staff fulminated that, in their opinion, the secret had been prematurely sprung.

The year 1917 would show who was right—the British for their thorough preparation and early disclosure of the secret; the French for improvization and absolute secrecy; or the Germans for brushing the whole thing aside as if it were only a passing nightmare.

Chapter 3

BATTLES IN INFANTRY STYLE

Although they had expended much blood and material in 1916 and had little to show for it, the Allies approached 1917 with confidence. Putting aside the threat of the implicit weakening of Russia, the Central Powers could be evaluated as frail by comparison with the Western Allies. Indeed, throughout 1916 the Central Powers had endured in an atmosphere of crisis and had only narrowly avoided collapse. Their predilection for close combat had led them to fight stubborn battles in the heart of the artillery holocaust and the cream of their armies had been thrown away. A period of reconstruction was needed and with it a new elastic defence, sited in greater depth so that the artillery storm could be avoided as much as possible.

Tanks had done little to discomfort the Germans and in early 1917 the British could pursue only limited experiments with what few machines and crewmen were available until the next wave of production came forward. Many lessons could be absorbed, such as the undesirability of using the tanks only in pairs, but when next they went into action at Arras on 9 April only 60 of the early, fragile vehicles could be assembled and, in the event, a mere 26 got into action on the first day—fewer than had attacked on 15 September 1916. Some, like the trio which took Monchy-le-Preux, would earn rich credit, but the majority merely discovered what hardening resistance could be expected in the future. They were up against the Hindenburg Line, a fortified zone of deep trenches into which the Germans had just withdrawn. It was not originally designed to be tank-proof, but its deep belts of wire and ditches, closely co-ordinated machine-gun nests (most of them firing armour-piercing bullets) and skilfully located field guns all combined to canalize, hamper and finally kill the slow-moving and partially blind tanks.

The infantry, pleased though they were to have help from tanks, could not wish them farther away when it was discovered that the fire aimed at the tanks also engulfed those nearby. Observers would watch a single tank, groping forward, the centre of a whirlpool of hostile fire, its plates glowing with strikes while its guns pecked back at tormentors rarely visible. Soon the tank would stop firing, halt, smoke pouring from it, and the survivors would leap out as exploding ammunition and petrol erupted. Arras gave false confidence to the Germans; forgetting that experimental weapons could be improved, they took to ridiculing tanks.

On the Chemin des Dames on 16 April, where the French employed a mass of 180 tanks, the Somme pattern was repeated, although here the Germans were forewarned of the attack and prepared to let it enter a trap. The defences were penetrated, though in one instance only one out of 15 St Chamonds got through, but exploitation was impossible. In a wilderness of shell-holes, deep trenches, which had been widened specially to frustrate tanks, and thick wire, the French Holt-type tanks failed for mechanical reasons, just like their equivalents nearly two years before on the trial course in England. Yet if it was pitiful it was not wholly discouraging. Some tanks accompanied by élite infantry parties actually fought their way deep into the German lines, only there to become isolated from their infantry and decimated after holding out in the same manner as the British at Monchy. But this doleful failure contradicted the arguments of those who had cried out for the surprise use of massed, untested vehicles and men, for more than half the vehicles and a quarter of the crews were lost in an offensive which never had the slightest chance of success.

And so it was to go on throughout that summer.

Russia was pulling out of the war, her place to be taken by an America which, for well over a year, would be unable to make a worthwhile military contribution. The American Army was deficient of everything, from men to weapons, and had no tank force because, early in 1917, on scanty evidence from France, they rated tanks a failure. The Americans came in as the need for their manpower became urgent. The French Army mutinied and for some months was incapable of offensive action. It was left to the British to do all the attacking, to retain some degree of initiative and—faint hope—bring the Germans to terms. Through a wet and miserable summer they stormed Messines Ridge (a siege action in which tanks had only a walking-on part) and then plunged deep into the artillery-made bog of the Ypres salient where not only tanks but men and horses sank and died in swarms. At Passchendaele the final irony of machine warfare was exposed: the guns which made the ground impassable could not have been supplied with more than £20 million worth of ammunition had not fleets of lorries been used. Soon, in a muddy waste, nothing could move. This was the ultimate stalemate.

Nevertheless a handful of profitable tank attacks took place in the grisly approaches to the Passchendaele Ridge—sparks flying up in the darkness briefly to show the way without setting light to a wholesale conflagration. Yet each rare success and every frequent failure added experience to be carefully sifted by the tank experts. While Estiénne was persuading the French Army and industry to drop his first gun-tanks in favour of a swarm of lightly armoured, two-man, turreted machine-gun carriers (to be called the Renault FT), the British Tank Corps, under Brigadier Hugh Elles, was hammering out a drill to make more efficient use of the rhomboidal tank—above all the new Mark IV with its thicker armour.

In due course tanks would avoid being thrown haphazard into battle. Although they might remain subordinate to infantry and would nearly always depend on artillery preparation and, to a certain extent, air attack to pave their way by neutralizing the enemy, each operation, no matter how small, would be planned in minutest detail. It was more than a question of saving men and machines in perennial short supply; it was a problem of improving relations between tankmen and the rest of the army. Devoid of adequate communications, once battle had been joined, every attack had to be controlled by a detailed and preconceived plan attempting to take account of every eventuality—and this would continue until each tank had its own radio. To change plans just before, or during, battle was almost invariably fatal—as had been shown at Monchy and on other occasions. Accurate briefing, however, depended upon information supplied to the tanks by the most meticulous pre-battle reconnaissance and, since it was tank men who could best do this work, their activities had to be carefully concealed in case news of their presence in a particular zone gave warning of an impending tank attack. Technical intelligence was also vital since this gave warning and time to counteract enemy counter-measures. The thicker armour on the British Mark IV tank, introduced in the summer of 1917, put the British a jump ahead of the German armour-piercing bullet—something the German infantry were to remain unaware of until they had suffered a heavy defeat at the hands of tanks they could not easily destroy. In this way the age-old race between protection and striking power got further into its stride.

The wide anti-tank ditches the Germans were constructing to strengthen their Hindenburg Line were closely examined on aerial photographs and by patrols. The antidote to them—a great roll of bracken carried on top of the tank to be dropped into the ditch as a causeway, was devised long before it would be needed. Tanks created a new industry, not only in the factories, but also close behind the front, and demanded a vast new army of technicians—a breed in short supply—and enormous depots and workshops. These gave blood to the body of the new mechanical armies.

The Germans too had to expend increased resources to defeat Allied methods—though they persisted in the fatuous declaration that they would resist a 'war of material'. At the Somme they had defied the British in a narrow belt of trenches by sacrificing men whom they packed tight in the forward zone. In 1917 they relented and deepened the defensive area to dilute manpower in the actual front line and save it from the worst of the artillery barrage. Thus centres of resistance were gradually substituted for a continuous line and therefore attackers were forced to plan their assaults in greater depth—pushing through wave after wave to take on each successive position in turn. Tanks, rather than unprotected flesh and blood, would be needed more than ever as greater mobility was encouraged by this slackening of the rigid trench line. The scene was being set for great changes in every interpretation of the Art of War.

Hugh Elles was the sort of folk heroic figure who, without seeming greatly to exert himself, persuades diverse personalities to act in accord. Handsome, brave, a mere 36 years old, and not a brilliant thinker, he epitomized the younger type of senior officer to whom the fighting soldiers could look with a gleam of hope in their eyes. His sort, perhaps, had the best chance to bridge the gap between the men at the front and those older generals who isolated themselves from the reality of war. Elles certainly had the confidence of the latter because, as an ambitious Royal Engineer with no intentions of blighting his career, he deferred unpopular schemes and spoke the language of tact by biding his time.

His senior staff officer, Major J. F. C. Fuller, was quite the opposite. A sceptical military intellectual and brilliant analyst, he prosecuted an unrelenting pursuit of whatever he believed in, regardless of personalities or seniority. To him the less mentally endowed in superior places were a target for scorn. He was the first genius the tanks acquired, but in advocating their case with untiring asperity he was to make many enemies.

Yet Fuller who, before the war, had written a paper foretelling the trench stalemate, was at first doubtful of the tanks' potential, though once he had studied the problem and seen how machine power could be substituted for muscle power his conversion was swift. To him, moreover, time was never to spare but judgment at a premium.

At the height of the Passchendaele campaign Elles felt bound to ask Fuller to remove a notice saying 'Don't be pessimistic. This is the last Great Artillery Battle', because he did not want to give offence to the Gunners and their friends. But the flood of training pamphlets pouring from Fuller's office could leave nobody in doubt that he was writing a new military doctrine. By the end of July 1917 he had consolidated the lessons of the Somme with those of Arras (where tanks had failed in the minor role but demonstrated the conditions needed for success) and Bullecourt (where tanks had gone astray because of misunderstandings with the Australian infantry and artillery).

In attack Fuller demanded two waves of tanks; the first to lead the way, dominate the enemy points of resistance and engage those guns which had escaped the artillery barrage; the second to move in close accord with the infantry and mop up those of the enemy overrun by the first wave. More reliable communications were devised, not only visually between tanks and infantry but by radio from special tanks moving behind the van and reporting what they saw to the headquarters in rear. Until an opportunity to use tanks in mass could be found these instructions were probably read only by tankmen. The rest of the army, so recently simple civilians, were rightly too busy trying to master the older, basic arts of fighting.

Seeking an opportunity to practise his new-found methods, Fuller suggested, on 8 August, a raid on an 8,000-yard front employing 216 tanks along with one or two infantry or cavalry divisions, and supported by artillery and strafing aircraft. This raid, he went on, should be only the first of many such as would unsettle the Germans along the entire front while the Passchendaele offensive proceeded. He wrote: 'The essence of the entire operation is surprise and rapidity of movement. Three hours after zero the retirement might well begin, the tanks and aeroplanes acting as a rearguard to the dismounted cavalry returning with their prisoners. Guns captured might be dragged in behind the tanks.' Yet though this audacious plan may have taken inspiration from the great cavalry raids of old it also exposed Fuller's misunderstanding of the incipient unreliability of tanks. Most tank operations so far had suffered at least 50 per cent casualties: the retirement from a raid such as he proposed would probably have presented the Germans with the scores of tanks their own industry had failed to provide.

Fuller's plan, though not received with the acclaim he felt it deserved, nevertheless stayed clear of the waste-paper basket. If GHQ was cool, General Sir Julian Byng, commanding Third Army (and with less to do because he had no part in the major offensive), was warm and on 5 September it was Byng who revived GHQ interest by suggesting an attack across ground which would allow tanks the greatest possible freedom of movement. By the middle of October (when failure at Passchendaele was undeniable) Fuller's raid had been transformed into a full-blown offensive the like of which had never been attempted before. The chosen ground was good, hard going to the south-west of Cambrai —a terrain of long spurs intersected by waterways and fortified with every ounce of German ingenuity. Here stood the Hindenburg Line at its strongest—three lines of 12-foot-wide trenches linking strong points containing nests of machine-guns which fronted skilfully placed artillery on the sheltered rearward slopes. Just to destroy the great avenues of barbed wire, some estimated, would cost £20 million by artillery fire and still leave the infantry with a stiff fight against an intact opponent.

The Tank Corps' tactical plan, accepted in principle and mostly in detail by all but one infantry formation commander, laid down systematic drills to be adopted by the 476 tanks (every available machine but including a mechanical reserve) and the rest of the force. A hurricane bombardment by 1003 guns, without previous registration (a technique which had been brought to its highest pitch only that year—an innovation as important as the tank) would begin at zero hour as the tanks began to advance. Aircraft would then supplement the artillery fire by strafing the German lines of communication and, above all, their gun positions, and while the tanks crushed the wire and filled in the ditches beyond with fascines, the infantry were asked to move in file, instead of line, to follow smoothly in the wake of the leading tanks without bunching while passing through gaps in the wire. These were the common-sense lessons distilled by Fuller from many months' study, but his extrapolation of old ideas to construe revolutionary methods was hard for others to digest. Fuller wanted to concentrate tanks only against known German strongpoints. But the infantry, having given way on the question of the advance in file instead of the old fashioned line, could not stretch their credulity further. Their movements were founded on a parade-ground training based on the mislearnt battle drills of a bygone age. They could think only in straight lines and of covering a wide frontage and they insisted the tanks conform and also disperse their effort.

But if among the infantry there were doubters, within the cavalry exploitation force there was little confidence that a genuine gap would be made in the German lines. The failure to penetrate a vast gap at Arras in April was too recent and well remembered. Therefore, though the nearest horsed units were kept in close proximity to the line, the Cavalry Corps commander established his HQ office six miles back, though retaining detailed operational control over the slightest movement by his men at the front. In theory all reports would be channelled to him at once but by staying indoors he was denied the immense benefit of a *coup d'oeil* such as benefited all the great cavalrymen of old. Tank Corps HQ, on the other hand, would have good radio communications almost from the forefront of battle. Yet Elles took it upon himself to travel in a normal fighting tank, cut off from all contact with his staff and commanders. He did it, so he said, to enhance the morale of his men, but he might have been absent when crucial decisions had to be made even though the commitment of every tank into action to the detriment of an operational reserve made this unlikely.

Though the exploitation scheme was clouded in pessimism, the rest of Third Army's plan was rooted in cautious optimism. It expected the front line to be breached on the first day, and the swift isolation of Cambrai by the cavalry after they had seized crossings over the River Sensée. It then hoped for a steady advance towards Valenciennes made easier by the ensuing collapse of all German forces in the Plain of Douai. Five cavalry divisions were ready—little enough on their own, but nobody could foretell the effect on the Germans of a really sudden and total rupture of their front. It was known that German infantry now gave up more easily than of old—and the bulk of their forces was said to be facing the Ypres Salient.

Stealth was to be the keynote of the British preparations—the secret and rapid transportation of guns and tanks to their assembly areas in thick woodland conveniently located close behind the firing line. The crews themselves, briefed in detail as never before for this their supreme chance to make good, were tense with the normal pre-battle apprehension plus the intense excitement of partaking in something quite revolutionary and, to them, entirely feasible. Some there were in high places who, justifiably, wondered if after the pounding the crews had received in the Ypres Salient they would have the will to press on. But afterwards, when all had been resolved, a commander wrote:

> Section after section . . . they crawled forward in long columns that split up after a while into smaller ones . . . until toward five o'clock on 20 November, the whole were deployed into a single line six miles long. So silently had this approach been carried out that many of the infantry . . . heard no tanks at all. . . . The night was very dark, with a dense ground mist. . . . From five o'clock until zero the whole front was quiet. At 0610 tanks and infantry began to move; and at 0620 . . . the barrage exploded with a shattering crash along the German outpost line.

In the rising dawn white tape guided the drivers to start points. One saw:

> The whole panorama . . . just like a set-piece of thousands of fountains of fire spurting from the solid earth. There was, as yet, very little response from the enemy artillery. . . . I noticed that the infantry . . . were now at grips with batches of German

soldiery . . . who were already throwing down their weapons
and surrendering. We fought our way to the wire and then
. . . I opened the throttle to the fullest extent and . . . plunged
through. Our tracks flattened out a clear pathway through
which the infantry followed.

Follow they did along the length of the front except before the
Flesquières ridge, where foundered the solitary infantry division
which had rejected the file system and insisted on the infantry
staying clear of the tanks. This method certainly saved the
infantry from weathering the fire directed at the tanks, but in
practice it fatally deprived them of intimate tank support in the
next wave. In consequence they suffered all the more and the
leading wave of tanks had to cross the Flesquières ridge in
isolation, to be immediately hammered at close range by German
field guns emplaced on the far slope. The crest was smudged
by the pyres of burning tanks: only here did the day's objectives
remain untaken. Nevertheless one tank commander called it 'a
cake walk' and, compared with the past, it was.

In the southern sector there were scenes reminiscent of a picnic,
albeit after some stiff fighting. Tanks had been destroyed or had
broken down, but they had achieved, on time, what Swinton had
hoped for in 1916. A commander wrote:

> We passed several batteries of field guns abandoned except for
> odd individuals who ran away as they saw us coming. . . . On
> reaching Marçoing we found French people . . . all very excited
> and happy and waiting to kiss us. . . . Captain W. Bailey ran
> all the way and came up just in time to prevent a party of
> Germans blowing up the bridge. When I saw Bailey he was
> crossing the bridge with a French woman hanging round his
> neck. He had one arm round her; they were both laughing and
> shouting.

Clearly a breakthrough *had* been achieved.

Now it should have been the cavalry's turn. But not until
shortly before midday—long after it was obvious that the German
front was broken—had the Cavalry Corps started to move. The
front stood still—waiting when all the omens of success could
be seen. The urgent drive of ruthless leadership was missing.
Traffic chaos, congesting gaps through the wire, uncertainty of

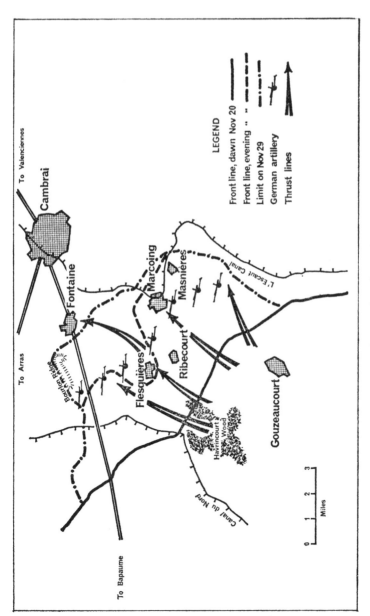

LEGEND

Front line, dawn Nov 20
Front line, evening " "
Limit on Nov 29
German artillery
Thrust lines

To Valenciennes

Cambrai

Fontaine

Marcoing

Masnières

L'Escaut Canal

To Arras

Bourlon Ridge

Flesquières

Ribecourt

Gouzeaucourt

Havrincourt Wood

Canal du Nord

To Bapaume

0 1 2 3
Miles

Map 1 The Battle of Cambrai

German reaction at Flesquières, ignorance of the existence of intact bridges near Marçoing and Masnières—all were offered as excuses to throw a cloak of doubt over the leaders of corps and senior cavalry commanders who, warily recalling the devastating effect of even one machine-gun, were reluctant to commit men and horses unless perfection—a completely clear run—could be guaranteed. Yet a squadron of Canadian cavalry, rich with the impetuosity of youth and ignoring the restraint from above, crossed the canal near Masnières to round up German guns and infantry on the opposite side. The remainder of their brigade declined to follow 'because there were machine-guns there'; the tanks could not cross because the bridges had collapsed under their weight and there were no portable bridges provided.

Across the front complete freedom of movement had been won. Even if Flesquières remained strongly German-held (though almost surrounded), British infantry patrols were able to by-pass and reach the outskirts of Bourlon Wood, thus cutting the Bapaume road and posing an immediate threat to the still more important Cambrai to Arras road beyond. Two officers actually rode on a mule and a horse from Marçoing into the outskirts of Cambrai. For 24 hours the Germans felt helpless. Facing panic at the front along with a dearth of information, they could only tentatively move reinforcements in the general direction of Cambrai without being precise as to where they ought to be used. Recurrent symptoms of disease disturbed the apprehensive and nervous Ludendorff, the German Chief of Staff. Previously he had persistently decried the tank threat. Now he blamed his subordinates for their failure to hold, but he could neither reincarnate the three divisions which had been wiped out nor the confidence of the men at the front who, at first hand, wilted before the implacable sight of tanks on the rampage. The speed of the British advance was itself baffling and led to hasty and ill-conceived orders for the demolition of bridges and the false deployment of reserves. The latter, groping across unfamiliar ground in the mist, were prey more to their own exaggerated fears than to the enemy threat. Gun ammunition—particularly solid shot for use against tanks—was in short local supply. If the British could have pushed forward strongly on the 21st all these difficulties would have multiplied with untold effect upon German fortunes.

On the 21st, however, the British were in no state, psychological

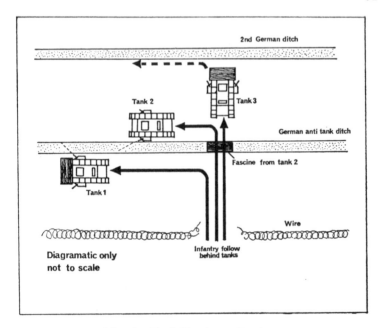

2nd German ditch

Tank 2

Tank 3

German anti tank ditch

Fascine from tank 2

Tank 1

Wire

Diagramatic only
not to scale

Infantry follow
behind tanks

Map 2   Tank Tactics at Cambrai

or physical, to push on. Unaccustomed to open warfare after two
and a half years in the trenches, infantry held back, perhaps
fearing a trap. Moreover neither infantry nor cavalry would
willingly advance without tanks and of tanks fewer than a
hundred could be readied for action. The other 376 were destroyed or broken down, though it should be added that losses in
men from all causes barely exceeded 4,000—a remarkable diminu-
tion of what had occurred in previous offensives. It even prompted
one witness to comment on the 'astounding lack of dead lying
about'.

The time which witnessed the lagging of the original impetus of
the attack gave the Germans an unexpected opportunity to
re-establish a front and then launch an exculpating counter-
offensive which retrieved much of what they had lost. But this
in no way underrated the importance of what had been accomplished by the first major demonstration of tank power. It had
been shown that tanks, operating by surprise on firm ground
and fully supported by artillery and infantry, could achieve com-

plete and instant domination over the strongest dug defences.
Rapidity of advance had outdistanced the mental processes of
trench-bound foes—and friends—but, contrarily, it had been
shown that neither tanks, for want of reliability, nor cavalry, for
lack of immunity, could maintain the initial momentum. If the
German system of control in defence had broken down, that of
the British in attack had done little better. Progress at the front
had been adequately reported by the wireless tanks, but the conversion of those reports into fresh and expanding lines of action
had been inhibited by the hesitant passing of orders towards
the front. Fuller, admittedly not the most unbiased of witnesses,
quoted the example of a corps HQ issuing orders for the next
day's attack in the almost certain knowledge that 'the attacking
troops would never get there in time ... with the result that the
attack had to be put forward to the early afternoon, then it was
put forward again, and finally cancelled'.

Tanks, however, were no longer a doubtful jest. Henceforward
Siegfried Sassoon's bitter verse would strike a sympathetic chord:

> The House is crammed: tier beyond tier they grin
> And cackle at the Show while prancing ranks
> Of harlots shrill the chorus, drunk with din;
> 'We're sure the Kaiser loves our dear old Tanks!'
>
> I'd like to see a Tank come down the stalls,
> Lurching to rag-time tunes, or 'Home, sweet Home',
> And there'd be no more jokes in Music-halls
> To mock the riddled corpses round Bapaume.

Chapter 4

THE SEEDS OF CONVICTION

Cambrai did more than vindicate a new weapon system: it began a violent revolution in tactics, coming as it did when technology itself was at a crossroads—when improved materials were being turned into better tools to crack the trench barrier. The French were completely convinced and ordered 3,500 Renault tanks. The Americans, too, joined the rush though with less to offer in the way of an industrial contribution. On the battlefield there was another sort of crisis, however, brought about by Russia's defection from the Allied side. For the first time the Germans could concentrate practically their entire might against the Western Front.

Still believing that superior numbers were of themselves decisive, the Germans nevertheless recognized that new skills had to be employed to give those numbers opportunity. Surprise by the unleashing of unheralded and titanic artillery bombardments, as abrupt and even fiercer than the one used by the British at Cambrai, was to pave the way in 1918 for infantry attacks on a new model. The infantry would advance by infiltration, bypassing centres of tough resistance and always trying to press on deep into the enemy rear, maintaining momentum by imparting depth to attack with an endless torrent of reserves. Of equal, if not greater, importance in the light of the subsequent developments, the Germans took to improvizing local battle groups, formed from all arms, so that each could give another intimate support in a rapidly changing battle when speed of reaction had to be faster than the old-fashioned and time-consuming major regrouping.

Of tanks, however, the Germans had but few of their own plus a number captured from the British and rearmed with guns of Belgian manufacture. And the German machine was a clumsy land-fortress, weighing 30 tons and crewed by no fewer than 18 men. Only a handful were to be used at the outset of the great offensive in March at St Quentin, and their impact was to pass almost unnoticed in the colossal turmoil which engulfed the front. Nevertheless the British Official History, picking out what it could from scrappy evidence, would have to admit: 'Wherever tanks appeared the British line was broken.'

A symptom of the Allies' strategic doctrine and weariness was their supine passivity before the storm. Fully aware of what was brewing they spent much time and effort after Cambrai exhausting limited manpower in digging more holes, instead of training in new methods. Forced by manpower shortages to begin the disbandment of units and the dilution of formations, and hagridden by experience which told them defence was superior to attack, both the French and British did little or nothing by raids to attempt the disruption of the German plans. Their tank force was a weapon well suited to raiding, but it was also threatened by having to share in the overall reductions on the principle of last to come, first to go. Yet it was a sign of the times that Staff proposals to cut tank strengths were invariably thwarted at the highest command level. Some historians have played up the various tank-limitation proposals as representative of a wholesale anti-tank school of thought—a means to retain priority for the older arms. But such proposals *had* to be made in staff papers in order that commanders might fully appreciate a difficult problem. In actuality the tank forces were steadily *increased* at the expense of the older arms because sheer necessity left no other alternative.

Economically, however, even the tank forces had to make concessions. With logical thoroughness the British had examined a project for a shell-proof tank, but the pilot model, called 'Flying Elephant', came out at 100 tons and was abandoned early in 1917 as being too expensive, particularly since improved rhomboidal tanks showed promise. A lighter tank—the Whippet— found favour, however, since here was a faster machine with longer range (40 miles) which might take up the pursuit after the rhomboidal tanks had opened a gap. Whippet, in fact, was meant as a mechanical horse for cavalrymen—if they would only ride in it.

The French, while themselves investigating a heavy tank, put most of their money on the little two-man Renault FTs, and these were coming off the production line in worthwhile numbers before the German offensive began. The incoming tidal wave of United States manpower was as yet a mere ripple, the Americans' situation the reverse of their Allies, for while the former had vast manpower to offer they possessed hardly any equipment—least of all tanks. But they did now recognize tanks officially as 'a factor which is destined to become an important element in this war'.

Unhappily for the Allies they had not devised the art of using tanks in defence. Not only was their rejection of raids an abrogation of the tanks' offensive virtues but official policy of dotting tanks in 'hides', strung out behind the front, merely denied them the opportunity to attack in the manner most natural. Once again, it seems, tanks suffered from Swinton's earliest guesswork when he had suggested a method such as this—though he would have been the first, in 1918, to have withdrawn his original suggestion. Thus when the Germans attacked on 21 March it was mostly to find tanks in isolation, to win a brief local encounter and capture machines which had either run out of fuel or had broken down for lack of technical support. But not everywhere.

On the first day at Doignes a whole company of tanks attacked in conjunction with two infantry battalions and temporarily stopped the Germans. On 22 March, at Vaulx Vraucourt, 30 British tanks attacked in unison, with whatever infantry they could gather nearby, and staved off the collapse of the front. Instinctively some tank commanders rejected the 'pill-box' concept and grouped together to attack before being attacked. At Serre, on 26 March, the Germans were in the act of pushing two infantry battalions through a four-mile gap in the British front— a situation which if permitted, would have led to a renewed major German breakthrough since no fresh British troops could be assembled to fill the hole. None, that is, except for twelve of the new Whippets which, pushed up from Bray, charged headlong into the advancing enemy, put them to flight and so disorganized the German advance that, before they could reform, British infantry reinforcements had arrived to fill the gap. Always speed of tank reaction had been decisive when linked with a surprise appearance, and nowhere was this more obvious than at Cachy near Villers-Bretonneux on 24 April, when all available German-built tanks—all 13 of them—were launched in support of a three-division attack. Here, in thick early morning fog, they suffered the problems once undergone by their opponents in 1916, and became detached from their infantry. But progress was made until, about 11 o'clock, three of the German machines, each armed with a 57mm gun, found themselves confronted by three British Mark IVs at 200-metre range. At first all went the Germans' way: they hit and drove off the two 'female' enemy tanks which were armed only with machine-guns. But a British male and its cannon, handled with aggression, jinked round the German flank, opened fire, scoring hits, and finally drove one German to topple on its side over a steep bank. And when, a moment later, two more German machines joined in, these too were repelled—the crew of one abandoning ship after the loss of five men killed.

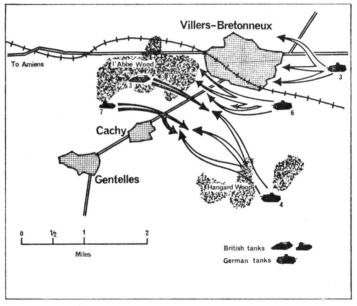

Map 3   Tank versus Tank at Cachy – 24 April 1918

Action now shifted a few hundred yards south where seven British Whippets suddenly appeared in response to a message dropped from an aeroplane which had observed the German infantry advance. For a while they had it all their own way, though it is unlikely they accounted for the 400 Germans enshrined in legend. But the Whippets might have done even better had not a single German tank intercepted them, knocked out one and hit others before following the rest to the outskirts of Cachy where the German attack petered out.*

The French also enjoyed their local successes, like the time at Vertefeuille Farm on 3 June, when they employed a high proportion of Renaults to infantry for a quick local riposte to disrupt a German thrust. Here verbal orders for the attack were given at 1800 hours; at 1830 hours the tanks had started; at 1900 hours they were on their objective and had killed many Germans and by 1930 hours they were back at the start point with 28 prisoners. A commander's laconic report summed it up:

> We crossed the Soissons road in column of half sections . . . where we moved east deployed. The surprised Germans received us at first with machine-gun fire. A bullet came through the left visor and wounded my driver in the shoulder. The section by this time opened fire on the enemy who ran away panic stricken. . . . Meanwhile the infantry occupied the farm.

These tank skirmishes, though mere pinpricks, were the essential harbingers of hammer-blows to come. Though bureaucratic moves persisted at British GHQ to cut back the Tank Corps as a means to propitiate the infantry and cavalry, the Allied Supreme Command, and above all General Foch, who had been made Commander-in-Chief of the Allied Armies on 14 April, demanded there should be a vast increase. Foch was convinced that tanks saved infantry lives and he looked to the British to contribute 3,500 machines manned by 45,000 men towards an Allied total of 10,000 tanks in 1919—a proposal which had originated in the mind of D'Eyncourt in December 1917.

Soon Foch's wisdom would be justified. As each successive German offensive ran out of impetus its end would be the signal for a tank riposte. On the ridge of Hamel, just north of Villers-Bretonneux, on 4 July, 60 British tanks, new Mark Vs which needed only one man instead of four to drive them, supported by the now customary surprise bombardment, suddenly led ten Australian infantry battalions and four American companies in a limited but violent assault on the lightly-held German positions.

---

* It is noteworthy that British accounts of the action, including that in *The Tanks*, do not say why the Whippet was lost, partly because the British were unaware of the reason at the time.

At once there was a local débâcle, the Germans losing 1,500 prisoners besides 171 machine-guns, while their latest anti-tank weapon—a clumsy 13mm rifle—proved a sad failure. And if the Allied infantry losses were just under a thousand—very high in proportion to the tanks, who lost only 13 wounded, this could be set against the good accord created between tanks and Australian infantry—an accord of importance to the future.

Far more serious from the German point of view, however, was the fate of their 15 July offensive against the French to the west of Reims. On the 16th it had been summarily halted after bloody losses, but on the 18th, quite unexpectedly, the flank of its salient, close by the Retz Forest, had been struck not merely by three score tanks rolling out of the dawn after a heavy rain storm but by 211 St Chamonds and Schneiders plus 135 of the little Renaults—all pouring eastwards without even the courtesy of a moment's preliminary artillery bombardment. That day the French advanced four miles and could have gone much farther had their tanks been more reliable. But by nightfall a hundred machines were out of action (mostly due to breakdowns), the rest short of fuel, and the French and American infantry in General Mangin's Tenth Army, strive though they might, could go no farther without tanks. And the Germans, poorer by another 25,000 men, were beginning to realize that the game might be up.

It was not always so easy, of course. At Moreuil on 23 July, when British tanks and French infantry attacked together, the tanks, driving too far ahead of the infantry, ran head-on against German artillery and suffered cruel losses. But now it was at last being brought home even to Ludendorff that he was losing the initiative and, though he was not to know that the Allies had more than a thousand tanks in reserve and were on the eve of a great comeback, his resolution was being undermined by tank successes while that of his men was in still sharper decline.

Chapter 5

THE TANKS' OFFENSIVE

Baffled by tanks in the approaches to Amiens and Paris, Ludendorff once more switched his attention to overcoming the British in Flanders, his great artillery battering train beginning its journey northward on 18 July as the build-up of ammunition dumps to satisfy its hunger began. Elsewhere his defeated troops crouched in newly dug shelters on freshly won ground—but nowhere could they construct so strong a defence as existed within the Hindenburg Line they had left behind. Rumour now spoke of impending defeat: letters from home reiterated the plight of starving families and the rumblings of civil disaffection. With the flight from confidence in victory came a fascination with the likelihood of defeat. In these circumstances a suspicion by the fighting men that the High Command did not understand their fears brought devastation to morale. Ludendorff's attitude to the tank threat was one cause of dissent. It was true that front-line troops frequently imagined non-existent tanks: east of Amiens it was said a hundred had been observed on 6 August when none was actually there. But a German staff officer, complaining of the prevailing attitude, wrote: 'Not even a request to keep a sharp look-out. . . . The Army Staff were astonishingly indifferent.'

The erroneous report of 6 August was, nevertheless, grimly prophetic and but 24 hours adrift. Already 604 tanks and 2,000 guns, along with three British infantry corps and a French Army, were being smuggled into hides in the vicinity of Amiens. On 8 August they would throw themselves at eleven emaciated German divisions. No German aeroplane could hope to spot this vast concentration for none had penetrated beyond the front line since 26 June and, in any case, the presence of the tanks could not be seen until the last moment since their sudden arrival on a stream of special railway trains could be withheld until the very last. Though the basic Allied plan resembled the Cambrai method, in application and sophistication it was different. This time the entire force would be set in motion from the start. Tanks and infantry would move as the artillery opened fire:

cavalry, accompanied by Whippet tanks, would follow closely on the assumption that success was assured. Canadian, Australian and British infantry would be instructed meticulously in how to co-operate with the armour—tanks dealing primarily with enemy machine-guns and wire and infantry with enemy artillery. On a rolling plain, innocent of deep ditches, a free run would be enjoyed by machines: even armoured cars were expecting to be let loose down the roads once a few felled trees had been removed.

The attack was scheduled to achieve great depth—rapidly—and thus would outrun the main artillery support before the guns could 'up trails' and advance to new positions. Undeterred, Fuller pressed for tanks to go even farther, beyond the range of most artillery from the outset, passing through the German positions on their own, to deposit machine-gun teams in the enemy rear before turning back to strike the bypassed enemy from behind. In essence Fuller sought a fulfilment of the ubiquitous fighting man—one who could fight mounted or dismounted without re-course to whether he were labelled infantry, cavalry or tankman.

Nobody seriously doubted that the German front line would be overrun and when C. E. Montague wrote, the night previously, 'Could it be coming at last...the battle unlike other battles?' his dream was almost reality. All eyes were fixed on the horizon of the final objectives and this was justified for, in thick early-morning mist, the rupture of the German front was complete and there was no pause in the advance even though, in places, German resistance destroyed many tanks. Repeatedly gruelling duels developed between tanks and guns, while the infantry of both sides could only wait and wilt. At one spot nine out of ten tanks were knocked out by one German battery and at another seven were wrecked. But everywhere the German gun line was finally crushed and the 225th Division had to report by 10 a.m.: 'The entire divisional artillery was lost; of the front line and support battalions practically nothing had come back; and the resting battalions thrown in piecemeal had either been thrown back or had not got into action at all...there yawned a gap, completely unoccupied.'

Shortly that gap was eleven miles wide. Churchill drove into it and saw 'cavalry cantering as gaily over the reconquered terri-tory as if they were themselves the cause of victory', when in fact they were mostly hampering its full accomplishment. For whenever the horsemen came under fire they had to retire to a flank to allow the Whippets to catch up, find, seek and destroy the menace. Hence the Whippets, held back by horses with tails between their legs, were deprived of several opportunities to dash ahead into the enemy rear. Horsed cavalry no longer even had the ability to be useful dismounted infantry.

Not all tanks—nor cavalry for that matter—were thus inhibited, of course, and a few ran amok far in the enemy rear, joined by armoured cars, which had been towed through the enemy road-blocks by tanks, in an orgy of destruction which engulfed gun positions, infantry columns, railway trains and supply installa-tions, besides reaching out to pepper commanders and staff in the fading safety of their HQs. German command and control began to collapse and with it Ludendorff's composure. On 11 August he wrote: 'Troops allowed themselves to be surprised... and lost all cohesion when the tanks suddenly appeared behind them.' He went on: 'As a weapon against Tanks, the prepared defence of the ground must play a larger part than ever, and the aversion of the men to the pick and shovel must be overcome at all hazards.' In aid he could offer nothing better than the old dogma, 'A Tank is easy prey for artillery of all calibres....' More to the point was news of German troops refusing to fight and this led him to recommend that an end of the war must be sought.

Vital to the issue was a German message which stated that 'no defence could be made in time against the Tanks'. Speed had certainly been of the essence, and the tanks' thrust faster than it had been at Cambrai, while the German parry was slower to take effect. Nevertheless, within 24 hours, orders from British HQs were again falling behind events and the German reinforcements were beginning to stabilize the line. But if the prime failing was in battlefield communications another important contributory cause was the sweeping reduction by casualties in tank strengths and artillery concentration. Only 145 tanks were available on the 9th and but 85 on the 10th, while the mass of artillery had still to catch up at the front. Therefore the infantry were driven to ground since they could not prevail on their own. The fact that the French, with far fewer tanks on the right flank, had never quite achieved the British rate of advance was just another reason behind the failure to widen the breach and turn a puncture into an irreparable rent. This attack, like so many before it, narrowed its front to follow the line of greatest enemy expectation—not even tanks could yet eradicate that fatal tendency—but the Allied chance of full exploitation was doomed when the British deferred the commitment of a single fresh formation until the 10th—after the Germans had already fed in a mass of reserves.

The battle was called off by Haig on the 11th when he convinced Foch of the futility of following a dead scent, a decision taken after one last promising experiment to maintain momentum had failed—a tank attack by night. The idea had been for 'columns to move along defined roads leaving the objectives well to the flanks and then encircle the enemy positions. Each column was accompanied by tanks. . . .' Unhappily the approach march was hampered by German air bombing and then by heavy machine-gun fire. In the dark the tank gunners could not detect the enemy weapons and the infantry were driven back, protected as they retired by a blaze of unaimed machine-gun fire from the tanks. It was an unlucky setback which was to stick in tank officers' black memories for many years to come.

Allied offensive policy now pandered to the inadequacies of mechanically unreliable tanks and inflexible battlefield command and control procedures. Because tanks might still suffer 50 per cent losses (mostly by breakdown) with inversely proportional casualties from enemy fire to the decreasing number of tanks they could concentrate in time and space, each fresh offensive had to await the delivery of worthwhile numbers of new or repaired tanks. New offensives on separate fronts became mandatory since, in the secondary phases of an attack, the higher command could neither impose its will at the advancing point of contact nor obtain timely information of enemy weaknesses. Nevertheless, the days of the step-by-step trench battle were passing. Fewer men and machines would need to be committed to a break-in but many more, pressing forward with greater ingenuity at the hail of those commanders who made a practice of staying close to the front, would have to follow up. Jab followed jab—first on one Allied front and then on another, as Foch and Haig alternated their blows. Like a boxer caught in the clinch by an expert 'in' fighter, the Germans began gradually to lose their stamina. But they were never floored—there was no knockout.

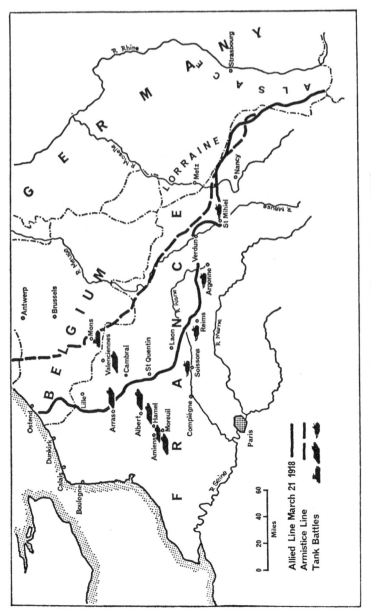

R. Rhine

G E R M A N Y

A L S A C E

Strasbourg

L O R R A I N E

Antwerp

Brussels

B E L G I U M

R. Meuse

R. Moselle

Metz

Nancy

Ostend

Mons

R. Meuse

Valenciennes

Cambrai

St Quentin

Laon

R. Aisne

Verdun

St Mihiel

Argonne

Dunkirk

Lille

Arras

Albert

Hamel

Amiens

Moreuil

Compiègne

Soissons

Reims

R. Marne

Calais

Boulogne

F R A N C E

R. Seine

Paris

60

40

20

0

Miles

Allied Line March 21 1918

Armistice Line

Tank Battles

Map 4   Tank battles on the Western Front in 1918

Immediately following Amiens there came renewed French attacks near Soissons, each supported by its skirmishing line of tanks. Then on 21 August the British lifted their tank force north as once the Germans used to redeploy their train of siege guns. Two hundred tanks struck out near Albert, cutting into the rear of the Germans who only recently had sealed off the penetration near Amiens. Once again early-morning mist, such as had hidden the initial moves at Cambrai, during several German attacks and at Amiens, hid the leaders of the attack more effectively than any smoke-screen. Keeping direction by compass, the tanks swept almost unopposed through the outposts and were hitting the main German position with its specially located anti-tank field guns before the occupants were prepared. Another few minutes and the tanks would have been among the guns at short range. But then the mist lifted like a theatre curtain, the German gunners were presented with targets galore in sharp silhouette and the tanks could not lay their own artificial fog. Each tank became the centre of a vortex of exploding shells it could not long avoid. Machines were ripped apart and turned into blazing coffins. On a hot summer day the survivors fought on, but 37 of their number had been destroyed and progress was halted in the main position. It had been a great day for the German gunners—so good that only a hundred tanks could be scraped together on 23 August to assist in a renewed attack south of Albert.

The German Army fought on—but erratically. Some gave up to tanks without firing a shot. Of them a German wrote: 'Their sense of duty is sufficient to make them fight against infantry, but when tanks appear many feel they are justified in surrendering.' Other Germans did better—though more by the expenditure of material than courage. Ernst Jünger saw: 'As though drawn by strings, four tanks crept over the crest of a rise. In a few minutes our artillery had trodden them into the ground. One broke across like a tin engine.' But in the same vicinity a tank commander claimed the destruction of 30 machine-guns, and a major cause of complaint among the crews was of exhaustion in the suffocating heat of poorly-ventilated vehicles rather than enemy action.

Tactical improvizations abounded. At Albert there had been a moonlight attack by tanks and later, in daylight, some Whippets, discovering that the artillery barrage was timed to move too slowly to suit their speed, took the law into their own hands and advanced right through and ahead of the barrage. Some Germans fled and were cut down: others fought on and peppered the tanks with machine-gun fire. With tanks well in the lead and exposed to every enemy field gun which could get into action unhindered by British artillery fire, the work of bombing aircraft took on a vital roll—though some airmen saw no point in bombing a target which was already visible to artillery. But not only did these aircraft bomb and machine-gun batteries in the open, they also passed on reports of progress which might otherwise have taken hours. Co-operation was rudimentary, occasionally decisive but always inspirational to the pundits.

But by 26 August the British Tank Corps was momentarily at the end of its tether, and still the Hindenburg Line loomed close ahead, as yet untouched. Attacking out of Arras, to close up to the Drocourt-Quéant Switch line, the Canadians were rationed to only 30 tanks, and told to use them sparingly only in the second wave of attack, in order to keep casualties to a minimum. Then one supreme effort on 2 September dredged up 75 tanks for the attack on the Switch, but once that had been broken (and this position, once considered impregnable, fell in 24 hours), there had to be a tank pause. Neither men nor machines could do more. Of the 1,200 machines available on 8 August, nearly all had been used up and it was to be three weeks before more than 200 could be assembled again. The British offensive died down.

Now it was the turn of the French and Americans at the other end of the front. First there was the attack against the St Mihiel Salient—an assault which, to all intents, hit thin air since the Germans were already in the process of withdrawal. Here only one Allied tank was destroyed, though 22 became bogged and 14 broke down. Much more was expected of the offensive between Reims and Verdun on 26 September since this aimed to split the hinge on which the German armies to the north were pivoting in their general withdrawal. Five hundred and fifteen Renaults, many crewed by Americans, were used in this, the greatest effort ever made by American-manned tanks in the First World War. That they got into action at all was a miracle of determination, for they had formed their Tank Corps only the previous November and since then had lived on borrowed tanks and goodwill. The commander was Brigadier-General S. D. Rockenbach—his command but three battalions, one equipped with British Mark Vs and the rest French Renaults. Indeed, for the 35 companies formed in the USA there were no tanks to be seen, let alone for use in training. The commander of the tanks committed to the Argonne was Colonel George Patton who had been Rockenbach's right-hand man in France, but he was wounded and leadership fell to Major S. Brett—though it has to be admitted that his task was more akin to a juggler of resources to the infantry, along with stringent administrative duties. In a nutshell, the brigade did not fight as such but in scattered groups until, by 5 October, it was exhausted.

Meanwhile the British had started again and on 27 September had crossed the Canal du Nord in an attack which gave fresh insight into future tactics. Here the breach was made on a narrow front which was then widened by the subsequent exploitation fanning outward behind the unassaulted front. Once the trench shackles had been removed it seemed as if imaginations blossomed forth with ideas such as had lain dormant for years. Another glance at the future was given near Niergnies, on 8 October, when the Germans had scraped together 11 tanks—one of their own and ten captured British Mark IVs—and launched them in a counter-attack. There was a lot of smoke hanging about and the light was poor, so although the British crew of L16 saw strange machines approaching it was not until the range had shortened to 50 yards that the danger was recognized.

> One 6-pounder round was fired at the enemy, but almost simul-
> taneously L16 received two direct hits. Captain Roe, believing
> his tank to be disabled, went to L9 and led it back towards
> the German tanks. L9 already had five wounded, had been on
> fire and, having no gunners left, could not use its 6-pounder, but
> engaged the enemy with its Lewis gun until it received a direct
> hit setting it on fire again. Meanwhile L12 was hit twice and
> disabled before its commander had discovered that the strange
> tanks were unfriendly. L8 was damaged and almost out of
> action.

In fact the British were being badly worsted until L8's com-mander went with an artillery officer and turned a captured German field gun on the nearest German tank, knocking it out. Honours were evened when two German female tanks next put in an appearance to be smartly destroyed by six-pounder tanks. The importance of the action lay in the lesson that tank-versus-tank fighting was inevitable and might one day dominate the battlefield. In this action, as at Cachy in April, the infantry of both sides had dived for cover as the monsters fought it out—and it was quite apparent that a tank without a cannon was a handicap. If the latter lesson took many years to digest, the knowledge that the Germans were good tank fighters did not.

The war was coming to its end as the German Army staged its come-back—a recovery made easier by a slackening of tank attacks since unreliable Allied machines operating at increasingly long distances from their workshops broke down more frequently and therefore could not be deployed in large numbers. Near the Forest of Mormal three Whippets fought a final duel with a German battery and chased some infantry through the hedges. But on 11 November the shooting stopped, the attempts to patch a peace began—and the soldiers turned to examine armies which had altered out of all imagination since 1914. Somehow the ungainly monsters thrown up by war had to be fitted into a peacetime setting.

The Peace, such as it was to be, brought little relaxation to the armed forces of any one of the warring nations. Fighting was still widespread—throughout Russia where White forces, using British and French advisers and equipment (including tanks) were engaged in a failing rearguard action against the Reds; in Asia Minor, the Middle East, Afghanistan and along several frontiers then being policed by the colonial Powers. Hardly one of these campaigns took place without seeing armoured cars or tanks in action. Sometimes, as for instance when a hostile crowd in occupied Germany had to be dispersed, the use of tanks might seem rather like a hammer to crack a nut, but when the shooting began, as with the North-West Persia Force when they came into action at Kasvin, the remark of the British commander, Ironside, that 'three moderately efficient tanks could have dispensed with three battalions of infantry' was not without importance in the debate on the future of the new arm. And in Iraq, Colonel Lindsay, the commander of an armoured-car force, was to take time off to practise tactics of the future with his cars—experiments which helped to formulate his views and then those of others about the nature of organizations and tactics.

After the war the praise or denigration of tanks and other partially-proven weapons was ostensibly intended only to affect those who had fought in them. Most statements from higher authority were calculated contributions to ceaseless inter-arm bargaining in the reshaping of peacetime armies. In his Despatch Haig might write 'the importance of the part played by them [tanks] can scarcely be exaggerated', but as a cavalryman in committee he would not take their part when it came to deciding which would be disbanded—a horsed or a tanked regiment. The British and, perhaps to a larger degree, the French, were anxious to return, so far as possible, to the same internal balance of forces as had ruled in 1914. Article 171 of the Versailles Treaty, which forbade the Germans offensive weapons such as tanks, aircraft and gas, lent force to this argument since it prevented the Germans from developing a strong offensive capability. Thus the Allies were deifying defensive strategy and tactics—to the enhancement, in fact, of a strong deterrent against Germany whose prospects of waging a profitable, lightning war of aggression were being emasculated.

But when Ludendorff and the principal body of German generals now referred to the ill effects of tank panic, they were actually trying to re-inject vitality into German national morale. The claim of General von Zwell, that 'it was not the genius of Marshal Foch that defeated us, but General Tank', was a gross exaggeration and partly in defence of the inadequacies of the German General Staff, who realized that the tank was but one of several factors which had brought them down. General von Seeckt, the architect of the truncated army, limited by Versailles to only 100,000 men, saw in this sanction the opportunity to build a *corps d'élite*; as he wrote: 'a small army excellently trained'. And a Captain Heinz Guderian, studying the motorization of future armies, drew the conclusion that, with only a small army, Germany would have to defend herself by mobile warfare since the system of lining an endless barrier was no longer feasible even if desirable.

On fundamental tank philosophy the British and Germans were at variance. Persistently the Germans regarded the role of the tank as an attack on morale, while the British, copied by the French, continued to regard it as the material means to attack material as the essential preliminary action to a reopening of mobile war. To the Allies the tank had been an important tool in shaping the final victory. To the Germans it was something more—a weapon with a magic of its own—and they reasoned that, since they had been unable to defeat it, they would have to acquire it for themselves in the future. Unfortunately for clarity of understanding, the factor of morale was intangible while the arguments of the pragmatists could be expressed more convincingly. There could be no immediate resolution of the argument then even had there been an immediate call to do so.

People who had endured enough of war, heavy taxation and monetary inflation yearned for peace and higher standards of living. The politicians and the League of Nations agreed and pressed for vast armament reductions. The soldiers, backed against the wall of every committee room, fought to retain all they could, the officers of each arm endeavouring to save themselves (in the interests, quite often, of promotion) regardless of what might happen to the others. Pressures recurred similar to those of early 1918 but with redoubled force, when the cavalry and infantry had quite naturally tried to soften the cuts to themselves at the expense of each other, and of the tanks and artillery. Then Haig had been on the horns of a dilemma. Beseeched in war by his subordinates for more tanks than he could have and convinced of their decisive effect, he would have been the last in peace to agree readily to the cavalry giving up one horse for a motor vehicle. It would have been astonishing had he done so, for he was the doyen of the cavalry and his desertion of the cause would have been a betrayal of the equine aristocracy to which he owed ingrained loyalty. His was an attitude that fairly represented those who took over from him after the war—and not in the British Army alone.

The strength of the case for the tank could not, however, be gainsaid and tanks—even machines which were not moderately efficient—survived. Yet for the majority in 1919 who yearned for a holiday from professional soldiers who clamoured for modernization, and for leisure in a peace for which they had striven, it was infuriatingly irksome that a small caucus of enthusiasts would not let matters rest.

Chapter 6

A CLASH OF IDEAS

The first outrageously futuristic but educated paper on tank warfare was written by a member of the British Tank Corps staff in November 1916, Captain G. le O. Martel. He foretold 'that future great wars were almost sure to start with a duel between the tank armies of the respective sides', and went on to discuss types of tank, including a vehicle with a speed of 20 mph, a quick-firing gun and armour half-an-inch thick. Martel envisaged tank armies working from special bases and saw as their whole object 'the destruction of the enemy's tanks'.

This paper undoubtedly had an influence on Fuller, and Fuller was to be the arch-apostle of tank warfare; indeed, his influence extends to the present day. As the great German offensive ground forward in May 1918, Fuller had taken his first definitive look at the future in a paper entitled 'The Tactics of the Attack as affected by the Speed and Circuit of the Medium D Tank'—a document first written as a sort of military novelette and then expanded into the paper which Foch was to welcome as the basis of an Allied Plan for 1919—and usually remembered as *Plan 1919*. The central feature of this paper was, in fact, an improved Whippet—the Medium C—which had been put into production in 1918. The specifications for Medium D—an improved C—evolved at a conference between Fuller and the Engineering Department of the Tank Corps. It was to have a speed of 20 mph, a range of 150-200 miles and the ability to cross wide gaps unassisted. This tank was to be the spearhead of the attack.

> ... without any warning whatsoever, fleets of Medium D tanks should proceed at top speed ... directly on the various [enemy] Headquarters lying in the primary tactical zone.... Meanwhile every available bombing aeroplane should concentrate on the various supply and road centres.... As soon as orders and counter-orders have been given a little time to become epidemic, a carefully mounted tank, infantry and artillery attack should be launched, the objective of which is the zone

of the enemy's guns; namely the secondary tactical zone some 10,000 yards deep.

Subsequently there would be a pursuit '... of at least 20 miles a day for a period of five to seven days' in which the cavalry and Medium Ds would collaborate though Fuller later declared that he mentioned the cavalry 'to propitiate the horse worshippers. Tractor-drawn light infantry would have been more effective'.

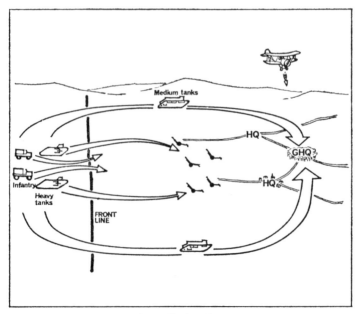

Map 5   Fuller's Plan 1919

Fuller wanted an offensive in three distinct phases—*Infiltration*, leading to *Disorganization* (followed by break-through) and then *Pursuit*. The object of attack was to be the enemy's morale—their resolution to wage war. While the paper was quite precise in demanding the number of tanks required for an attack on a 90-mile front—2,592 heavy tanks (for breaching) and 2,400 mediums—the sub-division of this vast army of tanks remained vague. Broken down into 30 brigades and 90 battalions though it was, there was no suggestion of the creation of tank divisions of all arms—though this was clearly intended.

Later, when Fuller wrote the sequel to *Plan 1919*, in 1919—a prize-winning essay in response to the subject 'The application of recent developments in mechanics and other scientific knowledge to preparation and training for future war on land'—he was working with Elles in the War Office and hotly engaged helping, though sometimes hindering by his tactlessness, in a protracted struggle to save the Tank Corps from extinction. But, although Fuller's advocacy of mechanization was strong it was not entirely uninhibited when he merely suggested the creation of a new model division of 12 infantry battalions each with a company of tanks, supported by four regiments of horse-drawn and two batteries of mechanized medium artillery, along with a mixed cavalry brigade of two horsed and one tank regiment. He actually restrained the habitual irony, which later characterized his writing, in order to soften the blow against the traditionalists and included as 'mere speculation' the prospects of a wholly-armoured formation.

Yet when the essay was published in May 1920 it gave a violent boost to the current debate on the future of war. Not only in Britain but throughout every nation with a continental style army, a flood of articles and lectures set forth to give ample evidence, not only that the traditionalists were frightened but that some in the younger generation were demanding progress because they, more than the older generals, had suffered personally from outmoded tactical plans in battle.

However, it was only in Britain, where the debate was hottest and where Elles's influence was decisive, that a separate Tank Corps survived. The French Army had never felt the need for one since its tanks had been developed either as self-propelled artillery or mechanized infantry machine-gunners and manned by a congregation of sailors, cavalrymen and others. In 1922 Estiénne proposed the formation of a division comprising tanks, infantry and artillery, but without inspiring a sympathetic response. France had endured enough of war. Moreover her arsenals were overflowing with the weapons of 1918, and new developments were constricted by a tight military budget which precluded the purchase of fresh and expensive equipment.

Committed to keeping an eye on Germany and maintaining the sanctity of her frontiers, France's military doctrine in 1921 hung on defence, a diametric swing from the policy of 1914, and enshrined in the *Provisional Instructions Concerning the Tactical Utilization of Larger Units*, a document produced by a commission under Marshal Pétain, the saviour of Verdun, whose reputation had been won by practising the art of defensive tactics. The *Instructions* declared that a continuous front would be invulnerable in the future, and could be broken 'only in favourable conditions after the assembling of powerful means, artillery, tanks, munitions. . . .' Tanks 'are destined to increase the offensive power of the infantry by facilitating its advance into combat', and infantry 'preceded, protected and accompanied by artillery fire, and possibly aided by tanks and aviation . . . conquers terrain, occupies, organizes and preserves it'. It was inevitable, therefore, that the French tank units, backed by a stockpile of 3,000 obsolescent Renault FTs, should become an integral part of the infantry in 1920. For more than a decade progressive military thought stood still in France, in part because there was nobody with intellectual fire and genius, or with the moral courage of a Fuller, to give a jerk to controversy and ingenuity. A few experiments there would be with motorized infantry units involving Renault tanks, but nothing more ambitious than that.

A similar apathy gripped the Americans. With them the combination of a stark political isolation of pure Monroe origin went tightly hand in glove with stringent financial parsimony when, after the war, they found themselves lumbered with a stockpile of 450 American-built Renaults and 128 British-type heavies. None had seen service and the estimated value was $32 million. The hope of manning them was remote, for in 1919 the struggling Tank Corps was limited by Congress to only 154 officers and 2,508 men despite the protests of Rockenbach—who had returned from France to take charge. Rockenbach's stated principal concern, like Elles's, was not that of increasing size but of saving the corps from total extinction—though among his colleagues there was a suspicion that his heart was not in the fight.

When a Congressman remarked '. . . I am unable absolutely to see any reason during peacetime for the creation of the overhead that would have to be established to give you a separate organization', he reflected the views of General Pershing and that of an Army Committee which, while admitting the value of tanks, refuted any claim they might have to independence. It was recommended that 'the Tank Service should be placed under the general supervision of the Chief of Infantry. . . .' Without appearing to struggle too hard, Rockenbach acquiesced and in 1920 Congress amended the National Defence Act and allocated the tanks to the infantry. Nothing was done by halves. The cavalry were excluded from having tanks and in 1921 expenditure on tanks was cut to $79,000—hardly enough to buy petrol, effect running repairs and carry out training.

The Americans having denied themselves a forward policy on armour, their infantry now proceeded to brainwash the progressives. A paper in favour of tanks, written by Captain Dwight Eisenhower, an infantryman, was derided. Patton, a cavalryman, and Brett, among the genuine experts, voiced faith in the future of tanks through the pages of military journals, but even Patton was later blinded to the future. In 1929 he was to express strong doubts as to the feasibility of operating large tank armies on the grounds that long-range, high-speed operations would lead to disaster because it would be impossible to maintain supply lines through hostile territory.

In Germany, where there were no tanks, there was no need either for an evangelical like Fuller. There, as a sharp reaction from their neglect of the tank in 1918, the tank creed had become strongly rooted in official circles—though German military circles, under the suppression of post-war surveillance, had to keep their councils secret. Circumvention of the peace conditions was the order of the day. The 100,000-man army would recruit a high proportion of officers and technically orientated men; defence of Germany would have to be based on a mobile strategy, and clandestine methods would be employed to acquire experience of tanks—the weapon which legend, as well as study, said had won the war. The LKII, a German tank similar to the British Whippet, was sold to Bofors in Sweden and arrangements made for Swedish industrial co-operation with Krupps. Under General von Tschishwitz, an Inspectorate of Transport Troops was set up and Captain Heinz Guderian appointed to it as a General Staff Officer in 1922. Within two years he was an ardent advocate of the tank, studying everything he could lay his hands on, arguing tank tactics, writing articles on mechanization, and promoting simulated exercises—even though there was not one real tank available for practice.

Other nations played with tanks—but only as novelties, skirting the heart of the problem. The Russians, convulsed by revolution and among the least mechanically educated of people, could barely keep a handful of the 300 French and British machines off the scrap heap—and her own efforts to copy the Renault were for prestige alone. Italy also copied the French designs and built a heavy tank as well, while Japan examined a few First World War models. The year 1925, however, seemed to reverse what, until then, had been mounting tension between France and Germany.

The signing of the Treaty of Locarno, on the surface, appeared to do more than reduce the chances of a collision by imposing conditions on France, Germany and Britain that they should come to one another's aid in the event of aggression. It was then hoped to open the way for the talks on disarmament to which the League of Nations was pledged: to outlaw offensive weapons, such as tanks, aeroplanes and gas, not only to the Germans but every other nation as well. In fact, far from being a palliative, Locarno and its disarmament aftermath were an immediate provocation. The French and British, among others, awoke to the reality that if disarmament was seriously imposed, they would remain in ignorance of advanced knowledge of modern weapons and at a disadvantage unless they investigated them at once. Seven years without much research and development had now to be compensated in the interests of national safety by intensive thought and experiment—a haste which would create unwanted pressures on soldiers' consciences.

The French, however, put armoured vehicles and formations in second priority to the fortification of their common frontier with Germany with a massive pile-up of concrete and steel fortresses— the inception of the Maginot Line and the birth of a psychology which was diametrically opposite to the philosophy of tank mobility. Obliged by Locarno to help either France or Germany if they were the victims of aggression, the British turned to examine mobile troops—the direction in which they had been pointed (with little enthusiasm) by Churchill when he was Secretary of State for War in 1919. In any case the British felt secure in the belief that a major war was out of prospect and military stagnation was sanctified by a statement of government policy that 'the British Empire will not be involved in any great war during the next ten years, and that no Expeditionary Force will be required'—a policy which, in part, now ran contrary to the mutual assistance spirit of Locarno.

The British, however, had run down their tank stockpile and, with all the enthusiasm of post-war retrenchment, disbanded the official Tank Design Establishment in 1922—and with it signed the death warrant of the Medium D before all its expensive snags had been ironed out. Both events turned out to short-term advantage. For a start the Tank Design Establishment was not as sound as some have made out; it was slow on the job and its main product, the Medium D, was too far ahead of its time and something of a technological white elephant. Next, the cuts came as the first post-war economic recession was gaining momentum, egged on by traditional kinds of Government deflationary measures which usually make financial matters worse.

One victim of the recession was the armaments firm of Vickers —to whom the Government felt an obligation—and it was Vickers who were now given the monopoly in British tank design and construction. Monopoly it might have been, but private enterprise did, at least, get on with the job and produce, by 1923, a light tank which, with its speed of 16 mph, range of 150 miles and 47mm gun in a rotating turret, came close to the specifications of Medium D—though the pathetically thin 6.5mm armour was less than that of the original vulnerable Little Willie.

The Vickers Light Tank—or Medium as it was soon called for reasons of status—was clearly not battleworthy. Yet it was the first post-war tank to be put into quantity production—more than 160 were made—and it was the only tank in the world at that time which could realistically put Fuller's concepts to the test in field trials. Thus the Vickers Medium gave the British a pre-eminent position, not only in technical but also in tactical advancement. Some of the guesswork would soon be removed from the more contentious assumptions thrown about in the fierce debate on tank futures—though how soon was to depend on the financiers and the Army Council.

Locarno did the trick. Less than a year after its signature—in March 1926—the British CIGS, General Sir George Milne, obtained financial approval for an Experimental Mechanical Force of all arms. Such was then the haste, in fact, that the essential preliminary groundwork had not been done when the announcement was made and it was to be another year before the terms of reference and the composition of the force could be settled. Since all arms were involved, each had to have its say in case influence was forfeit in the ensuing reorganization.

Eventually a mixed battalion of armoured cars and tracked machine-gun carriers (for reconnaissance), a battalion of medium tanks, a motorized machine-gun battalion and some mechanized artillery and engineers were assembled on Salisbury Plain. But Fuller, the man first and most naturally nominated to command, was not among them. Disenchanted with the arrangements to support the trial, finding that, in addition to leading the Experimental Force, he was also to command a conventional infantry brigade *and* act as a garrison commander, he had protested to Milne, pointing out that he would be unable to concentrate on the primary job and 'if I am not successful every soldier opposed to modernization will at once proclaim the newer arms to have failed'. But Milne would not listen and General Burnett-Stuart, who commanded the division nominated to sponsor the exercises, having at first asked for 'as many enthusiastic experts and visionaries as you can; it doesn't matter how wild their views are if only they have a touch of the divine fire', was also unbending.

It looks as if both Milne and Burnett-Stuart were determined to subjugate Fuller before launching him into the unknown—but theirs was a miscalculation, since Fuller resigned his commission rather than give way. All three were in the wrong, Fuller not least of all. Instead of resigning he could have acquiesced, taken up the appointment and then expended indirect subtlety in twisting and amplifying the original deficient arrangements to his purposes. Fuller, however, recognized the strength of the opposition his virulent advocacy of armour had stirred up, and he probably believed he would never be allowed a free rein. And, in fact, although he was soon persuaded to withdraw his resignation and serve on, by then an infantry officer, Colonel Collins, had been given the job with improved terms of reference.

In no small part this relaxation of control had come about because the newly-appointed Military Correspondent of the *Daily Telegraph*, Captain B. H. Liddell Hart, had taken up the cudgels and publicized the failings of Milne's original organization. The whole business smacked of intrigue and a miscalculation by the frustrated Fuller. In the event the decision to drop him may have been wise: he had never held command and there may have been something in his make-up which would have precluded him from combining his gifts of originality with the need to lead men less well endowed with vision. In his own words, 'My metier is to build substantial dreams'. From now on his influence within the Army was on the wane (though his subsequent lectures and writings, freed from official supervision, were to be among his most profound works) and the role of provocateur-in-chief in the struggle for modernization was assumed by Liddell Hart in the pages of the Press.

Liddell Hart had recently been retired from the Army, on the grounds of ill-health, and perforce had to earn a living. Already he was a recognized authority as the author of infantry training pamphlets and, among other writings, a penetrating forecast of the future of war. But until Fuller had convinced him that infantry were unlikely to defeat tanks, he was dedicated to infantry as Queen of the Battlefield and he had evolved a system of infantry tactics designed to restore their momentum in the advance—a method he entitled 'The Expanding Torrent'.

Better adapted, as he was to admit later, to armoured troops than to any other, this system, in fact, was historic. There is very little new in the Art of War and Sun Tzu had described an expanding torrent in 500 BC; the Germans were close to using it in 1918, and Fuller had already clearly perceived it. Liddell Hart agreed in fact that Fuller was his master in tactics, though doubting if Fuller understood the full strategic implications of tank forces. In those days, however, Liddell Hart expressed his ideas in terms more palatable to an authoritative section of the military hierarchy. His style, clear cut and modern, not only outmatched the stultified pamphlets of the day but became attractive to young and enquiring minds—the very minds which were already working to draw the British Army, ahead of others, into the future. Ever ready to criticize the men in power, Liddell Hart also made sure that he kept close influential friends who were either already in high places or on their way to them—friends who recognized his genius as an advocate and his susceptibility to flattery and kept him well supplied with information of the projects they were sponsoring. Thus his role was that of disseminator of ideas in coherent form—the collector of a mass of thought and its conversion into an understandable doctrine the like of which neither existed then nor, in such simplicity, exists today.

The manoeuvring of the Experimental Mechanized Force at times seems to have been nothing like so intricate as the manoeuvres behind the scenes. They began in the summer of 1927 from first principles—each step in movement and tactical deployment scheduled to be examined from the bottom upwards. To the participants and watchers it seemed, at first, very primitive and the pace inordinately slow. Colonel Collins was criticized for allowing infantry on their feet to slow down the fluent pace of which the force looked capable, but in breaking new ground with vehicles and men respectively ill-matched and unversed in each other's characteristics and outlook, he could be forgiven for keeping them under strict control and within close limits.

Collins had been instructed to examine the use of the Force for strategic reconnaissance as a substitution, possibly, for independent cavalry; in co-operation with main forces, and on an independent mission. With only rudimentary radio communications down to battalion level, control of the first and third class of exercise was sure to be slow and vague. In fact Collins had been asked to undertake far too much at once and without sufficient time for adaptation. Those, including Liddell Hart, who criticized him for acting like a banker—'no advance without security'—seemed to overlook the problems of control or to be unaware of the primary aims of the exercises. Air attacks played a prominent part throughout and though it was conceded that these would do little harm to tanks, their effects on supply columns were not overlooked; Collins later stated, however, that he would not be keen to command ground forces from the air.

Quite naturally the exercise which attracted most attention was the most dramatic one—the pitting of the armoured force in an independent mission against a conventional force of infantry and cavalry which, significantly, was without anti-tank guns. Not surprisingly the untrammelled depredations of fast-moving armoured columns paralyzed their opponents, though the results of the exercise, it had to be remembered, depended upon the awards made by umpires, few of whom understood tanks and many of whom could not keep up with the mechanized action on horseback. If the opposing infantry had been credited with the high-velocity anti-tank guns, which were already being produced by enterprizing manufacturers, the results could have been the reverse of what they were.

Some tank actions would have warmed the cockles of cavalry hearts when tanks charged straight to the mouth of the guns, sustaining, in the umpires' opinions, losses up to 25 per cent. Yet a debate on the cavalry was appropriate if cavalry was to find a way of retaining its identity. Not only the general public but also the soldiers had, in their minds, outlawed the horse from a serious role in future war. In lectures at the Quetta Staff College in 1926, Colonel Percy Hobart, a Tank Corps officer who took part in the 1927 experiment and who was to be one of the leading tank exponents in the next two decades, had envisaged the day when a separate Tank Corps could wither away as the entire Army became armoured.

Liddell Hart had written in 1926, 'The tank attack is the modern revival of the cavalry charge' and in 1928: 'The best hope of using armoured fighting vehicles aright is to put more cavalrymen in charge of them. The infantryman or gunner gifted with unusual imagination may acquire the art. The good cavalryman is, by his past training, a ready made artist'. Unfortunately Liddell Hart seems to have overlooked the fact that cavalry were, by 1928, little more than mounted infantry and that their spirit of mobility had been sapped in 1917—and in the light of his later disenchantment with the cavalry for their conservatism, force is lent to this contention.

The cavalry were not as averse to modernization as some of their leaders gave people to suppose. Their professional thinkers saw no prospect in serving a dying arm; the rank-and-file welcomed motorization because they learnt skills which would be of practical use when they left the service—and anyway they were not as enamoured of the horse as were their officers, probably because they had to live in closer proximity to the beasts. The heart of opposition to modernization lay, in fact, among the infantry, who went on deluding themselves in thinking they had won the last war. Artillery and tank men the world over had no doubt that it was *they* who had been the decisive elements, while the cavalry were all too aware in their hearts that they had failed, despite the few last-minute successes won by British horsemen against demoralized Turks in Palestine. For the cavalry there could be no false illusions, only an inner resolve among the realists to save themselves from extinction—if they could not beat mechanization they had better join it, as had the French cavalry by taking to armoured cars as far back as 1914!

False lessons were learnt from the 1927 experiment—above all an over-valuation of light tanks which were embraced as match-winners because the setting of the exercises and unrealistic umpiring had allowed them too free a run. Fuller, lecturing to officers, could dilate on the light tanks' value, forgetting that their small size made them poor cross-country vehicles. (In 1917 he had derided the little French Renault FT and then, in 1942, was to recant, castigating those who, in the thirties, pursued the folly of making light tanks. Clearly as much confusion was generated by the tank experts as by their opponents.)

In those days it was fashionable to compare tank warfare with a naval engagement and to equate light tanks with torpedo boats. This was highly misleading because whilst the torpedo was a weapon which could sink the biggest warship, the machine-gun or light cannon on a light tank gave no such guarantee of superiority. Liddell Hart saw light tanks in the mode of cavalry and postulated: 'The light tanks would lead, to pave the way by drawing the enemy's fire and testing his defence. If found to be weak they would go through it "all out". . . . If strong they would halt on any suitable close-up fire position, thus turning themselves into a screen of minute pill-boxes.'* Successive generations of light-tank men who played that gambit were soon removed from the board and as one critic said: 'The sheer speed of the bird does not prevent a good shot from hitting it.'

A feeling of euphoria was whipped up by Liddell Hart's eloquence and his action in persuading General Milne to give publicity to a speech which gave a far-ranging insight into the future of war. These ideas, when joined by imagination to the sight of an armoured force in being, seemed to offer the chance of reinstating the ability of an aggressive nation to win a quick decision. If war by stalemate was to be outmoded, a complete rethinking of each nation's defence policy was due. Suddenly, to keen minds, it seemed possible that faith in the existing deterrent to war—the inevitability of stalemates caused by an

---

* Writing after the Second World War, Liddell Hart, in quoting this passage, omitted the portion dealing with going through 'all out' though maintaining his advocacy of the 'close-up fire position'.

impenetrable defence—might be misplaced. Typical of this brand of thought was a passage in a paper Hobart had written setting out the requirements for a 'Light Division of the Future' (in fact one of many such proposals dating from this time for an armoured division). 'If a blow removes the heart or brain combat would be over.... Thus a *supreme effort* and heavy casualties are worth while if a campaign's duration can be shortened.'

Lightning, pre-emptive campaigns were again in prospect— and the representatives of America, France, Russia, Italy and Germany who watched the British experiment rushed off to jump on the band-wagon. If, a little later, Liddell Hart was to be found laying down that in the *tactical* field the defensive was superior to the attack, it was too late: the genie was out of the bottle and the tank idea he had espoused at first was to over-whelm his second thoughts. World war within the next decade became much more likely. Maybe the innovators did not actually provide a cause for war but they certainly encouraged those who might welcome it.

Some nations moved more quickly than others. The US Secretary for War, Dwight Davis, who immediately ordered the creation of a similar force to that of the British, had approved an organization by the end of 1927 and witnessed its concentration in July 1928 at Fort Meade. But its hesitant steps up the path of advancement were made inevitable by slow, First World War tanks, whose pace and reliability could not match the requirement and whose system of internal communications was archaic. At times tank company commanders were to be seen controlling their sub-units with coloured flags while walking among them on foot. Nevertheless before the Force was disbanded in September (according to programme and not, as some historians have stated, because of technical failings) a file of useful information had been gathered and the debate between those who, like one infantry officer, Captain Colby, resisted mechanization because 'we will be enmeshed in a mass of extraordinarily complicated and possibly antiquated machinery', could be set against the official view of General Parker that mechanized firepower and mobility would be required to achieve success in modern war.

In France there was less recognizable enthusiasm than anywhere else. General Doumenc proclaimed the need for armoured divisions and a few uninfluential writers backed him up but it was to be another four years before suitable French tanks were available to compose a formation with the range and speed to act on a long-range mission beyond the confines of an infantry-paced battle.

The odd men out—the Russians and Germans—had already started military collaboration in 1922: Russia because she simply had to obtain modern military know-how from somewhere and only the Germans would help, Germany because Russia offered a haven for secret experiment outside the surveillance of the Western Powers. The year 1927 was important for, by then, a tank school had opened at Kazan where Germans and Russians examined new tactics and tried out a whole collection of prototype tanks, several of which were founded upon British Vickers designs. Here the future trainers of the German and Russian tank forces learnt their trade while the designers analyzed a new technology. That year, too, Guderian was conducting exercises in Germany with 'tanks' which were only motor-cars covered with canvas and sheet-metal.

The Russians were on the eve of launching their first Five Year Plan in which industrialization was to be boosted beyond anything dreamed of in the past: an epoch was opening for them in which the peasant class was to be painfully subjugated to a new tractor regime and in which the Army, driven hard by the young and fanatical Chief of Staff, Marshal M. Tukhachevski, was to strive for every modern facility it could acquire. In Russia and Germany, as elsewhere, the forces of old-fashioned conservatives who could not comprehend, and therefore feared, the introduction of complex machines and organization, were to raise intrigues of opposition. But the education of a new technocracy had begun and from 1928 onwards the pace was to increase. In 1929 the Russians copied the other nations (as was to be their habit for a decade hence) and assembled an Experimental Brigade from those few old armoured vehicles they could get running. Germany, meanwhile, followed the lead from Britain and France, while America hid behind the Monroe Doctrine in isolation.

But it was from America that there came the most important innovation with the demonstration in 1928 by a maverick tank designer, J. Walter Christie, of a nine-ton tank chassis capable of speeds up to 30 mph. Though the first model was thoroughly unreliable it offered a complete breakthrough in the field of tank design. This, in fact, was the father of many of the great main-battle tanks to come except, significantly enough, in America and Germany. Tactical thought which, for a while, had led technical progress was once more to be stimulated by a technical revolution.

Chapter 7

FUGUES AND FEUDS IN
THE THIRTIES

The growth of tank philosophy in the 1930s resembled the composition of an international fugue—the theme devised by British composers and the voices and episodes from other nations piled one on another, until a surging consonance of ideas combined with the main political score leading to war. Yet while the fugue seemed to be an orchestral composition, discordant notes came from individual performers.

In Britain the publication in 1929 of an official manual entitled *Mechanized and Armoured Formations* consolidated the experience of the 1927–28 experiments. Armoured divisions were mentioned but the emphasis was laid at brigade level and below. Despite the title, cavalry formations were included 'for tasks more efficiently carried out by horsemen than by AFVs'. An infantry brigade, which included machine-gunners in armoured carriers, and a battalion of light tanks, plus an armoured brigade which included artillery, were also described—nothing in fact to provoke those who feared the Tank Corps was trying to create a separate armoured army. Yet behind the scenes this very innovation was being proposed when Colonel Charles Broad, the author of the pamphlet and a stormy petrel of the Tank Corps, suggested to Milne that an Armoured Corps should be created comprising ten cavalry regiments, two infantry battalions and the four existing Tank Corps battalions to make up four brigades.

The essence of Broad's proposals was the raising of standards to turn selected but representative parts of the Army into a *corps d'élite,* equipped with the most modern weapons and thinking progressively instead of dragging its feet, held back by the complacent laggards. Not that Broad's pamphlet rejected all but armour, for he was careful to point out that tanks were better used in open ground and with infantry in close support. Finally he was at pains to justify the acquisition of voice-radio to be fitted in each tank and armoured car—an improvement which was judged to be only just feasible using crystal frequency-controlled radios.

The pamphlet was marked 'not to be communicated either . . . to the Press or to any person not authorized to receive it', but it was soon plain that not only were members of the Press fully aware of its contents but, far less savoury, a Captain Baillie Stuart had sold a copy to the Germans. With a translation before them the job of Lutz, Guderian and the other German enthusiasts was made considerably easier. That year Guderian became convinced 'that tanks working on their own or in conjunction with infantry would never achieve decisive importance'. In 1937 he wrote: 'It was decided to rely mainly on English experience until we had more experience ourselves' and 'tanks are no longer a supporting weapon of infantry—almost the opposite—tanks must not be held back by old-fashioned infantry pace. Therefore infantry should best be carried in vehicles'. He went even further to claim 'it would be wrong to include tanks in infantry divisions . . .' though actual German practice was to deny this point in the end.*

In Britain the infantry were under strong pressure to change. No longer did *Field Service Regulations* support them as the decisive arm and Fuller, lecturing the officers of his infantry brigade, pointed out the inconsistencies of FSR when, in one paragraph, they demanded that infantry should 'close with the enemy and destroy him' and later, 'infantry in defence are stronger than infantry in the attack'. Realizing this, enlightened British infantrymen such as Wavell and Dorman Smith were developing armoured carriers to carry the important infantry weapons—the machine-gun and anti-tank gun—through enemy fire into key positions. The carriers were rather feeble relatives, in fact, of Estiénne's original light tank, yet the enthusiasts seized on them not only as the vehicle to propel the infantry deep into the armoured battle but as a means of ensuring the infantry's future existence.

* After 1945 Guderian proclaimed himself as a disciple of Liddell Hart and was among those who said the Germans attached little importance to the writings of de Gaulle. Yet it is instructive to note that in the bibliography of *Achtung Panzer* in 1937, the works of Fuller, Martel and de Gaulle are quoted but none of Liddell Hart's. Furthermore while Guderian's son remembers his father met Fuller, and often spoke of him, there was little mention before the war of Liddell Hart.

The infantry's doubters—those who feared the future and the prospect that mechanized operations would outpace their own, slow reactions—resisted doggedly by pouring scorn on the carriers and, obtusely, passing them off as 'tanks' and therefore the business of the Tank Corps. One moment they accused the Tank Corps of daring to create a new army; the next they rejected a weapon which could only encourage that very act. In due course, however, the light carriers were to be up-scaled into turreted light tanks, such as the 1927 experiment had suggested would be important. These would be sent to fight in the rugged terrain of the Indian North-West Frontier, where their thin armour and machine-guns were more than a match for tribesmen with antiquated rifles and where, on rough tracks and forbidding slopes, the ability of tracked vehicles to climb like goats demolished the contention that tanks need be confined to open country to achieve their full effect.

The French remained steadfast to their original beliefs, agreeing that infantry would be powerless without tanks in close attendance while conceding that the slower machines would be highly vulnerable to anti-tank guns. This they attempted to resolve by designing stronger tanks with armour between 30 and 60mm thick that made them proof against the newest 37mm and 47mm guns. Here was the gun–armour race at full tilt again and also the competition between quality, of a sort, and quantity, for heavily armoured tanks were costly products and so more difficult to make. Thus the onset of the great financial blizzard of 1930 ran counter to mechanization when, by tradition, the financiers met a recession with deflationary measures and by cutting military expenditure to the bone—measures which ran happily in tune with the idealists' attempts to apply general disarmament.

Yet progress with the tank experiments never quite stood still. The British had a new medium tank on trial—but it cost £16,000. As important, they were in possession of a practical crystal frequency-controlled radio set which gave direct short-range voice communications between tank commanders. In 1931 Broad conducted the first wireless controlled exercise of a whole brigade of tanks and it was a revelation, even though it occurred to some doubters who watched the intricate manoeuvring of the machines that they might be witnessing an elaborate hoax, so precisely ordered were the manoeuvres! Yet the basic arrange-

ments were simple enough for, to quote Broad, 'every drill movement should be based on a probable tactical requirement' and this
lent swift, practical simplicity to what might otherwise have
been hesitant and time-consuming deployment on the ponderous
infantry pattern. The result was a free flow of movement—'a
spectacle', as Liddell Hart wrote, 'that had never before been
seen—a mass of 180 tanks, marching and counter-marching,
wheeling and deploying, as a single body controlled by a single
voice'. Radio was thus powerfully demonstrated as a weapon
more potent than the gun since it could instantly shift the centre
of gravity—the fighting machines—from one part of a front to
the other and thereby to multiply or diversify their destructive
output.

Once more those who feared the growth of an all-tank Army
became alarmed, though in Britain the 1931 episode inspired
far less comment than its predecessor in 1927. Security cannot
have been the cause for this reticence, for in November 1931
Liddell Hart was already quoting in the *Daily Telegraph* from
the latest edition of *Mechanized and Armoured Formations,*
re-entitled *Modern Formations.* But this edition, though admitting
that mechanization 'must be accepted as an inevitable stage in
the evolution of army organization', was qualified in Milne's
introduction by the words, 'Though published by command of
the Army Council, this pamphlet does not represent the considered views of that body...'. Liddell Hart said what they
could not: 'Large mounted forces are no longer worth their
upkeep. The armies of the future will be small and highly
mechanized.'

There was now an awakening even in France when, in the 1932
exercises, mechanized cavalry and infantry were combined in one
formation, leading to the creation in 1933 of a faster moving
Division Legère Mécanique (DLM). But having taken two steps
forward by forming a true armoured division as well as raising
the possibility of establishing a separate armoured corps, General
Weygand, the Vice-President of the Army Council, recoiled a
pace, proclaiming 'Two armies, not at any price...nothing need
be created, everything exists'—in rather the same way as the
French thought every gaiter button had been provided prior to the
débâcle of 1870.

In France more than anywhere else the anti-tank school

received an almost unchallenged public hearing. Loudest in his cries was General Narcisse Chauvineau (a man of literary ability without the foresight of a Liddell Hart) who received the overt approbation of Pétain. Chauvineau twisted historical evidence and economic calculations his way to argue for the sanctity of a continuous line of static defences held by infantry and artillery. Yet by the time his major work had been published in 1938, official French Army policy had reverted to the 1914 theme of aggression—even if their officers' instincts remained unalterably passive. *Instructions on the Tactical Utilization of Larger Units 1936* had stated 'The offensive is the supreme form of action' and, to give it teeth, construction began of a fleet of well-armoured light, medium and heavy tanks to fill the DLMs and infantry support battalions.

In 1932 the Disarmament Conference assembled in Geneva. On an agenda, which nobody really trusted, were tanks, but in the wings each nation was endeavouring to bamboozle the delegates of the acceptable weight at which a tank should be deemed an offensive weapon. Some soldiers would denigrate tanks as contrary to accepted practice, but when faced with the possibility of losing them altogether they sang a different song. Light tanks were, deviously, evaluated as defensive and therefore retainable —though current philosophy hardly bore that out. At first it was suggested that six or eight tons might be a suitable top weight, but Britain, having just produced her first 16-tonner, was anxious to develop the breed. On the suggestion of Pile, a Tank Corps officer involved with mechanization in the War Office, the British delegates argued for an upper limit of 20 tons, and this, to quote Liddell Hart, 'encouraged the French, who wanted to preserve a few experimental 70-ton monsters, to advocate that the weight limit should go up to that figure'. This ludicrous quibbling dragged on into 1933—the year Hitler came to power in Germany —and Hitler's future programme would soon be shown as respecting neither treaties old, treaties in draft, nor the Disarmament Conference itself.

The strains of fugues and feuds grew louder. Russia had become involved in battle with Chinese Nationalist troops in Manchuria in 1929—an encounter which ended in victory for the Russians by sheer weight of numbers but which taught the salutary lesson that their attenuated tank forces had hesitated and not combined well with cavalry, infantry and artillery. Japan, too, was soon making threatening noises in Manchuria and turning aggressively against China. Peaceful trials began to give way to the real thing. In 1935 Mussolini invaded Abyssinia with an infantry army assisted by 300 machine-gun carriers copied from those produced by Vickers, but even tribesmen were unawed by these frail machines with their thin armour and forward pointing guns. Several were knocked out, though the ability of these vehicles to go almost anywhere the infantry could go (given engineer assistance) went not unnoticed.

It was in Russia and Germany where expansion on the perceptive and grand scale in every department of war made most progress. Skipping freely through the examination and early experimental stages because they could draw deeply upon the information so freely supplied by the British, both nations at first co-operated in increasing their armaments.

In 1930 the Russians persuaded the Germans to grant them full access to their knowledge of armaments, though of tank technology the Germans knew, if anything, less than the Russians. Both had drawn heavily upon Vickers—the Russians even more than the Germans. So for tanks Russia turned also to America to copy Christie whose fast tank of 1928 had made such an impression and which, by 1931, had been radically improved. From then on Vickers and Christie models, suitably modified to suit Russian terrain and climate, were the basic tanks in their armoured forces. They were also the inspiration for a team of budding tank technologists bent on developing a new breed of simple, sturdy tanks, powered by good diesel engines instead of the original petrol engines. By the mid-thirties the Russians were invading the frontiers of tank technology.

They were only just abreast in philosophy and tactical techniques, however. Kryshanowski, reflecting, no doubt, the opinions of Tukhachevski, the Chief of Staff, wrote: 'A decisive success can only be achieved by annihilation of the main enemy armies in depth as well as on the strategic and tactical plain. It is necessary to use powerful, fully mobile combat elements with great momentum.' The combat elements were certainly coming along well in 1932 at the end of the First Five Year Plan:

that year 3,300 tanks—mostly of Vickers derivation—were built, and work had begun on the Christies, and called BTs.

The 'mobile elements' were to be BTs and organized in three tank battalions within an armoured brigade; brigades, in turn, would be grouped in so-called mechanized corps which, by Western terminology, equated to armoured divisions. But when, in 1936, foreign observers were given a first sight of the Russian armoured mammoth they became aware of striking anomalies. Mixed tank and infantry masses raced here and there to exhibit enviable standards of reliability. At one demonstration a thousand tanks swept by without a breakdown. This must have been an extreme effort for its like was never achieved again. Nevertheless tactical handling contradicted the high-sounding philosophy and wasted the tanks which tended to charge to the mouth of the guns like old-fashioned cavalry. Subtlety, in fact, was at a premium and although Tukhachevski had already begun the training of a modern thinking officer corps this corps threatened to be the very element which might later unseat the Head of State, Josef Stalin, and undermine the authority of the old guard revolutionary infantry and cavalry generals such as Voroshilov, Timoshenko and Budenny. Already the latter were intriguing with Stalin and a drastic purge, designed to eliminate the educated élite, was in preparation. In Russia modernization was to give way to the calls of political survival: tank forces were to provoke a pogrom.

Russia's threat to the West—if threat it then was—never stood apart from Hitler's calculations while he plotted the expansion of German hegemony. To solve the power equation Hitler needed a new coercive factor—the ability to reach decisions by lightning war. In 1933 Hitler's Germany cancelled her pact with Russia, closed the tank school at Kazan and began the secret construction of tanks and aircraft on her own soil based on the prototypes evolved in Russia—a painfully slow process despite the mass of theoretical work already done. Nevertheless, that same year, General von Blomberg, the War Minister, was able to demonstrate to Hitler a combat team comprising a motor-cycle platoon, an anti-tank platoon and some experimental light tanks and armoured cars. 'That,' exclaimed Hitler, 'is what I need.' In 1934 the first German tank battalion—long visualized in skilfully phased plans—came into existence. At the same time the cavalry also began serious mechanization.

From this moment the British and French began rapidly to fall into arrears. Although 1934 was the year in which the French consolidated the existence of their DLMs and the British gave permanence to their Tank Brigade and first tried out an embryonic Armoured Division by temporarily manoeuvring the tank brigade in co-operation with a motorized infantry brigade and artillery, it was the Russians who were streaking ahead in sheer numbers and the Germans taking the lead in perception. Neither the British nor the Germans had yet confirmed their choice of tanks suitable for combat, but the Germans were on the verge of making that crucial decision based on British policy amended by Guderian. Germany's studies of the lessons from the First World War had led to the conclusion that it was better to fight *from* rather than *for* specific positions. Put another way this meant using remote firepower against weakness. Guderian wrote: 'We intend to make a breakthrough and roll up the enemy front in order to exploit the characteristics of the tank in co-operation with other weapons.' Here, for anybody to read, was the essence of Panzer divisions—formations of all arms but predominantly tanks, which could execute every operation in the book of war from reconnaissance, attack, defence and withdrawal, using machines in 'suitable country', by which Guderian meant almost any terrain to be encountered in Europe. The Panzer divisions were meant to be the centrepiece of other formations and to 'attack on a broad front so that the heart of the attack could be left free on its flanks'. Then would come the blow to the enemy brain, the drive against reserves and HQs, the destruction of his HQs, the engagement of his infantry in the combat zone and still the maintenance of a reserve to deal with contingencies. Written as they were in that order in 1937, they were lifted almost straight from Fuller's *Plan 1919*.

Guderian also accepted the British definition of the type of tank required, asking for a light, a medium and a close support tank —the latter to provide fire support to the other tanks from within the moving phalanx of machines.* But in 1933 he hit the snag

* These were Guderian's views as written in *Achtung Panzer* in 1937. After the Second World War, in *Panzer Leader*, he glossed over his requirement for the close support tank, perhaps because it smacked

which was always to cramp Panzer divisions: the dependence of the German economy on other nations for raw materials which unavoidably limited production of tanks. Moreover production was bound to be slow in view of the leeway in design and manufacturing techniques which had to be made up. At first only a light, training tank (Mark I) could be made, to be followed in 1934 by a better light tank (Mark II) with a 20mm gun and the medium-cum-close support Mark IV with its 75mm gun. Not until 1935–36 did a genuine medium (Mark III) with its 37mm gun appear, and even then Guderian was dissatisfied because it did not have a 50mm high-velocity gun. By September 1939 only 98 Mark IIIs and 211 Mark IVs had been put into service.

Mainly because tanks would always be in short supply, Guderian fought to keep them concentrated only in the Panzer divisions—of which three were established in 1935 after Hitler had rejected Versailles by the announcement of conscription in March of that year. In any case Guderian was not to have it all his own way for at various times both General von Fritsch, the Chief of the Army Command, and General Beck, Chief of the General Staff, put obstacles in his way while the cavalry generals behaved like cavalry generals in other armies and got in on the act by infiltrating cavalry units into the Panzer divisions.

Fritsch was sympathetic to the tank idea and embraced the opportunities it gave for rapid decision, but he was a snob and would have preferred the older arms to use them and not the 'upstarts' who were taking over. Nevertheless, Fritsch gave Hitler crucial help in his early days as Chancellor. Beck however was the opposite. Violently anti-Nazi, he also resisted every move to create Panzer divisions,* but for military and personal reasons. 'You move too fast for me,' Guderian (who supported the Nazis) quotes him as saying, and under his influence the new Armoured Troops Command was denied full status as an arm, the traditional

---

too much of the All Tank Idea. Some historians have accepted his post-war view, but when it is remembered that the short 75mm gun fitted to the Mark IV tank had a muzzle velocity as low as 1260 feet per second it becomes obvious that this gun was best used for close support since its accuracy could not have been sufficient for pinpoint engagement such as a tank-versus-tank fight demanded.

* The theory that he did so in order to deprive Hitler of such a powerful weapon is not substantiated by evidence.

subjugation of tanks to the infantry was maintained, and the peeling off of a Panzer brigade for close co-operation with infantry divisions carried out despite Guderian's protests.

Yet the disagreements between Guderian and the older arms, while giving victory to neither side, engineered a better balanced Army than if one or the other had achieved total dominance. To leave the infantry divisions devoid of motorized anti-tank guns—as might have happened if they had remained bottom of the list of Guderian's priorities, would have demolished what little strength and hope remained to the marching infantry. To have spread the tanks throughout the Army would have been equally wrong. Similarly, not to have found up-to-date employment for the existing cavalry would have been as wasteful and destructive of confidence in the Army as to let them keep horses. The infantry got their anti-tank guns and, for some of their formations, an improvement in status with the creation of four motorized infantry divisions to work in close collaboration with the Panzer divisions and, eventually, to be grouped into Panzer corps. Panzer divisions alone had tanks but the cavalry were moved in, first, to become the motorized reconnaissance units with armoured cars and later as the nucleus of four so-called Light divisions which were, in fact, motorized rifle formations with the inclusion of a tank battalion. It was always intended that these Light divisions should be converted to Panzer divisions when sufficient equipment could be made, but this interim organization had its advantages as part of the weaning of horsemen to motor vehicles.

Meanwhile, in 1935, to the amusement of a sceptical German Army, the tankmen went on appearing at exercises in motor-cars covered by wire-and-cloth screens. And even when the first Mark Is began to appear they were far from convincing. Guderian's tanks were badly in need of a way to show their strength in battle. The opportunity was not long in coming.

Chapter 8

MISLEADING REHEARSALS

Civil war broke out in Spain in July 1936, and quickly the
Germans, followed not long afterwards by the Russians, rushed in
to stake their ideological claims and to use the Spanish battle-
ground as the proving ground for their untried weapons. Com-
munist Russia took the Republican Government side and within
18 months, among many other weapons and stores, had shipped
in more than 700 Vickers and Christie-type tanks, along with
trained men. Fascist Germany and Italy backed the opposing
Nationalist cause under General Franco, sending men and a
representative selection of weapons. In the Italians' case, however, there were only machine-gun carriers to come (call them
tanks though they might) and the Germans, with their little
Mark I tanks, sent nothing better.

On the Russian side Generals Pavlov, a tank expert, Rokossovsky,
Koniev and Malinovski made appearances; all, with one exception, would later win reputations as exponents in tank warfare. On
the German side, in the Condor Legion, Colonel von Thoma
commanded the ground forces and tanks. Regardless of
nationality or partisanship, each doubled his rôle as adviser to
the Spaniards with that of leader in combat. Each nation,
particularly the Russians and Germans, welcomed the opportunity to acclimatize relays of soldiers to combat, but when it came
to actual practice neither was able to employ the most sophisticated tank theories—and for a variety of intractable reasons
which tended to make post-operational analysis confused.

At first, due to shipping difficulties, there were only a few
tanks available to either side. The first major tank battle occurred
on 29 October when fewer than 50 of Pavlov's tanks engaged
Nationalist cavalry, head on, at Esquivas. The harsh fate of the
horsemen in a street battle against tanks was never in doubt, but
in victory the Russians woefully exhibited the cloying limitations
of their tank education. Trying to emulate British theory without
possessing the proper means, they thrust ahead with their tanks,
leaving their infantry well behind. Tanks found it difficult to hold

ground on their own however, and, in any case, had soon to turn
back for shortage of fuel. Thus they forfeited the advantage of
mobility when that alone could give success.

Then near Madrid on 5 January 1937 it was the turn of German
tanks, preceded by air and artillery bombardment, to break
through the Republican lines and at first it was Amiens all over
again. The assault surged forward, following the line of greatest
expectation, until it stopped on the 9th after the thin-skinned
Mark I tanks had let in more shots from the Republican anti-
tank guns than the survivors cared to count. Pavlov's swiftly
ensuing counter-attack on that day certainly showed the speed
at which the new arm could react but it also demonstrated again
the fallibility of Russian methods. In the old-fashioned cavalry
way they sought an eyeball-to-eyeball battle, the tanks homing on
enemy centres of resistance and thrashing around in an orgy of
mutual destruction instead of selecting some strategic target
and making for it via the areas of least resistance. But in every
case tanks still left their infantry behind, mostly because the
pedestrian unprotected mass could not survive in the open in the
midst of a tank battle.

Next it was the Italians' turn to take the offensive near Guadala-
jara—an attack designed to demonstrate the supposed prowess
of Mussolini's newly invigorated countrymen. Two hundred and
fifty machine-gun carriers joined action with armoured cars to
breach the Republican lines and flood south along the main road
to Madrid on 8 March 1937. Inevitably, of course, they telegraphed their obvious and only line of strategic approach and
so it was easy for Pavlov to position his tanks for a counter-stroke.
When the Russians charged the Italians broke, many surrendering
at call, but, yet again, when in hot pursuit, the Russian tanks ran
out of infantry and then of fuel. Such an obstinate repetition of
the same mistake was unhealthy but the reaction, when it came,
was even worse, for Pavlov and other officers returned home
to spread an impression that modern theories had failed and that
the French were right in claiming that only when tanks attacked
deliberately with infantry in close attendance were they likely
to prevail.

The opposing armies in Spain were a heterogeneous lot—all
nationalities mixed up with and against each other. Idealism was
rife and discipline inconstant: sometimes a motion to attack was

decided on a show of hands. Organizations such as these did equate with the sort of small, highly professional tank force, envisaged in Britain and Germany, in which mutually disciplined co-operation by all arms was to be mandatory. Fervour in modern warfare was not enough. But while the Republicans took full advantage of the better Russian tanks, von Thoma had to replace as many of his Mark Is as possible and did so by offering a reward of 500 pesetas for each Russian tank captured in good order. 'The Moors,' he said, 'bagged quite a lot' until eventually he managed to equip four out of his 12 companies with these superior machines. In the short term this invigorated the depressed German crews—for it is miserable to fight in a tank battle crewing a positively inferior machine—but the underlying factor was more important, though not recognized at its true value just then.

Infantry might be cowed by individual tanks on first acquaintance—as might an entire army; but once they had the measure of a tank by recognizing its vulnerable points the tank lost much of its psychological advantage. So while the men in the firing line made personal and practical adjustments to hard facts, those at the top stuck to preconceived ideas. Von Thoma complained of Franco who 'wished to parcel out tanks among the infantry.... I had to fight this tendency constantly in the endeavour to use the tanks in a concentrated way. The Francoists' successes were largely due to this'. On the other hand it was Thoma, in his report, who threw doubt on the need for each tank to have its own wireless-set—at the very moment when Lutz and Guderian were struggling to acquire this vital facility from a parsimonious War Ministry in Berlin.

From Berlin Guderian watched Thoma's activities in the Spanish war with anxiety. Under constant pressure from his rivals, he wrote *Achtung Panzer* in 1937 on the instruction of General Lutz, the Armoured Troops commander, intending it as a propaganda defence of tanks against the critics. Guderian had to stonewall over Spain on the grounds that false lessons were being learnt, but he made the best of a bad job, pointing out how, up to 1937, never more than 50 tanks had been used at once, the Spanish soldiers were poorly trained and the ground imposed difficulties. He also seemed aware that tank fighting in the environs of a city such as Madrid would be costly and a bad thing. Tenaciously the German tank theorists managed to hold out and the Panzer divisions were increased in number until by 1938 six were in existence with a theoretical strength of about 320 tanks and a greatly increased infantry component compared with the original organization. Now each had 12 tank and 12 infantry companies, whereas previously it had been 16 to nine, and at the same time the scale of wireless-sets was being increased.

The Russians, on the other hand, veered towards French practice, though their reasons for doing so may not have been so heavily influenced by Spanish experience as some historians would suggest. In any case, Russian tanks were to do well enough against the Japanese in Manchuria when the Japanese provoked a series of frontier incidents between the sea of Japan and Outer Mongolia.

In August 1938 matters had come to a head when a large body of Japanese infantry and tanks invaded Russian territory in the direction of Vladivostok. Soon they were in head-on collision with Russian tanks and infantry in the sort of bull-headed fight which each thoroughly understood. A slogging match lasted a fortnight, heavy casualties were incurred and the Japanese forced back. The Russians had been orthodox and the Japanese had kept their tanks close to the infantry. It had been straightforward, unimaginative practice with neither side making a serious attempt to use tanks as the primary weapon of decision. Japanese tanks, in fact, were well up to Western standard in 1938 but were soon to fall behind, while their tactical techniques made hardly any advance at all. In the field of armoured warfare they were never of much influence.

As his reward for the Russian victory, Marshal Blukher was recalled to Moscow by Stalin and liquidated—at any rate he was never heard of again— and in his place came Generals Shtern and Koniev and, later, General Zhukov. It was Zhukov who had next to deal with the Japanese when they sought revenge in May 1939—and one wonders what his feelings were as, on the one hand, he devised a striking manoeuvre on the battlefield while, on the other, he strove to retain the confidence of his political leader in Moscow. Be that as it may, the Japanese opened proceedings by seizing a piece of Outer Mongolia jutting into Manchuria. Both sides now undertook a remorseless build-up of forces in the contested area. The Japanese gathered 180 tanks, 500 guns and 450 aircraft; the Russians did even better with 498 tanks and 580 aircraft—some of their tanks spread among the infantry but the 6th Tank Brigade kept independent for a decisive manoeuvre.

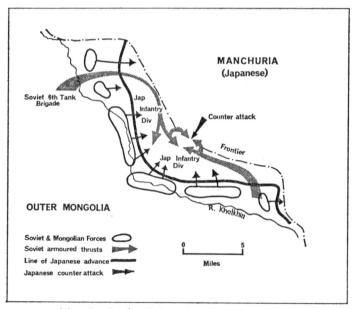

Map 6   Battle of the River Khalkhin – 1939

When Zhukov attacked along the River Khalkin on 20 August, he began with heavy bombing and then launched his forces along the length of the front against furious Japanese resistance. But the really significant feature of Zhukov's conduct of operations was his launching of 6th Tank Brigade round the northern Japanese flank to fall on the rear of a Japanese division—a clear rebuttal of reports that the Russians had forsworn the use of independent tank forces. There were no hesitations here as there had been in Spain. The Russian tanks interposed a tough strategic barrier across their opposite communications to the rear and held the ring against all breakout attempts from within and relief attempts from outside. The encircled Japanese lost more than 40,000: the Russians only 10,000. 'The Japanese,' said Zhukov some years later, 'are not very good against armour.' Nevertheless it had taken him ten days to beat them.

Renewed confidence was injected into the Red Army, Zhukov survived to do greater things, and in Moscow diplomats negotiating a dubious non-aggression pact with Hitler took heart. Voroshilov boasted, 'The Fascist powers will never break through the Soviet western frontier!' He probably believed it too.

Chapter 9

ON THE EVE OF THE
GREAT TANK WAR

On 1 September 1939 Hitler threw six years' work—the rejuvenation of Germany—to the winds. Perhaps egotism was at the root of his aggression, but no less assuredly that aggression could be fostered only by the new tank and air forces which capitalized on psychological warfare and paved the way to undermine each victim's internal resistance. Should the unproven forces falter the penalty for Germany must inevitably be the weakening of an economy which, to rationalists in 1939, seemed incapable of sustaining a protracted war.

Addressing his military leaders on 22 August, Hitler laid stress on the need to solve the Polish problem—by force if necessary. Here too, he said, was the fascinating and, indeed, essential opportunity to test the Wehrmacht upon which so much expense and intense care had been lavished, for if, later, there was to be scope for more ambitious adventures it had to be known if a quick decisive war was feasible. Goering could loudly claim the omnipotence of air power, but Spain had not established an unanswerable case for it, while Lutz and Guderian's Panzer divisions had even smaller grounds for recognition as the elixir of victory. But Goering's Luftwaffe had absolute priority over German manpower and industrial resources, and because of this the Panzer arm suffered shortages, along with the rest of the Army.

The Spanish imbroglio had been inconclusive and the bloodless annexations of Austria and the Sudetenland in 1938, followed by the occupation of the remainder of Czechoslovakia in March 1939, had exposed serious weaknesses and deficiencies in the Panzer arm. Mechanical failures alone kept 30 per cent of the tanks off the road at any one time: the repair services languished from few technicians and the absence of a field-workshops organization (major repairs could be carried out only in factories within Germany); there had been breakdowns in supply when tanks ran out of petrol; inadequate control had caused traffic jams—particularly when tank tracks cut road surfaces to pieces. Any one of these shortcomings could not only cripple the tank forces but hamstring the entire Germany Army —for the Panzer Arm contained the cream of that army; if that failed all else failed. It was therefore not surprising that the other German commanders showed healthy scepticism of the new arms despite the work which had been put into rectifying the more obvious faults.

With six Panzer divisions and four light divisions containing, between them, 3,195 tanks to spearhead 44 infantry divisions and a cavalry brigade into Poland, Germany was not, in fact, as overwhelmingly strong as her propaganda stated. Of the tanks 2,886 were light Mark Is or IIs and all but four of the infantry divisions for the most part depended on horsed traction. On the other hand the Polish Army was almost entirely horse drawn, and its 30 infantry divisions and eleven cavalry brigades boasted but a low content of anti-tank guns. The 13 battalions of light tanks were mainly spread thin among the infantry with the exception of a single brigade kept concentrated in Central Reserve.

A fatal threat to Germany could thus come only from Britain or France if they chose to go to war on behalf of Poland. Russia, the greatest potential threat, had been temporarily neutralized by the August pact with Germany. Britain, however, was even weaker than Poland, though the Germans sceptically refused to believe it when told that the antiquated medium tanks they had seen on manoeuvres in England were, in fact, the first-line strength.

The reconstruction of the British Army had begun tardily in 1935 and had been concentrated on the motorization, at great industrial effort, of the cavalry, infantry and artillery with, mostly, unarmoured wheeled vehicles. Over tanks there was vacillation made acrimonious by the generals' resentment of prodding by such critics as Fuller and Liddell Hart and Tank Corps officers such as Lindsay, Broad and Hobart.

General Elles had become Master General of Ordnance (MGO) in 1934 and thereby responsible for the procurement of tanks with an authoritative voice, as the original Tank Corps Commander, in the Army Council. But the Army Council was set on creating an infantry Army of the 1918 model and Elles was not the kind to challenge a majority in committee, in any case he genuinely doubted the future of the tank except as a slow, heavily-armoured machine to accompany the infantry. But it had to be made cheaply.

Martel, who had seen the massed BT and light tanks in Russia in 1936, thought that there was the need for a medium 'with 25mm armour and a speed of 25 mph'. Hobart wanted a medium tank as the cornerstone of the tank brigades which would be the hitting element in the forthcoming Armoured Divisions. Talk of the actual hardware required was merely academic, however, in the long-prevailing atmosphere of financial stringency. Although the Ten Year Rule had been abrogated in 1932 this had done anything but release a flood of money for tank construction, and even after 1936, when the Treasury loosened the purse strings, the Chamberlain Government's policy of appeasement overlay every decision and put a hidden brake on rearmament.

Another joker was the state of British industry which, in 1935, was far better adapted to producing wheeled vehicles of basically civilian design than specialized tracked vehicles for which no large-scale production facilities existed. To make tanks in quantity would demand enormous capital outlay and this was a factor in Elles's considerations. Eventually Elles had his way over the cheap infantry tank and kept priority low on the mediums since they would be expensive and 'a long shot'. By the time Elles had been removed from office in 1938 the damage had been done, for it takes a long time to design a tank and set up production facilities—as the Germans were discovering.

The prototype of the first new British medium, decided in 1936, was not coming into production until 1939—something like a year behind the German Mark IIIs and IVs. The British had lost their lead and in September 1939 could raise but a few regiments of unbattleworthy light tanks and a single battalion of Elles's infantry tanks to accompany an Expeditionary Force to France. Not only were the British short in quantity, they were poor in quality too.

France, on paper, looked extremely strong. The Maginot Line bolstered confidence even if it terminated at the Ardennes and left the frontier with Belgium practically undefended, covered by a tenuous string of pill-boxes then hardly under construction. The quantity and quality of the French tanks were formidable compared with Germany's, however. In May 1940 there would be more than 3,000 machines well armed and better protected than the German tanks, not one of which had armour more than 30mm thick. True, most French tanks were slower than those of their future opponents and their operational range was short, but this simply complied with the strict infantry support role to which they were committed. Even so, the 400-plus 20-ton Somua tanks, to be found mostly in the DLMs, possessed several characteristics of a good cruiser tank.

The basic defects in the French tank forces could be found not so much in their machines as with their organization and in the spirit engendered by an out-moded system. In 1938 no additions had been made to the three DLMs, which went on being restricted to the unambitious roles of a screening force, plus, in favourable circumstances (undefined), the pursuit. Specifically they were not to be used to break a front, to concentrate to counter a penetration or to raid deeply and independently as might the Panzer divisions and their level of training and system of communications reflected this official doctrine. They would seek strength and offer weakness to it; they could not transmit messages when on the move. In effect and outlook they were an adolescent force without sense of parental direction or outward seeking ambition.

A sort of godfather, Colonel Charles de Gaulle would have made more and had more of them as he described in his book, *Vers l'Armée de métier*, published in 1934. But de Gaulle was isolated by party political considerations in an Army that was riddled by politics. Some interpreted his demand for an armoured élite as undermining the morale of the remainder of the Army; others regarded it as a threat to the security of the Republic. There was intense opposition to de Gaulle and yet, indirectly, he was supported in high places by no less a personage than General Gamelin, the President of the Army Council.

After Germany had remilitarized the Rhineland in 1936 Gamelin had pleaded: 'We do not have the instrument of attack [as was French policy again]. . . . We need an instrument stronger than the Panzer division.' He was overborne in Council and the Minister for War (a soldier by training), putting on his political hat, declaimed: '. . . when we have lavished so much effort in building a fortified barrier, who could believe us foolish enough to sally out in front . . . in search of heaven knows what adventure?' He forgot that offensive operations might include the counter-attack of penetrations of the fortified barrier, and discounted the possibility of French forces having to move north to succour Belgium and Holland.

Then Chauvineau chimed in with carefully selected historical passages in support of his contention that the continuous line of defence was omnipotent. Forgetting the less palatable lessons of 1918—those occasions when infantry had wilted in the midst of an armoured affray—he stipulated that, 'like little mice which ran into their holes when threatened', infantry could evade tanks by taking cover and waiting until the passing monsters could be taken in rear. He seems to have overlooked French doctrine demanding that tanks ought to be closely accompanied by infantry who, in attack, could claw the mice out of their holes. When Chauvineau claimed that 'strong nerves and good discipline' were good anti-tank weapons he certainly came closer to a solution, providing he equated it with Ludendorff's unavailing exhortations of a similar kind in 1918 and then linked it with the detectable decline of French morale in 1938. For unhappily thoughts of aggressive action could not later be implanted in the main body of an army, whose will was rotting.

Annually Gamelin returned to the charge. In 1937 when it became known that Germany was to build a western defensive barrier—the Siegfried Line—he asked 'whether it is better to group with the general reserves the battalions of heavy tanks [the tough Char Bs] already existing or to be formed, or to bring them together in a large unit'—and the Army Council deferred the matter for study and thereby, inadvertently, did nothing. 'Inadvertent' it was: the French General Staff had proliferated into such a beautifully balanced, headless bureaucracy that by giving almost equal credence to every conceivable point of view it automatically cancelled any new controversial proposal put to it. It was almost proof against implementing a command decision. After the Sudetenland crisis in September 1938, the Army Council at last agreed in principle to create two armoured divisions, but the staff system was unable to settle on their composition and a year later when war broke out nothing had been done.

Russia, Hitler's preordained opponent in the east, looked the toughest opposition of all and stood last on Germany's list of victims. On paper the Russian Army, with its mass of tanks and artillery, appeared formidable and its performance in Spain was not beneath contempt. Yet since 1937 there had been vicious purges of the officer corps and so it could be argued that, with the elimination of the Army's educated élite and by the addition of fear and uncertainty in the hearts and minds of the survivors, the psychology and prowess of the fighting men would be undermined.

By her own choice Russia remained an enigma, regarded by the German generals of 1939 as an opponent better contained than attacked. The greatest imponderable to the Germans simply remained the question as to whether the psychological effect of the new weapons could compensate for their deficiency in numbers. Would fast-moving modern forces pursue the slower old-fashioned armies to comprehensive destruction? Would the impact of massed tank and air attacks overwhelm the British and French (who *never* before had to withstand massed tank attacks on the Amiens model) as they had overwhelmed the Germans in August and September 1918, or would they resist with asperity as had the Germans in October 1918? Would Western infantry hunt tanks with the same enthusiasm as had the Moors in Spain? These were fundamental questions Germany had to answer if she gambled on war with Poland. If the new weapons made an initially poor showing (*complete* failure against so weak an enemy as Poland was most unlikely) Hitler's chances of extending his conquests would be nullified to the benefit of all his neighbours and, possibly, to Germany herself. If they crushed Poland in a short campaign and demonstrated every conceivable military virtue, then Hitler's ambitions would be irresistible. In either case the danger of British and French involvement with the onset of another world war was appalling. For that reason both abject failure and glittering success were frightening, for with failure the subjugation of Germany by hostile Powers might be assumed and after success a long, all-consuming struggle which must eventually engulf Germany would be assured.

Small wonder that the main body of German generals doubted the wisdom of gambling on war in 1939, particularly since the armed forces would not reach their optimum strength until 1941. As Guderian wrote on the eve of war, 'We did not go light-heartedly to war and there was not one general who would not have advocated peace'. There is more than a sneaking suspicion, however, that the tank generals, with Guderian at their head, had an insatiable curiosity to justify themselves and see how their creation would work out in practice. The mere existence of untried powerful tank forces was a contributory cause of war.

Chapter 10

THE DESTRUCTION OF POLAND

The strategy shaping the German invasion of Poland epitomized the mixed feelings of their General Staff by making both conventional and unconventional approaches to battle. The direction of the main thrusts were entirely conventional in principle —in the north convergent thrusts from Germany and East Prussia to eliminate the Polish Corridor; in the centre the preponderant lunge by two armies striking at Warsaw, the political heart of the country; and in the south the flank drive by a single army through the Carpathian range into Galicia. In accordance with long-standing German practice every ounce was extracted from surprise—the propaganda war of nerves, the unannounced invasion before Polish mobilization was complete, the use of overwhelming force against critical but weakened sectors and the ruthless exploitation of immense territorial spaces neighbouring a long frontier which the Poles loyally attempted to guard by a linear strategy.

Unconventional, and yet foretold by Guderian's published opinions, the Panzer divisions were frequently concentrated and at the tip of each break-in and advance, while the Light and Motorized Infantry divisions were in close attendance. Tanks formed the sharp point of deep wedges: infantry divisions expanded the initial puncture at the base, and always there were waves of medium and dive bombers striking far and wide at communications, or closer in at fortifications. In fact the most surprising facet of the so-called *Blitzkrieg* was to be the precise selection of thrust lines by individual tank formations. Thus von Thoma, commanding the tank brigade in the 2nd Panzer Division in the Carpathians, wrote: 'I was ordered to advance on the Jablunka Pass, but suggested instead that the motorized [infantry] brigade should be sent there while I carried out . . . a flanking move—through thick woods and over the ridge. On descending into the valley I arrived in a village to find the people all going to church. How astonished they were to see my tanks appearing! I had turned the enemy's defences without losing a single tank—after a night march of fifty miles.' Thereafter the southern prong of the German trident pushed almost uninterruptedly deep into Galicia, with 2nd and 5th Panzer Divisions well in the lead, and were instrumental in encircling the Polish High Command after it had moved into Lvov.

In the extreme north Guderian's XIX Corps, heading Fourth Army towards East Prussia, fell into far heavier close fighting because it was pitted against strong Polish fortifications guarding the corridor. Guderian's account is an intimate story of battle as seen from his armoured command vehicle moving in the forefront of the advance of 3rd Panzer, 2nd and 20th Motorized Divisions. It is also a reiteration of minor internal crises caused by inexperience among his men. 'Unfortunately the heavy artillery of the 3rd Panzer Division felt compelled to fire into the mist, despite having received precise orders not to do so;' as a result Guderian was 'bracketed' and his driver ditched the command vehicle. Around Gross-Klonia '...where the mist suddenly lifted, and the leading tanks suddenly found themselves face to face with Polish defensive positions, the Polish anti-tank gunners scored many direct hits'. And later when the advance was held up on the River Brahe and the commander of 6th Panzer Regiment took advantage of an order from the Army commander to take a rest: 'I walked angrily away and tried to decide what measures I should take to improve this.' Going to a bridge which remained crossable he discovered that nobody was there to take the lead—although staff officers were busy in confabulation while the opposing sides shot indiscriminately across the water. Organizing a swift infantry assault in rubber boats where enemy fire was non-existent Guderian then '...ordered the tanks over the bridge. They took the Polish bicycle company ...prisoner. Casualties were negligible.'

Everywhere, nevertheless, the Poles were fighting with the desperation of a people who recognized sheer survival as their war aim—the most compelling of all incentives to battle. They fought an historical oppressor with fervour and had to be prised out of almost every strongly fortified zone. Upon them the dive-bombing had only a marginal effect, striking terror as, at first, it did into the uninitiated, but causing far more damage to the 'soft' lines of communication than it could to 'hard', pinpoint targets at the front. The bombing was not, therefore, conclusive in its own right. For decisive effect it depended on a quick follow-up by ground forces—above all by tanks. For instance, in East Prussia, close to the Corridor where no tanks were committed at all, the Poles repulsed the German infantry assault with telling finality, but farther east, towards Mlava, the front was broken peremptorily by a tank spearhead.

Guderian concentrated his attention on eliminating nervousness and instilling confidence in young men who were in action for the first time (informed by 2nd Motorized Division that they were compelled to withdraw when threatened by cavalry 'I was speechless for a moment'). He sought ways to avoid direct opposition via unguarded sectors in the Polish line—sectors left virtually unguarded because the Poles believed them impassable to tanks, but he had to fight almost as hard to maintain petrol supplies when the tanks ran out of fuel on 2 September and the lorries had to be escorted to the tanks.

Instead of advancing through open country towards Bydgoszez, Guderian steered north through the Tuchola Forest and here 'the Polish Pomovska Cavalry Brigade . . . had charged [our tanks] with swords and lances and had suffered tremendous losses'. He goes on to recount the overrunning of artillery ('only two of its guns managed to fire at all'), the heavy Polish infantry losses, the capture of supply and bridging columns and the speedy disruption of the opposition as the battle of the Corridor rose to its climax.

Meanwhile the heavy blow by Eighth and Tenth Armies towards Warsaw had fallen with exemplary speed, directed by Army Group South's General von Rundstedt and his brilliant Chief-of-Staff, General von Manstein. They unreservedly embraced the doctrine of attack against weakness followed by ruthless exploitation in depth, and with two Panzer and three Light divisions as the spearhead of Tenth Army were able to deliver an irresistible punch through country left practically defenceless to tanks because, to the Poles, it was not of the traditionally recognized 'tank kind'.

While giving the air forces full credit for their contribution to the victory, both Manstein and Guderian were discriminating in their praise. Thus Manstein recorded that 'What decided the battles . . . was the almost complete elimination of the enemy's air force and the crippling of his staff communications and transport network by the effective attacks of our Luftwaffe'—in other words the stroke to brain but not to the body. And Guderian in answer to Hitler's question, 'Our dive-bombers did that?' as they passed a smashed artillery regiment replied, unhesitatingly, 'No, our Panzers!'

At any rate, by 6 September, Eighth and Tenth Armies were at large in the Polish Plain, preparing to meet the one remaining threat of a counter-attack from the north in the vicinity of Kutno, and sending 4th Panzer Division straight at Warsaw. Thousands of Poles were cut off and had yet to be herded in. The Panzer divisions in the lead had attracted most resistance and drawn the Polish Tank Brigade into combat and destruction—yet their advance had hardly been impeded, partly because the tanks had deflected enemy opposition from the infantry. The crisis arrived on 9 September. That day the Poles were staging a major counter-stroke along the River Bzura against the northern flank of Rundstedt's drive on Warsaw. That day too 4th Panzer Division became bitterly involved in the capital's suburbs, while Guderian, who had repositioned his corps through East Prussia in a matter of hours to place it speedily on the left of the penetration already effected near Mlava, was poised to hurtle south against Brest Litovsk in Warsaw's rear.

Now the overruling strengths and abiding weaknesses of tank forces were made plain. In Warsaw Staff Sergeant Ziegler, in a light Mark II tank, led his company HQ in action. Shots peppered the armour, but Ziegler, negotiating a minefield, led the advance through hedges, gardens and summer houses into the suburban streets. At first the Poles ran until suddenly Ziegler found himself alone, his gun jammed and a Pole in the act of hurling a grenade. A burst from the 20mm gun blew the Pole to bits, but the attack stalled, tanks were going up in flames and Ziegler was told by radio to take charge of the assault. He advanced again. A 75mm gun loosed off at 30 yards range—he fired back and the gun escaped. More tanks, including a Mark III, were in flames, smoke belched from 'candles' fastened to the backs of the tanks. Crewmen bailed out, fought on foot and then Polish fire intensified. Of 120 tanks engaged that day in street fighting no fewer than 57 were lost.

Slow at first to recognize the strength of the Polish counter-offensive against Eighth Army, Rundstedt's reaction when it came

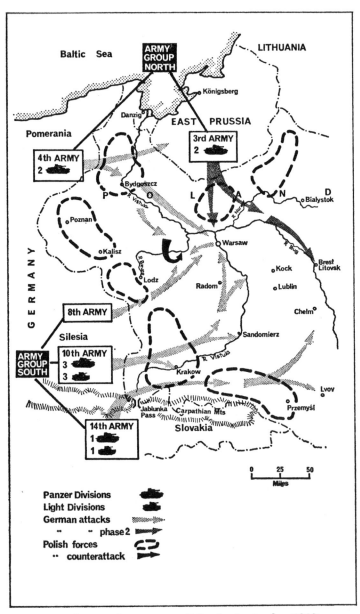

Map 7   Tank invasion in Poland – September 1939

was charged with significance. Resisting an orthodox request by Eighth Army for reinforcement by a Panzer corps to prevent a Polish breakthrough, Rundstedt and Manstein utilized the inherent speed and power of motorized units to swing Panzer and Light divisions back from Warsaw to take the Poles in flank and rear from the north and east. Moreover they took direct charge of operations themselves, thus reducing the number of command and signal links and hastening each phase of the operation. Such a mass of mobile forces was quickly assembled at the vital spot from far away that it became a simple matter to block each Polish attempt to slip through the net. Manstein was to write, 'The Battle of the Bzura was the largest [battle of encirclement] of its kind to date. It was not one which could be planned from the outset through penetration of the enemy front by powerful tank formations, but arose from counter-moves made on the German side when the enemy's own actions unexpectedly gave us our big opportunity'. Those few words describe to perfection the kind of flexible operation made possible by modern formations. The killing ground within the cordon of German forces marked the real grave of the Polish Army and by 15 September all resistance there had been rubbed out.

That same day Guderian had encircled Brest Litovsk. Grouping two Panzer and a motorized division in XIX Corps (the ideal combination by his reckoning) he had raced south on the 10th, skirting the main centres of Polish resistance, brushing aside isolated pockets and carving a narrow incision far to the east of Warsaw. There was local cut-and-thrust but the German movements were smoothly co-ordinated by Guderian riding with the leading tank units; the Poles were outpaced (several of their tanks were caught de-training in a siding), outmoded and, despite supreme bravery, out-fought.

This had been the strategic tank thrust in depth with extended flanks *par excellence*. The Russians' invasion of eastern Poland to link up with Guderian at Brest Litovsk merely took political advantage of a military accomplishment. Only Warsaw and one or two other pockets of resistance held out—but the arduous business of street-fighting had been shown as outside the scope of tanks.

In any case the tanks were urgently needed elsewhere, for although the French Army had made only a gesture of offensive action in the west to take pressure off the Poles, there was no saying what they might do once their mobilization was complete. Three weeks' hard motoring had left the Germans in a state of semi-dilapidation, however. Intensive maintenance was essential, not only by the crews but within the industrial base. It would be several weeks before Panzer divisions at strength could again go to war. Between victories the mechanical tools of victory, like the men, needed a pause for recuperation: this was immutable. That Hitler would interpret their pleas for time in which to effect repairs as excuses for evasion of action was perhaps no harder for the German tank leaders to swallow than a serious suggestion by the Army Command to increase the horsed cavalry and defer tank expansion, despite overwhelming evidence of victory by the tank arm and irrevocable proof of the horses' failure.

But what a victory it had been! German casualties had been a mere 40,000, including 8,000 dead and 217 tanks—and the casualties in the tank units had been strikingly low by comparisons with other units and their achievements. Polish losses were that of an entire Army of nearly 800,000 with all its equipment. A nation lay in ruins.

Hitler could now turn his attention to France and Britain—and with the greatest possible assurance too. Planning for an invasion of the West began in earnest, but first the mobile troops had to be put straight and the infantry reinforced. Mark II tanks were shown to be fit only for reconnaissance: Mark IIIs were battleworthy but, with only the 37mm, undergunned: Mark IV was the best tank available and it was for this machine in quantity which Guderian plumped. But industrial capacity, with top priority given to the Luftwaffe, was in no condition to meet his wishes—it was hard-pressed enough to supply sufficient spares to a tank force which had suffered 25 per cent breakdowns and in which maintenance had been inadequate.

New light 38t Czech tanks with a 37mm gun were coming into service and these, with increased production of German machines, could equip and turn the four Light divisions into Panzer divisions. Mark I tanks could also be taken progressively out of service and, on the insistence of infantrymen such as Manstein, reworked, given heavier guns on fixed armoured mountings and allocated to the infantry divisions as the foundation of their power in the close assault. For in attack the infantry divisions had been criticized for their paucity of initiative. Thus an infusion of armour was more than a victory by infantry in the struggle for possession of its own tanks—for the assault gun was merely a poor man's truncated tank—it was wholehearted recognition of the battlefield fact of life that without armour there was no cutting edge and little confidence.

There would be further organizational and tactical changes affecting the conduct of future battles too. Control of the battle by commanders moving and observing in the forefront of the battle would be insisted upon and provided for with better command vehicles and communication systems. Close air support of the leading troops would be studied in greater detail and improved systems for integration evolved, for at times the bombing had been inefficient and so ragged that friendly troops had suffered more than the enemy. There was much more besides—all drawn from lessons in a campaign which, by some, was rated an elaborate training exercise made more realistic by the spice of acute danger. Every phase of war, except for withdrawal, had been practised and a variety of organizational and tactical permutations put successively to the test against an enemy who was anything but timorous.

The German forces readying themselves for the invasion of western Europe would be more sinewy than those which had so recently won in the east—and the propaganda machines would make them seem far stronger than they actually were. But what of their future plans—would they be appropriate against so strong and yet so numerically vulnerable an organization as the German tank force? What, too, of the opposition? Would it be as fiery as in Poland and would it put its more numerous equipment to the most profitable use? Or would it collapse as it did in the April invasions of Denmark and Norway when but a few light tanks in critical places among the fjords and mountains had frequently dislodged what might otherwise have been staunch opposition?

Chapter 11

THE SHATTERING OF ILLUSIONS

There are many recognized strategic routes to the political nerve-centre of France—Paris—and by 1940 it was supposed that History had nothing further to teach on this subject. Invasions of the past had sometimes come from the east down narrow topographical corridors which are easily blocked: more often they had come from the north, where blocking is less easy since here the plains are broad and there is room for manoeuvre. Between the hereditary routes lie uplands and forests intersected by narrow lanes—militarily stagnant country avoided by grand armies of the past and which, to the majority of soldiers in 1940, seemed more inaccessible than ever to tank forces.

The Ardennes were classical examples of a strong natural, physical barrier backed by a sizeable water obstacle—the Meuse. Therefore, in theory, while the Maginot Line stopped up the eastern approaches to France the only remaining entrance was by way of the north, through Holland and Belgium. Thus thought and planned the Germans until Manstein, backed by Guderian, pointed out that the soft going and heavily built-up areas of the Low Countries were effective tank obstacles just as was the rest of the frontier to the east. Manstein therefore proposed a fundamental change—to make a feint in the north but to drive the main German blow through the Ardennes westward into the French plains—a complete strategic surprise aimed straight to the rear of the French armies holding the frontier—and to the heart of the nation.*

The complex story of the adoption of Manstein's well-reasoned plan in the teeth of conventional German military beliefs will not be discussed here. Suffice it to say that the original German

* Liddell Hart suggested in 1935 that the Ardennes could be easily penetrated by mechanized forces and it is said that Manstein got his idea from him. Yet Liddell Hart, writing in 1939, actually suggested that 'the Ardennes country east of the Meuse can be yielded to an invader without serious industrial or military risk'. It would be interesting to know which, if either, of these statements Manstein read and how he interpreted them.

plan, which itself bore only a superficial resemblance to the Schlieffen Plan of 1914, was rejected because it failed to aim at a total knockout and was, therefore, the antithesis of the modern conception of tank warfare. The new plan took a calculated risk, but was far from a gamble. The Ardennes and Meuse would be tackled by seven Panzer divisions unaided by other formations. After making the initial breach these divisions would shoot ahead towards the English Channel. In effect they would have taken a short cut to the best tank country. This was the apotheosis of tank warfare: it avoided frontal attacks on Allied strength and yet, by seizing vital territory, it promised to force the Allies into making hasty attacks on ground of German choosing (the fact that this only rarely occurred is beside the point) and once free in the open spaces of their enemy's rear the Germans could vary their direction of attack at will.

When the German armies simultaneously crossed the Dutch, Belgian and Luxembourg frontiers on 10 May 1940, with bombers and airborne troops preceding, it appeared for all the world as if Schlieffen had been reincarnated and that 1914 was to be repeated. Countering by historical reflex the Allies wheeled their mobile forces to the north, pivoting on the Ardennes and soon came the initial collision of tanks as two DLMs of General Prioux's Cavalry Corps, throwing out an extended, thin screen ahead of the French armies deploying on river lines in Belgium, met two Panzer divisions head on. Yet the tank-versus-tank battle did not develop as had been expected, for while French tanks deployed in shallow formation on a wide frontage the Germans chose to concentrate in depth on a narrow axis.

Near Gembloux strong German columns pierced a crust of Somuas and light tanks, the latter in armament a match for the Germans but tactically outmatched because of their unwieldy control system. Hence each penetration of the French line was abrupt and led to withdrawals of its flanks; dramatic changes of direction by units taught to rely on linear tactics could not be adopted overnight. Yet individually, General Prioux's crews fought quite well, though by the time they had been forced back to the main line of resistance under construction the men had lost heart: by using superior, controlled mobility the Panzers had hypnotized them. Not that the French leaders noticed nor understood. The premeditated task of screening had been accomplished and now the tanks could be relegated, under the infantry, as the main battle commenced. 'They have ... begun to dismember the Cavalry Corps,' complained Prioux on 14 May as his units were broken up and scattered in line as semi-mobile pill-boxes. Moreover, since they would never again be wholly reunited, dispersal evaporated the crews' last fighting spirit. Irrevocably the only French tank formation capable of matching a German Panzer corps had been destroyed by their adherence to an outmoded doctrine.

As the mobile Cavalry Corps dispersed, mobile warfare itself intensified. The seven Panzer divisions committed to the Ardennes, grouped in three separate Panzer corps—XIX under Guderian, XLI under Reinhardt and XV under Hoth—had threaded their way through the close country (with their infantry leading) and debouched across the Meuse on a 40-mile front on the morning of the 13th. Effortlessly they had brushed aside some Light Cavalry divisions screening the wooded areas (each actually containing a horsed brigade), had repaired demolitions and established orderly traffic control on the narrow lanes. Only a few low-quality French infantry divisions, without tanks, stood on the river line and such opposition as they could muster was likely to come only from their artillery, which was already desperately short of ammunition. But these guns were the main target of swarms of dive-bombers, and even if only a few were actually hit the terrorizing noise of an unknown weapon effectively neutralized the teams and stopped them firing during that critical period when the infantry bridgehead was being formed and as the work of ferrying tanks and building bridges began. By substituting dive-bombers for heavy artillery the Germans had relieved themselves of the administrative problem of moving and supplying a siege train, and had taken their enemy by surprise with the sheer speed of their movements.

Without a tank force of their own close to hand the French defenders of the Meuse stood footfast and gave up when encircled. All three DLMs had poured into Belgium and were committed to battle. There remained, in addition to those light tank units attached to some infantry divisions, four so-called armoured divisions (DCRs), the product of Gamelin's suggestions in 1936 but not created until the outcome of Poland no longer permitted bureaucratic delay. The equipment and philosophy of these divisions (only three of which had been fully assembled by May) were incompatible with their present task. Their Char B tanks were suitable for only short-ranged assaults at a measured tempo commanded by men whose mental processes were geared to the art of war as it had been in 1918. Also in Belgium behind the DLMs near Philippeville were 1st and 2nd DCR; 3rd was south of Sedan (and close to Guderian's break-in) while 4th (under de Gaulle—the first to demand armoured divisions and the last to be given command of one) was assembling away to the south.

All four DCRs moved to the sound of the battle but their contribution resembled *opera buffe*. Ordered to counter-attack General Rommel's 7th Panzer Division where it led XV Panzer Corps north of Dinant, 1st DCR ran out of petrol near the front and was overrun without making even a threatening gesture: abandoned tanks far outnumbered those destroyed in brief encounters. 'The French ceased fire and were fetched out of their tanks one by one by our men,' wrote Rommel. 'It being impossible to leave a guard, we took the undamaged tanks along with us in our column, still with their French drivers.' Caught, while detraining, 2nd DCR and its survivors were then dispersed to join the DLMs, spaced like a string of beads along the front. To 3rd DCR went the best chance to win glory for at Sedan on the 14th it was presented with a priceless opportunity to hit Guderian in flank when his corps veered westwards on its way to the Channel. But there was a complete absence of urgency in the French preparations: creaking battle drills to preclude a quickly launched attack even if the endemic shortage of fuel had been overcome at once; a trail of broken-down vehicles to reduce numbers in action, and, above all, palsied indecision at corps and divisional HQs which finally cancelled the attack and allowed this vital concentration of tanks to be dispersed like all the rest.

That left de Gaulle's 4th DCR struggling up, short of tanks and deficient of its infantry and artillery. 'I would attack next morning with whatever forces might reach me,' announced de Gaulle with the right spirit but in contradiction of the principle that armoured divisions should attack only when concentrated. De Gaulle staged his attack against Guderian's flank at Mont-cornet, but the latter dismissed the performance as all but comic: An enemy tank company which tried to enter the town from the south-west was taken prisoner.' Continuing to nip at Guderian's tail for a few days longer, de Gaulle only wasted his time; the battle had run out of French control and the ineffectuality of 4th DCR merely epitomized French operational failure as a whole.

In their advance to Abbeville, from 14 May to the 20th, the only crucial checks administered to the Germans came from their own indecision and worry in the highest echelons of command. The debate which preceded and ought to have been settled when Manstein's plan was finally accepted, revived and became prolonged when such unprecedented success created sinister fears of a French trap. The Germans could not believe that so experienced an opponent would succumb so easily. Manstein himself, in criticizing the original German plan, had written: 'One had no right to assume that such [French] leadership would be lacking, particularly in view of the reputation General Gamelin enjoyed with us.' In fact Gamelin had all but handed over conduct of the battle to the elderly and ailing General Georges, and Georges, on receiving news of Guderian's breakthrough at Sedan, had broken into tears. And when at last Gamelin intervened (far too late on the 19th, when Amiens was closely threatened) it was to preface his orders with 'Without wishing to interfere in the conduct of the battle . . .'. That day he was sacked and replaced by General Weygand.

So the German tanks enjoyed an almost free passage to the Channel, always moving by day and sometimes by night—XIX Panzer Corps at an average speed of 19 miles per day for seven days with a maximum of 56 miles on 20 May; Rommel's division averaged 13.75 miles per day including a spurt of 43 miles in one day and night—rates which would have been higher had not the German High Command fearfully but understandably imposed halts on the tanks to allow the much slower moving infantry divisions to catch up. To the Germans it was inconceivable that the French directing brain could die so suddenly—not even Guderian fully expected that—yet this was the logical product of tank warfare foretold by the handful of early enthusiastic thinkers in the 1920s.

Who now could not be impressed by the Panzer cavalcade rolling continuously westwards? Their battle drill was aimed at perpetual motion and their supply system was working like clockwork so that there were no fuel shortages—perhaps the greatest

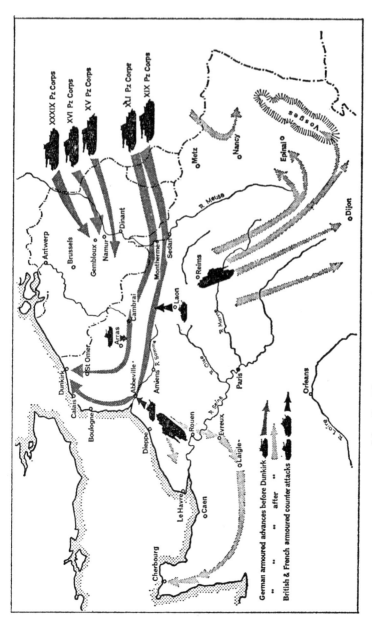

Map 8   The overrunning of France – 1940

XXXIX Pz Corps
XVI Pz Corps
XV Pz Corps
XLI Pz Corps
XIX Pz Corps

Antwerp
Brussels
Gembloux
Namur
Dinant
Metz
Nancy
Epinal
Vosges
Reims
Dijon
Montherme
Sedan
R. Meuse
Cambrai
Laon
Arras
St Omer
Dunkirk
Calais
Boulogne
Abbeville
Amiens   R. Somme
R. Oise
R. Marne
Paris
R. Seine
Dieppe
Rouen
Evreux
Laigle
Le Havre
Caen
Cherbourg
Orleans
R. Loire

German armoured advances before Dunkirk.
     "   "   "   after   "
British & French armoured counter attacks

triumph of all. First would appear armoured cars and motor-cyclists cautiously probing for opposition—dashing full speed for cover when fired upon and then reporting back all they could see. Next light tanks, helped forward by mediums with their bigger gun, would drive up and open fire while reserve tank sub-units tried to find ways round the flank, either to encircle the foe or plunge yet deeper into enemy territory.

If the opposition proved too strong, or could not be bypassed, more formal yet equally fluent measures would be taken. A local *ad hoc* battle group would assemble under command either of a tank or an infantry leader. Orders, endorsed and supplemented by the divisional commander, who was likely to arrive at first sign of a hold-up, would put a routine procedure into operation, with artillery unlimbering from prime movers and firing ranging shots, and infantry driving up to debus behind cover before joining the tanks. Nearby a Luftwaffe officer would be talking on the radio to guide Stuka dive-bombers like gannets on to their prey below. The fire plan from artillery, tanks, mortars and machine guns would build up, and as it reached a crescendo the leading wave of tanks would drive forward to break through the enemy lines and head for his artillery area. Meanwhile the second wave, composed of tanks and infantry, would methodically com-plete the crushing of the main front position. And if the situation was critical Heinz Guderian or his like might appear to urge on the laggards with a few curt words, or to praise high initiative—but chiefly to assess the situation and arrange supplementary movements to keep his corps' momentum going.

In France the German fighting men needed less urging than in Poland. Not only was the opposition of a lower calibre but the misfits in command had been weeded out and their successors imbued with the need—and economic good sense—for constant movement. When tanks and infantry kept moving in har-monious fluency the prospects of heavy opposition were reduced: taking quick risks reduced casualties in the long run. We detect this in Rommel's account of breaking the Maginot Line pill-box extension at Clairfayts and can picture his tanks moving forward, all guns firing, in the dusk, accompanied only by a few motor-cycle infantry because the lorried infantry had failed to keep up.

More than his contemporaries Rommel had a tendency to separate tanks from infantry—perhaps because he was an

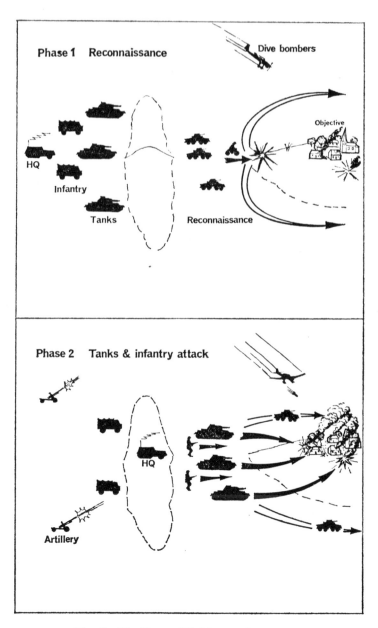

Map 9   The Panzer Division on the rampage

infantryman himself but more likely because he had the gift of smelling victory. Instinctively he detected the magnitude of the French collapse and took what might otherwise have been outrageous risks, but travelling in the forefront of battle he could weigh the chances better than another general at the end of a telephone miles in rear. This *coup d'oeil* was the true art of tank warfare as it had been with the great cavalry leaders of old.

Once Rommel did cut it rather fine—but then it was the only occasion when shock brought a temporary halt to all German progress. It happened on 21 May when British Matilda and French Somua tanks, swinging south from Arras as part of a reconnaissance in force, caught Rommel's infantry unescorted: his tanks, as usual, were miles ahead and out of touch. This encounter battle was saved for the Germans only by their 105mm field artillery, helped by 88mm dual purpose anti-aircraft guns knocking out Matildas after the 37mm anti-tank guns had utterly failed to penetrate the Matilda's thick armour. Significantly, however, when the less well protected German tanks reversed course to come to their infantry's assistance they lost more than 20 tanks—not against Allied tanks but against British 40mm anti-tank guns spread out to screen the flank of the British thrust. Arras witnessed one of those rare occasions when the Germans were forced into an attack against an enemy holding ground of his own choosing. Not only were the results strategically salutary, they also showed that decisions by shock tactics were not the prerogative of one side alone.

Defeat in the north caused the Allies to withdraw to Dunkirk in the hope of an evacuation by sea. But in victory the Germans renounced a fleeting chance to enter Dunkirk unopposed because the High Command, echoed by Hitler, again entertained reasoned doubts of their tank force's ability and endurance. The local setback at Arras (magnified in seriousness by the shock implied in Rommel's initial reports), when linked in mind to several stiff encounters with the British garrisons at Boulogne and Calais, was one cause for concern: high tank losses and 30 per cent of the force out of action (as many by breakdown as enemy action) were an even greater worry, particularly since the residue of France had yet to be conquered and the built-up areas in northern France and Belgium might exact an even heavier toll. The Panzer divisions were called off and the taking of Dunkirk left to the rest of the armed forces and, more particularly, the Luftwaffe. The Luftwaffe then demonstrated, by its failure to stop the evacuation, that air power in land warfare was only a complementary weapon to land forces—not a decisive weapon on its own.

On 24 May, when all eyes were riveted on Dunkirk and the German armour was mostly engaged on the northern flank of the corridor it had driven to the sea, Allied armour launched a single formal combined attack, with infantry, against a German bridgehead south of the Somme near Abbeville. Once more, however, tanks were pitted against only guns—the lightly armoured cruiser and light tanks of the British 1st Armoured Division advancing side by side with the heavier tanks of de Gaulle's 4th DCR in an attempt to eliminate the bridgehead before lunging northward. Even if, as a German wrote, 'a profound terror of the tanks had got into the bones of our soldiers . . .', this did not deter them resisting and causing the Allied tanks severe losses. In this set-piece attack, the sort in which the French were supposed to be expert, co-operation between tanks, artillery and infantry was hesitant—that is, the French infantry stopped once opposition appeared and their sparse artillery failed to give detailed support to the tanks.

Predictably the lightly armoured British cruiser and light tanks, highly vulnerable in such an obviously direct attack against unshaken enemy guns, suffered far more than the better protected French tanks. The plan had everything wrong with it and when the attack stalled, well short of the objective, this was taken by the French as another excuse to disperse the tanks into a cordon with the hope of shoring up a failing infantry defence.

Nothing could hold the Germans now. After patching up their tanks and replacing their losses they roared southward on 5 June without fear of meeting an Allied counter-force. Frenchmen in isolated 'hedgehogs' might hold on momentarily, but without a mobile reserve to dominate the gaps in between they were doomed to encirclement and destruction. Without armour in mobile warfare there was no salvation.

Soon the war in France would fizzle out and the Germans could preen themselves on having subjugated three highly industrialized countries—Holland, Belgium and France—along with the most vaunted military machine in the West. What was more important, they had done it with numerically inferior forces —compensating for that inferiority only by prowess. It had cost only 156,000 killed, wounded and missing in six weeks' fighting— a minute fraction of what had been suffered in the previous war for advances in a few days of only a few thousand yards. As a bonus of immeasurable importance was the booty—mountains of equipment, much of which could be turned to the advantage of the tank forces, and access to the facilities and stockpiles of a great manufacturing empire to help increase the meagre mechanical content of the Panzer and Infantry divisions. Soon, for instance, French tank chassis would be turned into self-propelled assault guns to bolster the German infantry divisions, while the supply echelons would be strengthened by a mass of captured lorries.

All of this was frightening enough to the British as they sheltered in their island and prepared to go it alone. More shattering to some was the destruction of so many illusions in so short a time. Warfare had entered a new epoch, understood by the Germans and, in 1940, the Germans alone.

The German tank forces had practised just about every manoeuvre in the book and their infantry, in suffering tank attacks themselves, had, except for the notable exception at Arras, withstood the strain. German conventional artillery had also done well although the trend to hand over much of its traditional function to bombers and tanks could be seen as a decline which, when accelerated, would have an important bearing on the future. The German gunners, eager to share the Panzers' glory, seized on armoured assault guns as a means of deploying artillery pieces in the lead to apply direct fire against the enemy; from that moment indirect methods and means of concentrating massed fire of many batteries fell into disrepute.

British infantry, though hardly ever exposed to massed German tank attacks, had come to depend more on artillery than tanks, partly because so few of the latter were ever available. Of large-scale tank-versus-tank battles there had been none of consequence—not even the screening action by the French DLMs against the Panzer divisions at Gembloux could be rated as a large-scale tank battle, while the actions at Arras and Abbeville had been almost entirely in the nature of tank-versus-gun combat. Nevertheless the invulnerability of the Char Bs and Matildas against 37mm guns, while convincing the Germans that they must re-equip with nothing less than a calibre of 50mm, both on field mountings and in tanks, led to a speeding-up of the gun-versus-armour race in which the British, also impressed by harsh experience, joined. British post-battle reports demanded:

1. Tank armour of between 40 and 80mm and a bigger gun of 57mm—measures which were slow to appear in the field because of production problems in the aftermath of Dunkirk, problems demanding the making of great quantities of existing types instead of bringing fewer new ones into use later.
2. Improved reliability—no less than 75 per cent of their tanks had been lost by mechanical failure.
3. A higher road speed so that tanks could be switched more quickly from one front to another.
4. An end to light tanks. Time and again these machines had fought at a gross disadvantage, being neither tough enough to deflect 37mm shot nor armed with a gun which could kill gun crews sheltering behind their shields. The idea of 'establishing fire positions close to the front' was proven as sheer suicide. The chances of moving fast in machines of inherently bad cross-country performance were negligible.

There was much else besides—insistence for control of tanks in battle by experts to eliminate abuse of machines by the uninitiated, such as occurred when the British Matildas were sent to run 300 abortive miles from one unimportant location to another in Belgium, and becoming worn out before being committed to battle in France. This sort of thing the Germans had avoided by putting their tanks in specialized divisions.

For all the intensity of their parochial concern, the British entered a backwater in tank warfare in the summer of 1940. There was scattered jousting with the Italians on the frontier of Egypt, but apart from that the war on land had virtually come to an end. The Luftwaffe tried to soften up Britain as the prerequisite for an invasion which never came, and in Germany the silence was broken mainly by celebration parades. But the mind of the Army was being turned stealthily and somewhat unwillingly in preparation for Hitler's next great venture—the invasion of Russia, for which he had opted as July ran out. From now on German tank forces would evolve at the bidding of a theatre of operations which would dominate the war in all its aspects. Great changes would be made in the German tank arm—but always because of Eastern Front demands: the other fronts would merely react in tune with the Russian front's lead.

The balance of world forces had been completely upset by the elimination of France. Russia waited in uncertainty. And, across the Atlantic, the American people also began anxiously to stir, their desire to stay uncommitted to Europe still strong and unsympathetic to President Roosevelt's realization, from as far back as 1938, that Germany and not Japan would be the principal threat. Roosevelt had already, in 1938, begun seriously to allocate increased funds to rearmament as part of his programme to reduce unemployment, but little material gain was yet to be seen. In 1940 the American Army possessed only 28 new tanks — 10 mediums and 18 lights—and already those were obsolescent. As Robert Grow, a cavalry officer, wrote in his diary, 'Things seem to be popping'—but that he wrote after ten lean years when American armour had progressed only gradually under conditions of isolation.

Chapter 12

AMERICA IN THE DOLDRUMS

The reasons for America's tank forces—indeed for her entire Army—remaining at a low ebb for so many years stemmed not simply from a policy of national isolation but, in addition, from the debilitating effects induced by the clash of branch rivalries and jealousies. It was true that the perennial money famine sentenced her soldiers to make do with obsolete equipment for years, and it is possible that this penurious environment stimulated the rivalry between sectional interests to seize every available crumb from the financial cake—but none of these entirely explained the fundamental rivalries which embittered relations between cavalry and infantry as to who should have tanks, and how they were to be used.

Sharp divisions appeared when the second mechanized force was raised in 1930, and at the root may have been the challenge by the Chief of Staff, General Summersall, in his pronouncement that 'the tank will become a weapon exercising offensive power in its own right'. This smacked of an independent policy for armour and seemed to challenge the infantry's congressional inheritance of the tanks. Infantry suspicions were then sharpened by intense cavalry interest in tanks when, in Washington, that ardent cavalryman, Chaffee, as head of the Troop Training Section, turned every tank development he could the cavalry way, regardless of how often the rules of Congress were revoked.

Paradoxically the 1930 force achieved little more than its predecessor because, when General MacArthur became Chief of Staff in November, he initiated studies which convinced him that, although tanks were the 'essence of mobility' and therefore within the traditional role of cavalry, the entire army, particularly the cavalry, should mechanize as far as possible. That was the rub, for by spreading the demand across the entire service no one branch could make outstanding progress. In any case, in the following year, when faced by a crippling shortage of funds and the choice of either increasing men's pay to raise the strength of the Army from its nadir, or to buy new tanks, MacArthur put men before machines.

In retrospect MacArthur's part in mechanization is enigmatic. He did not fight nearly as hard for tanks as he later made out, while his overall policy of 'gradualness', allied to a cavalry bias, made bitter the nascent inter-branch disputes for a decade hence. The cavalry were officially encouraged to circumvent Congress and the infantry by subterfuge: if they could not have tanks they would adopt the same machine and call it a 'combat car'. The Chief of Infantry, however, ingeniously defended his rights by appealing to cavalry emotions, suggesting that, if they swapped their horses for machines, it 'would be an irretrievable loss to the Army'—a sentiment which was far from lost on emotional cavalrymen. The Chief of Cavalry compromized, saying he was prepared to mix tanks with horses—seeing operational uses for both. To this the horse-loving cavalryman Robert Grow, who was already mixed up with mechanization, retorted (in his diary): 'You can't dig a fox-hole for a horse.'

Quite by chance the cavalry and infantry reached agreement on the kind of combat car or tank (call it what you will) they needed—and much to the relief of the Ordnance Department and Tank Board since it simplified their never-ending struggle to stretch dollars further than they could reasonably be expected to go. *They* had put their money on a light tank of only 8½ tons armed with machine-guns, but the appearance of Christie's fast tank, and the welcome given it by the members of the Tank Board, upset Ordnance. The outcome, they knew, would be a 15-ton vehicle costing $34,000—a far cry from financial reality in 1931.

In the event the cavalry, with tactical thoughts centred on reconnaissance and deep raiding, and the infantry, believing in a mass of small vehicles dispensing heavy machine-gun fire in support of men on foot, were as one in adopting the light tank armed only with machine-guns, while Christie's habitual intransigence in making a deal gradually lost him popular support. But once it was ordained that American tanks were to do without cannon it became necessary to carry these heavier weapons on another kind of tracked vehicle to enable artillery units to remain in touch with the mobile battle. This introduced a third branch-contender in the search for additional money. Yet between

1925 and 1939 only $60,000 could be spent on tank development at a time when Ordnance and others were insisting on expensive mechanical perfection. Small wonder that so little was produced.

Again MacArthur's purist views were crucial. 'Too often in the past,' he stated, 'organization has been attempted from the standpoint of equipment rather than from the standpoint of missions assigned.' From the standpoint of Army unification such a policy was admirable, but it flew in the face of the irrevocable tendency of traditional arms to stick to traditional methods and postulations. Those who hoped the tank might act as a unifying influence would be disappointed by General Croft, the new Director of Infantry, when in 1933 he remarked: 'Personally I doubt very much if in the next war tanks will be able to go charging about the battlefield in the face of anti-tank weapons ... the success of tanks in battle will be ... in co-operation with infantry.' Cavalry experiments seemed to indicate a middle path. Chaffee might demand that cavalry tanks should fight, but his cavalryman's eye was focused more on sweeping rides in the mode of Jeb Stuart.

Of course each side was close to the right track though slightly off centre and blinded by their prejudices. In war tanks actually became maids of all work—fighting alongside other arms one moment and dashing off on raids the next. It was hoped the arms branches might shelve their differences and, when engaged side by side in actual combat, discover that each owed the others a living.

Chaffee tried to be a liberalizing influence, free from preconception and eager to study every aspect of the new art—particularly the British approach. 'He loaded me down with a terrible list of things he wanted to know from over there,' wrote a colleague—but, of course, he also studied the reports of all military attachés in Russia, Germany, France and Italy. Not all Chaffee's compatriots were as thorough—Grow admitting that he never read Fuller or Liddell Hart at all: 'I was too busy doing other things.'

Throughout the thirties experiment followed experiment to a shrill chorus of dissent between the branches. But it was the cavalry who took the lead in practice, largely because Chaffee, then Chief of Budget and Legislative Planning of the War Department, deftly transferred spare funds to the aid of mechanized cavalry, be it for new equipment, training areas or living accommodation. Gradually more horsed regiments were turned over to vehicles—though not all of them necessarily with tanks—for each experiment, studied in context with reports from Europe, impressed the need for tanks to be closely co-ordinated with mounted infantry and artillery using cross-country vehicles with performances compatible with tanks. Gradually half-tracked carriers began to find favour with the ancillary arms: empirically an organization which was basically home-spun grew up. It was by no means as overwhelmed by German practice as some historians have suggested.

If 1938 was the year in which Roosevelt, as Commander-in-Chief, began to push the Armed Services into the future, it was also the year when a new Chief of Cavalry tried to put time into reverse. General Herr was a man of stubborn conviction with his mind obstinately closed to innovation. Almost his first act upon taking office was to attempt the reintroduction of the sabre, which had been disposed of in 1934. This was at least direct, unlike some other dealings of his at the time Poland fell. On 21 September 1939, to quote Grow's diary, 'He is going all the way in mechanization as being the best thing for cavalry. He wants one and, if possible, two "Panzer" divisions.' What he would not do was form those divisions at the expense of horsemen when manpower was at a premium and the cavalry branch seemed in peril. 'Not one horse will I give up,' was Herr's favourite cry, and so there could be no change while he presided.

Faced with double talk of this kind, Chaffee had at last to resort to measures which he had hoped, despite many warnings, to avoid. In 1931, Colonel van Voorhis, the Mechanized Force Commander, had warned how mechanization progress would be disrupted by branch jealousies. In 1937 General Craig, the Chief of Staff, had concluded that if the infantry and cavalry could not work harmoniously towards mechanization he would 'inaugurate a mechanized force without regard to arm of service in order to keep abreast of current developments'. His staff reported: 'Experience [in the Spanish Civil War and the 1936 Second Army Manoeuvres] has shown that the older arms will fight in the traditional way. . . .'

Briefly the factions drew back, but soon they were at it again, neither side being ready to throw their differences into the melting pot for the Army's sake. In practice the process of modernization continued to go the cavalry's way because Chaffee was a clever manipulator of men and money. Moreover he was being forced, by a growing popular movement in the Army, to take a stand on the side of creating a new arm of the service—an Armored Corps. By 1939, in fact, he had finally decided that this was the only way to solve the dilemma and from that moment onward he made sure that the 7th Mechanized Brigade, which by long trials possessed most experience of independent tank work, should concentrate on the independent role and become the cadre of the future corps.

A new Chief of Staff, General George Marshall, took office shortly before Germany invaded Poland. Among the most progressive and open-minded officers of his generation, Marshall had much more than the question of tank doctrine to solve if America was to take a leading place in world affairs—as Roosevelt by now intended. The solution of the tank controversy as to who did what may, in fact, have been one of his easier decisions since Chaffee had it almost ready-made and with strong outside support.

Early in 1940 Marshall ordered the formation of an experimental armoured division by combining mechanized cavalry and infantry—and these would be tried out in exercises in Louisiana in May. These exercises, six years in arrears of the European armies, brought together much more than the amalgamation of elements for a new division—they also prompted the gathering in a basement of the High School in Alexandria of Chaffee and other officers, including Brett and Patton, who were now convinced that only by creating a new arm, independent of the old arms, could a genuine armoured force on European lines be founded. The Louisiana Exercise rolled on—'the best controlled large manoeuvres which I have attended', wrote Chaffee, although it has to be mentioned that the emphasis could be only on movement without simulation of actual combat—and with so large an area left open for manoeuvre with few constraints applied, mobility was somewhat exaggerated.

Nevertheless this exercise provided the basic data for all future American tank battle drills: in years to come British officers were to be mystified by hearing officers of the 1st US Armored Division quoting the Louisiana Exercise rather as others quoted from the Bible. Yet Chaffee had by no means entirely forgotten the combat side of a fighting formation's mission. He demanded infantry half-tracked carriers 'to transport as many men and infantry weapons to battle as can be crowded above the axles'. And he saw the need for 'the inclusion of a proportion of medium tanks and the inclusion of the present 75mm self-propelled howitzer in the cavalry combat-car or tank elements of the armoured brigade of the armoured division'. One day a 75mm gun would be standard equipment in the latest American medium tank.

The results of this exercise and the resolution by the tank leaders to seek an independent Armored Branch reached Marshall as the German Panzer divisions were nearing Dunkirk. His dogmatic decision in Chaffee's favour was a foregone conclusion, yet taken in dignity. On 10 June the old guard were given their last chance to kick in defence of the old order. But the future was overbearing. 'Speed is essential,' said Chaffee—and in the end, for the sake of unity in the future, an agreed decision to support Marshall was passed. On the surface it looked most democratic.

The new arm came officially into being on 10 July. To begin with there were to be two armoured divisions—the first to be composed of the existing cavalry and infantry mechanized units, artillery and supporting services. In addition separate GHQ tank battalions were to be formed for direct support of infantry divisions.

For the moment it was simply a reshuffling of the cards, for it was to be more than a year before suitable equipment in worthwhile quantity would appear. But from now on, under Chaffee, American armour would increase at a rate geared to war-making even though America was not yet at war. Marshall, indeed, planned to be ready to fight in 1943, but elsewhere events, already ahead of him, were gaining speed and it would be touch and go whether the Americans would be ready for the test when it came.

Chapter 13

TANK VERSUS TANK IN THE DESERT

Ever since Mussolini's Abyssinian mission in 1935 the British had stood guard where Italian armies menaced the Suez Canal—that vital link in British grand strategy—and the oil-bearing lands of the Middle East where lay the coveted life-blood of modern warfare. Therefore of all the Italian forces the partially motorized Tenth Army stationed in Cyrenaica seemed to pose the greatest threat.

This Army, however, was but a shadow of what propaganda claimed it to be, for when Mussolini declared war on France and Britain in June 1940 it possessed only 70 poor quality medium M11/39 tanks plus an assortment of light tanks such as had proved useless in Spain. More serious for its future well-being, it clung in old-fashioned trepidation to fortified positions along the frontier with Egypt, close to the coastal road. Invite these Italians to diverge even a few miles deep in the desert and they would boggle, for they feared the waterless and, largely, uncharted wastes where every commodity had to be carried for survival and they were at hazard with their poor weapons in a zone where combat survival depended, above all, on tanks. Italy, having begun rearmament before her opponents and allies, found herself lumbered, less than a decade later, with obsolete, first-generation equipment, and lacking the capacity to create a second generation in quantity and in time.

In North Africa the British were inferior in numbers to the Italians, but in 1940 a small infusion of new cruiser tanks, unreliable though they might prove, had amply compensated for mere quantity when harnessed to the spirit of crews (even those in light tanks and armoured cars) who had been trained to live and navigate in the desert for prolonged periods. The balance fell cleanly in their favour as preliminary skirmishes along the Egyptian frontier rapidly imposed such a sense of inferiority upon the Italian soldiery, from top to bottom, that Mussolini found the greatest difficulty in goading Marshal Graziani to move timidly in mass, let alone aggressively like the British, in small groups.

At last, in September, Graziani was coerced into making a slow advance towards Mersa Matruh, his leading troops marching cautiously down the coastal strip in the hot sun, harassed at every defile, and from out of the desert, by a handful of British armoured vehicles darting, striking and then friskily retiring to safety where no Italian would follow.

As if by mutual consent, however, the competition closed when Graziani stopped well short of Mersa Matruh. Now he protested that his tired army was overstretched and would need a thorough reconstruction with a force of the newest tanks before the next hop. In Mersa Matruh itself General O'Connor, the commander of the British Western Desert Force, lay secure behind his main defensive position, satisfied with his men's performance but concerned about wear and tear to his vital fighting vehicles. Both sides, in fact, were temporarily done and the next moves would be prompted by the arrival of tank reinforcements.

By the end of November, while Graziani waited inert but engaged in hot procrastination with Rome, General Wavell, the British C-in-C, decided to take the initiative himself. His overriding strategic aim was the elimination of the Italian possessions in East Africa—a campaign in which tanks would play only a secondary role—but that must wait until Graziani had at least been neutralized. A tank raid—shades of Fuller—was his proposed solution, to be carried out by O'Connor with the 7th Armoured Division brought close to full strength by a regiment of cruisers from the UK, and the 4th Indian Infantry Division, reinforced by 50 heavy Matilda tanks which had also recently arrived from England. Even so, in terms of tank strength, this was hardly a big enough force for a prolonged desert campaign run over hundreds of miles if determined opposition was met. There were only 75 cruiser tanks in 7th Armoured and these would be the mainstay of sustained operations once the initial break-in had been made by the Matildas.

O'Connor, however, was a most ingenious general, who had been involved with mechanized experiments in the early 1920s. Richly endowed with profound tactical insight, he regularly took the advice of tank experts. Above all he sought surprise. Not unnaturally, therefore, his attack, launched on 9 December, contained those elements of which Fuller would have approved though O'Connor admits to having not read Fuller's books. The

Matildas, with the Indian infantry, executed a short hook through the desert to enter a row of Italian fortifications through the back door (instead of by frontal attack across a minefield) while, to quote a participant, the tanks of 7th Armoured Division '. . . hulls hidden in drifting clouds of dust, but with each turret standing out clear and black against the fading western sky, each with two muffled heads emerging and two pennants fluttering above from the wireless aerial', were sent in a wide sweep to descend far and deep on the Italian rear, to isolate the forward zone and create alarm and confusion.

This was a classic example of what the British tank pioneers had always envisaged armoured formations doing, even though they had not specifically designed their armoured division for desert war. A formation such as theirs, preponderant in tanks, had to achieve freedom of movement either by way of a permanently open flank or through a hole punched by other infantry formations and heavy tanks. On land it was the closest thing to naval warfare, yet far removed from a battle at sea since here, even in the desert, there were just a few places where forces might stand and fight in rolling ground, where ambush was possible and where the problems of supply overrode every other consideration. Hobart had foreseen this and had trained 7th Armoured for the role since 1938, and Hobart had been sacked for his pains by Wavell because it was judged that he placed 'too much reliance upon the invincibility of the tank to the exclusion of the employment of other arms in correct proportion'. Now a tank heavy army was to smash an infantry and artillery founded force with all the certitude of Hobart's defeats of infantry with tanks in exercises held in England during the thirties.

Of course the swift Italian débâcle—they lost their entire invading army with more than 20,000 prisoners in three days—was not simply a matter of modern tactical genius over old-fashioned absurdity. It was true that the Italian tanks, caught by surprise and with some of their crews in a state of undress, had been shot to pieces in a one-way engagement, but the crucial duel between Italian guns (which were fought with heroic determination) and the invulnerable Matildas having gone wholly the British way, there could be no redress in terrain which mostly offered little natural shelter to unaided infantry formations.

The Italians were demoralized as much by technical surprise as anything else, and to quote a senior British tank commander, 'they assembled their own lorries, refuelled them with their own fuel, and drove them full of their own prisoners ... all without escort of any kind'. But though the British crews revelled in the thrill of victory and their casualties were extremely light, the moments of horror inseparable from their particular calling stuck in their minds—the memory, for instance, of a light tank charging Italian guns, its dead driver's foot stuck on the throttle, the commander describing over the radio his predicament and how the tank, hit again, was on fire: then the rising cries of panic, broadcast to all by a set on 'send', telling of jammed hatches and the agony of men being burnt to death. Moments such as these superimpose themselves for ever on the minds of the real creators of tank history.

Again and again a tactical pattern was repeated—7th Armoured Division detouring through the desert, cutting in to isolate the garrisoned ports of Bardia and Tobruk, then holding the cordon prior to Matildas, artillery and Australian infantry approaching with implacable deliberation to make a renewed assault which, invariably, presaged another quick Italian collapse and the capture of a new influx of prisoners. Fundamental, however, in a desert war in which every item, including water, had to be transported over hundreds of miles to the front, was the possession of each port, for they provided the essential stepping stones for every subsequent advance.

It is worth recalling that by the time 7th Armoured Division had reached Tobruk it had travelled more than 250 miles in 30 days of almost continuous activity through completely undeveloped country. Compare that with the 190 miles covered by Guderian's XIX Corps through the well-developed lands of Northern France between the 10th of May and the 20th and it can be seen that British tank serviceability, over the longer period, was no worse than the German. Neither had suffered a breakdown in supplies and O'Connor had to suffer almost as much vacillation from above as Guderian had endured in France: each fresh leap forward followed renewed mental gymnastics by incredulous higher commanders who sceptically adjusted themselves to each unexpected twist of the situation. As a result the British never generated a continuous drive towards some recognizable political

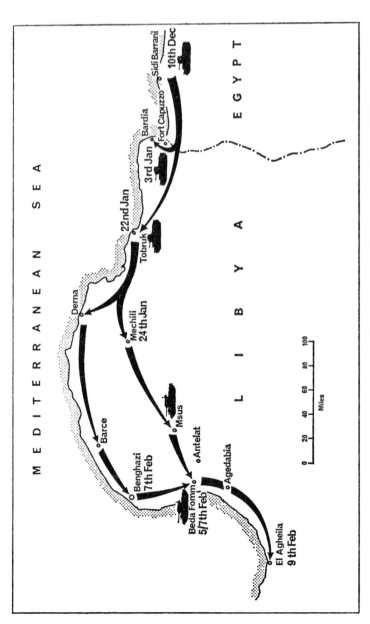

Map 10   Wavell's Desert Offensive – December 1940 – February 1941

strategic objective. Instead they projected a series of jerky opportunist tactical advances aimed primarily at the destruction of those Italian forces which appeared in range.

The overall will to eliminate an empire, such as had motivated Manstein, was not within Wavell's scope, partly because of his other commitments, it is true, but also, one suspects, because he had never envisaged such success being achieved by tanks. Yet the capture of all the Italian possessions in North Africa could well have brought the downfall of Mussolini's government and might easily have been within his scope. So thought Hitler, at least, when later he committed himself to sending troops to Tripoli.

After Tobruk had fallen on 22 January O'Connor set off again but with only 50 cruisers and 97 light tanks and leaving the now worn-out Matildas behind. Petrol was short and the strength and disposition of the Italians almost unknown but, in the hope of forcing his enemy into disclosing his intentions, O'Connor sent 7th Armoured Division by night to Mechili. Unfortunately the state of the moon had been miscalculated and so the division, starting too early, travelled in pitch darkness and, because radio silence had been imposed, could not be recalled. By daybreak the columns were lost and scattered in a poorly charted desert — and in the close presence, moreover, of a totally unexpected and strong force of the new Italian M13/40 medium tanks with their good 47mm gun. It says much for O'Connor's generalship that he kept his nerve and coolly went on planning the enemy's envelopment: it says nothing for the Italians that they failed to take their chance to press the British as they laboured in confusion. There was, in fact, a brisk skirmish as British light tanks were chased off by the M13s and then rescued when they drew their pursuers on to the guns of a squadron of friendly cruisers. Six M13s were knocked out, in what amounted to an ambush, and the rebuff was enough to deter the rest, who retired hurriedly that night unnoticed.

In criticizing his own tankmen, O'Connor put his finger on a prevailing British failing — one left over from the previous war — 'the disinclination of armoured forces to take any action at night'. He felt he had been robbed of an opportunity to destroy his opponent in detail, yet he also knew that, short of petrol, he was in the presence of elements of an Italian armoured division — Babini's Armoured Brigade, with more than a hundred medium tanks operating knowledgeably in home territory. Furthermore, already there were reports of impending German intervention and so O'Connor urgently wished to dispose of one enemy before the arrival of another more dangerous. He reasoned that a direct advance upon Benghazi was likely to be rebuffed, but that if he swung deeper than ever before into the desert, and drove cross-country to the junction at Msus, he could threaten his enemy from several directions in rear and might promote a battle on ground of his own choosing.

On 4 February 4th Armoured Brigade, with 29 cruiser and 54 light tanks, set off headed by Combeforce, consisting of armoured cars, anti-tank guns and motorized infantry. No sooner had they started, however, than news arrived of the Italians already evacuating Benghazi and making for Tripolitania in one vast column which stretched the length of the coastal road. With scanty fighting and administrative reserves the British threw discretion to the winds and tore ahead to the coast near Beda Fomm. O'Connor was taking an instinctive risk just like Rommel had done in France.

Combeforce was first to arrive—winning the race and setting up a road-block in a natural defensive position and bagging the first unwitting Italians who appeared a couple of hours later. Shortly the main Italian force, away to the north, became aware of its peril as British light tanks, cutting the column at high speed and firing their machine-guns left and right, began the proceedings—old-fashioned cavalry stuff by modernized cavalry tank-men. It was surprise at its zenith because the Italians were unprepared to defend from any direction, let alone from south and east. Moreover their armoured brigade was some distance off, still defending the tail of the column near Benghazi.

The night of the 5th/6th passed uneventfully in squally rain and it was not until well past dawn that forays out of the desert by British tanks on the halted and bewildered enemy began the battle in earnest. At 0830 hours the Italians made their first serious attempt to break through, using ten M13s supported by artillery. They were met by British cruisers firing from stationary, hull-down positions—only their turrets and guns protruding above a crestline. No sooner had eight of the Italian machines been shot into flames, however, than it became the turn of the British to evade trouble as more M13s appeared to a flank only, themselves, to be taken in flank by a countering British move.

This check and counter-check went on for nearly two days, with the Italians feeding in ill co-ordinated tank and artillery assaults as their units arrived piece-meal from the north (never waiting to concentrate all for one mighty heave) and the British hanging on with dwindling numbers, deprived of petrol and ammunition, with but a few scanty reinforcements yet to arrive from the east. Heavy cruiser tank versus medium tank fighting near Beda Fomm was punctuated with raid after raid by light tanks against the inert Italian column bunched up along the road.

Occasionally scattered Italian units would burst past Beda Fomm only to run against Combeforce to the south—there to be irrevocably stopped in close tank versus gun and armoured-car combat. Never once, however, did the Italian command come to terms with the rhythm and theme of the battle—the need to co-ordinate their attacks and to manoeuvre wide in the desert: mesmerized and with few radio sets, they did most things wrong and clung to the false safety of the road where they were cut to pieces. And here, too, the prewar British belief that tank-versus-tank fights must come was vindicated by the gunnery of the cruiser tank crews who, with simple graticuled telescopes, picked off 39 Italian tanks at 800-yard range or less while suffering the loss of a mere handful themselves. A further 60-odd Italian tanks were found destroyed by other causes or just abandoned: the end result was the same—total annihilation of the Italian tank force followed, inevitably, by the residue of their Tenth Army with more than 25,000 prisoners. One more weakling, out-moded army had been struck from the lists. Soon only the hard professionals would be left.

Chapter 14

MEDITERRANEAN DIGRESSIONS

The obsessional Hitlerian grand strategic bias against Russia became reality on 5 August 1940 with the issue of the first invasion instruction. Yet even while embarking, tentatively at first, on preparations for so all-consuming a project, Hitler simultaneously began to consider other operations—some in support of the main effort in the east, others in aid of Italy and against Britain. To a contingency plan for the occupation of the rump of Pétain's France, a seriously considered move through Spain to seize Gibraltar and a proposal to send reinforcement for Graziani in North Africa to hasten the capture of the Suez Canal had to be added supporting projects to secure control of Rumania and her vital oilfields, and gain the co-operation of the other Balkans countries in case they threatened the southern flank during the invasion of Russia. Invariably Hitler was absorbed by the megalomaniac desire to attempt everything—and almost all at once—regardless of economic practicability. The exultation induced by the tank and bomber triumph enhanced his delusions of grandeur and invincibility; it also persuaded him to alter the winning combinations of quality by demanding quantity in order to satisfy his expanding commitments.

In September the number of Panzer divisions was doubled by halving the tank content of those already in existence. At the same time the light tanks were finally relegated to reconnaissance and other special duties, and only up-gunned Mark IIIs and Mark IVs kept in the tank regiment. From now on, with wide variations in strength between different divisions, the basic Panzer division looked like this:

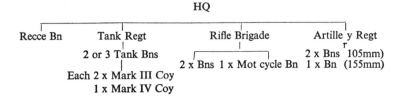

HQ

Recce Bn	Tank Regt	Rifle Brigade	Artillery Regt
	2 or 3 Tank Bns		2 x Bns 105mm)
	Each 2 x Mark III Coy	2 x Bns 1 x Mot cycle Bn	1 x Bn (155mm)
	1 x Mark IV Coy		

Soon would come the long-expected head-on battles, tank against tank, on a scale to put the light overture of Beda Fomm in the shade. Hence the dilution of tanks in the Panzer divisions came at a critical moment since their chief opponents were also in the process of making changes. In 1940 the Russians, prompted in part by the German successes with divisions of all arms, had ordered the formation of two new-type, all-arms formations. Their Tank Division, as its name implied, contained a preponderance of the fast early Christies and their successors, the powerful well-armoured T34s with a high velocity 76mm gun which could outclass the existing guns mounted on the German tanks. The organization looked like this:

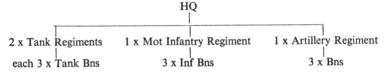

The other Russian division, called 'Mechanized', simply reversed the proportion of tank to motorized regiments. Either way these were original Russian conceptions which owed as little in detail to the German organizations as did their tanks to the German designs: with almost unlimited resources in men and machines the Russians had no reason to practise the same strict economy in specialization of functions.

The British just went on as before, seeing their tank-top-heavy armoured divisions as specialized complements of their infantry divisions, and remaining, for some time, heavily influenced by the desert environment in which tanks were certainly almost omnipotent. Their Armoured Division looked like this:

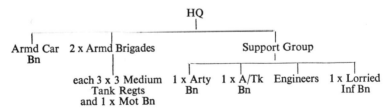

The Tank debate in Britain largely revolved around who should command and control. One school of thought, stolidly led by General Dill, the CIGS, and General Brooke, who a year later was to suceed Dill, maintained, in MacArthur's fashion, that while tank formations should be raised and trained by experts they must then be handed over for battle to conventionally-minded army and corps commanders regardless of whether those commanders understood tank techniques. Hobart, brought back from retirement by Churchill, led the faction which demanded an armoured Army composed of *all* arms (including its own artillery and air component), to be formed and commanded by specialists. This was a step ahead of the German system, but rather closer to what Chaffee had achieved in America. Hobart lost his argument with results that would be made plain in battle.

Chaffee's original Armoured Division would be modified too and in 1941 looked like this:

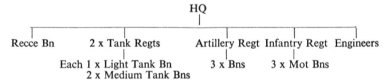

However, while the Germans persisted with their policy of forming *ad hoc* battle groups, Chaffee introduced a more formal system, establishing three autonomous combat command HQs within the division to lead variably composed groups of all arms —the variation to be decided by the demands of any particular tactical situation.

Whether tanks were increased or decreased in proportion to infantry the element of command and control with its network of signal links was everywhere sharply on the increase. In theory these were meant to improve operational flexibility and very often they did: in practice there was always the danger that this sort of proliferation would hamper decision-making in an environment which thrived on speed—a tendency made more likely with so few tank experts available to fill the increased number of key posts.

Although Hitler gave the impression in 1941 that Germany was irresistibly strong and could, with a strength of 20 Panzer divisions, safely venture in several directions at once, his various digressions from the main aim of attacking Russia were usually involuntary and invariably enacted within uncomfortably close margins.

The Balkan flank might well have been diplomatically pacified
had not Mussolini's invasion of Greece, in October 1940, mis-
fired. As it was, the threat of British bombers based in Greece
taking off within striking distance of the Rumanian oilfields,
followed by the provocation of Yugoslavia in taking it upon herself to reject his overtures, compelled Hitler to invade both
countries. So in April a German army, including five Panzer
divisions, turned south on an unpremeditated campaign, and in
the end two of those Panzer divisions were to drive so deep
into Greece that they would be effectually prevented from initial
participation in the Russian campaign. Since, already, two more
Panzer divisions had been diverted elsewhere—to Libya where
the foundering Italian Army could no longer be left to sink—the
German tank reserve had already been dispersed by about one-
sixth of its strength before the commencement of its next major
task.

The German invasion of Yugoslavia on 6 April overran a country
whose people were divided among themselves and whose army
was totally deficient of tank or adequate anti-tank forces. It
was all over by 17 April and taught no important lessons in tank
warfare. The bold advances by Panzer, supported by infantry
and mountain divisions through mountainous terrain normally
considered the worst of tank country went practically unopposed.
It was more a test of agility than of combat worthiness.

Major F. von Mellenthin, who has written one of the most
perceptive German personal accounts of tank warfare, called it
'virtually a military parade'. But he was not so off-hand about
the fighting in Greece, although even there the final result was
never in doubt. Exhausted by its fight against Italy, the Greek
Army was rapidly overwhelmed where it stood in defence of its
northern frontier, leaving just one intact but inadequate force
to oppose the Germans—the Australian and New Zealand
divisions with some additional artillery, light tanks and 52 old
British cruiser tanks. An immediate retreat towards Corinth down
the east coast of Greece was unavoidable, but in the passes, where
Greek heroes of old had fought for time, the British also stood
to delay. British tanks played a walking-off part: their crews
would have acted well had not the machines broken down. In
one day, to quote a survivor, 'five tanks were left lying with
hopelessly broken tracks, two more had fractured pistons. There

were no spare parts so the tanks were destroyed'. Soon no cruisers were left and the crews fought on foot: the remaining light tanks would be no match for the Germans.

Near Mount Olympus, on 15 April, the 2nd Panzer Division found the narrow coastal plain blocked by New Zealand infantry, supported by artillery but without anti-tank guns. The New Zealanders had been told the ground was impassable to tanks —and the German divisional commander agreed once his first tank assault had been repelled. He now told the tanks to demonstrate while the infantry worked through the hills to encircle the New Zealanders. By laborious struggles the Germans seized control of the position: it was slow work and at one point their tanks had to be towed over a ridge. Yet this was only a local action and, had the British the strength to extend their defences inland instead of being forced to leave an outpost with an open flank, a protracted stand might easily have been possible. As it was von Mellenthin comments that 'pursuit was out of the question as the riflemen were exhausted...and for the time being it was impossible to move tanks . . . along the atrocious cart track which served as a road'.

Again, at Thermopylae, German tanks ran into trouble. A contemporary account describes an advance by 19 tanks: '. . . shells burst on all sides . . . a heavy tank was hit direct . . . in the middle of the road are three others on fire . . . before long . . . only two able to shoot.' Tanks against strong opposition in narrow passes did little better than Persians versus Spartans. Unlike the Greek alliance of 480 BC, however, the Alliance of 1941 had no further powers of resistance and within days the campaign was over.

Simultaneously an unintended tank battle had broken out in Cyrenaica—unintentional because the Afrika Korps, sent there under General Rommel, primarily to prop up the Italians and only eventually to launch an offensive, had exceeded its instructions. Probing strongly forward, Rommel, having beaten a weakling British force of infantry and guns at Mersa Brega on 31 March, suddenly found his opponents melting away. No strong tank counter-attack took place. Indeed, as Rommel drove eastward he was to discover lying about old, broken down British cruiser tanks at the rate of one every ten miles. To begin with, Rommel himself had only 50 tanks and had been opposed by well over a hundred, but that British force, poor in its communications, faultily positioned, and ineptly led, fired only a few shots in anger before it was frittered away during long, unproductive manoeuvres. Recognizing the signs of his opponent's crippling weakness, Rommel pressed home his advantage and by 2 April was at Mechili, having rounded up almost the entire British mobile force along with most of its commanders, among them the richest prize of all, O'Connor himself, sent up by Wavell too late to restore the chaotic situation his predecessors had, in part, created.

Yet the very enormity of Rommel's success induced a fierce backlash. To the habitual breakdown rate attributable to German tanks had now to be added the attrition of desert travel—the wear and tear on inadequately filtered engines of dust which reduced engine life to a third of normal. In Germany, General Halder might complain 'Rommel had brought about a situation for which our present supply capabilities are insufficient', but he would have done well to investigate if they were likely to do any better during the really big test in Russia. For in Libya the separation of the German tank forces from their central supply and repair bases in the Fatherland was crippling; losses from breakdown became as serious with the Germans as they already were with the British. A fresh advance of a hundred miles to the defended perimeter at Tobruk, and to the Halfaya Pass over the frontier, cancelled out the numerical superiority which had so recently and quickly been won in battle. Within a few days Rommel was stalled by a frail but mobile British defence on the outskirts of Tobruk, his men and supplies exhausted, his tank strength at its nadir.

The war in the desert, being a war of material in which men's determination to master machines was of far greater importance than sheer numbers, frequently hinged upon the rate at which new tanks could be shipped to the Axis via Italy and to the British through the Mediterranean or, usually, via the Cape; also the speed at which worn-out vehicles could be repaired was of fundamental importance. Likewise the inherent reliability of each tank was a factor to be matched with their capability in giving and receiving blows. Hence the relative and growing munificence of the British Egyptian base partly offset the dis-

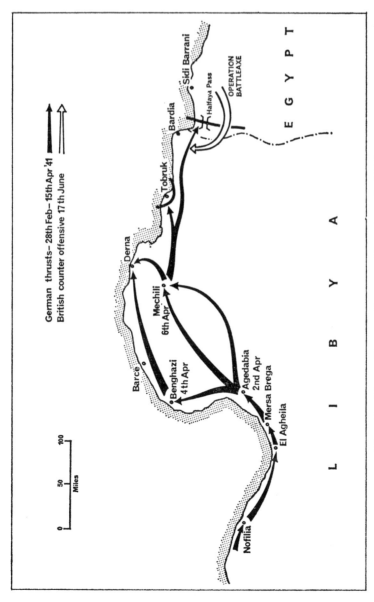

German thrusts– 28th Feb– 15th Apr '41
British counter offensive 17th June

Map 11   Desert thrust and counter thrust in early 1941

advantages of a long line of supply compared with the relative paucity of the Axis supply and repair organization in Libya.

Some concept of the state to which both sides had been reduced can be found in their tank strengths at the time of Operation Brevity, launched by Wavell on the Egyptian frontier on 14 May 1941. The British had only 26 Matildas and 29 assorted cruisers of doubtful reliability; the Germans had somewhat less and were short of petrol. At first the British overran the local Axis frontier garrisons (which were without tanks) but the appearance of a Panzer regiment driving up from Tobruk persuaded the British leader, Brigadier Gott, to withdraw in the night—passing close to the Germans who were in the act of running out of petrol. Almost with a sense of relief, it seems, both parties accidentally averted a serious tank-versus-tank engagement.

At the next attempt, 'Battleaxe', Wavell brought on a tank battle the outcome of which he knew to be finely in balance from the start. Reinforced most daringly by a convoy of new tanks pushed straight through the Mediterranean in a special convoy at the insistence of Mr Churchill, Wavell was made to feel obliged to use them at once—and ill-prepared—in a large-scale replica of Brevity. There was to be another—cruiser wheel round the desert flank while Matildas and infantry tackled the Axis garrison holding the frontier at Halfaya, but this time Wavell intended to relieve the garrison at Tobruk if he could, although his primary aim was the destruction of Rommel's forces. In effect he challenged Rommel to a tank duel, pitting his 200 tanks against Rommel's 170—though at the time both sides actually exaggerated the other's strength.

The British advanced on a wide front on 15 June, with command exercised by General Beresford Peirse from an HQ well in rear since from there he felt he could best co-ordinate operations with the air force. This faith in air power was unwarranted for neither air force was strong enough to impose decisions, whereas the tank battle which broke out that afternoon was dominant. Rommel, at the apex of action in person, could give sensitive orders on the instant: Beresford Peirse, leaving it to two or three subordinates to co-ordinate the battle among themselves, had no grip on events. And throughout the entire engagement Rommel enjoyed the priceless asset of being able to monitor the

British radio conversations carried in uncoded speech between Beresford Peirse and his junior commanders—an ability which not only told him exactly when the attack was coming but where and also such variations as attended its development.

This was the other edge of the radio link for quick command and control, and it introduced nice questions of judgment. On the assumption that the enemy would always listen in, a calculation had to be made as to whether an order might be obeyed before the enemy could react or whether a laborious process of enciphering and deciphering would end in the message arriving too late for its purpose. Subterfuge, such as speaking by innuendo in so-called 'guarded language' was inevitably comprehended by an intelligent monitor and the use of Hindustani, as reverted to by Beresford Peirse during 'Battleaxe', was unlikely to serve for long as a cover.

In 'Battleaxe' when British tanks inadvertently charged German dug-in guns they were slaughtered—particularly so the Matildas against 88s at Halfaya, but also the cruisers at Hafid Ridge. Nevertheless when Rommel riposted, sending his tanks in a direct attack against the British tanks west of Bardia on the evening of the 15th and early on the 16th, he, too, sustained heavy losses—50 of 80 out of action at one moment, though not all were destroyed.

Only by wide manoeuvre could a positive result be achieved and it was a scything sweep south and then east by Rommel through the desert towards the British rear which impelled them to make a precipitate withdrawal to escape encirclement. Again the British were saved by imposing their tanks directly in Rommel's predicted course to fend him off at point-blank range, but once more their total losses of 87 were largely composed of broken-down machines—some, as with the new Crusaders, from only trivial causes. Apart from this, honours were fairly even in the tank-versus-tank confrontation, for the German crews had been most reticent to tackle the British in solo combat. Rightly they had been taught to avoid strength and it was unsettling when they could not. They would have to evolve new methods against the days when they could no longer avert a stand-up fight.

Chapter 15

BATTLES AGAINST ODDS IN RUSSIA

When the Germans invaded Russia on 22 June 1941 it was their opponent's unpreparedness which simplified and eased the task. Telegrams from Marshal Timoshenko, the Russian Commissar for Defence, warning his armies of the coming blow, went out too late because Stalin declined to credit irrefutable evidence of what was in store—it is extremely difficult to conceal the concentration of a modern army. The German Panzer divisions, driving fast and far on the first day, overran Russian units that were immobile in their peacetime locations. By striking on a Sunday morning, when the Russians were sleeping off Saturday night entertainments, the Germans achieved an additional measure of surprise in places, but in most other respects, too, the Russian units were unready. 'We had not finished reforming and had not managed to find all our equipment and spare parts,' wrote one officer of the VIII Mechanized Corps. 'We didn't even have orders.' And the Soviet Official History admits that only a quarter of Russian tanks were actually in running order—'. . . many tank men had only 1½ to 2 hours' experience in actual driving. Many officers, even, were not fully qualified to drive them.'

There had been prolonged debate and disagreement among the Germans concerning the correct strategy to adopt against Russia —whether to seize political and economic objectives to paralyse the nation's government, as Hitler wished, or to concentrate on seeking and destroying the Red Army as many German generals demanded. Manstein, whose plan against France in 1940 had amounted to a stroke to the brain, now thought mainly along the lines of attacking the enemy's body—his Armed Forces— reasoning that national collapse would automatically follow. Guderian also seemed obsessed with physical combat while fearing the enormity of the task: his book deals with strategy but balks at the grand strategic issues.

In effect these divergences of opinion were not as schismatic as post-war memoirs by German generals have suggested; all believed in delivering a central punch directed against Moscow;

even Hitler's 'General Intention' for Operation Barbarossa stipulated 'destruction of the Russian Army located in western Russia by ... deep penetrations by armoured spearheads'. The debate centred chiefly upon the proportion of effort demanded by each of three lines of strategic approach—whether in the north against Leningrad, in the south against the Ukraine or in the centre against Moscow—and in the timing of the start. All three approaches took precedence at different times with the result that the entire Red Army was brought to battle since it was never wholly committed to the defence of Moscow. Each German thrust provoked a corresponding Russian reaction: where Panzer divisions attacked, tank and mechanized divisions struck back.

The enormous German acceleration at the outset outpaced the Russian response in all departments. Preponderant in quantity though they were, strategically the Russian tank forces were slow and poorly co-ordinated though boldly, if ineffectually, handled in combat. The standard German tactics of swift tank thrust and ambitious encirclement of a slower enemy, preceding a hard squeeze by gathering hosts of infantry divisions, carried all before them until isolated pockets of Russian resistance had to be digested. To stop was a contradiction of tank tactical philosophy, however. Manstein wrote: 'The farther a single Panzer corps ... ventured into the depths of the Russian hinterland, the greater the hazards became. Against this it may be said that the safety of a tank formation operating in the enemy's rear largely depends on its ability to keep moving. Once it comes to a halt it will immediately be assailed from all sides by the enemy's reserves.'

This summarized German experience in the summer of 1941. The Panzer groups at first rolled on at breakneck speed. When faced by only small, surprised groups of Russian tanks and guns, annihilation caused by the sheer speed and concentration of German force would ensue. While the weather remained fine, allowing the supply lorries to drive easily along dry roads and even across country, the safety of momentum was maintained. But when it rained and the lorries got stuck in unfounded roads degenerating into quagmires, or when the Russians interposed themselves solidly across a supply route, the advance would atrophy and the army fall into peril.

The experience of Manstein's 56th Corps in the preliminary

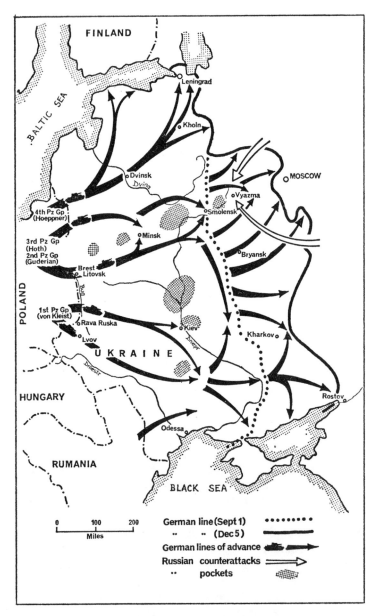

Map 12 Battles in Russia 1941

moves towards Leningrad was typical. By 26 June he had penetrated more than a hundred miles to seize a bridgehead across
the river at Dvinsk. By then his 8th Panzer, 3rd Motorized and
209th Infantry Divisions were more than 50 miles ahead of the
nearest German formation, and the Russians had failed to concentrate effectively against him. But already supply problems
were being caused by a single heavy Russian KV tank which
straddled the road for 48 hours and prevented all replenishment
at the front. The armour of this tank (106mm, sloped, at its
thickest) was quite impervious to anything other than an 88mm
gun, while its 76mm gun prevented the Germans getting one of
these guns into action until a vast diversion by no fewer than
50 German tanks could fully distract the KV's attention. This
interruption of the German mobility gave sufficient time for the
Russians to interpose their XIV Tank Corps between Manstein
and the remaining Germans following up.

Heavy tank-versus-tank fighting broke out over a wide expanse
of country, but, as in Spain, the Russian tanks moved too far
ahead of their infantry—or perhaps it would be truer to say that
the infantry hung too far back in greater safety and left things
to the tanks. At all events the better provided German all-arms
groups had it all their own way against the bulk of Russian light
tanks which comprised the majority of the XIV Tank Corps.
Only on those, as yet, rare occasions when the heavy KV or, later,
T34 tanks appeared did the Germans become reticent, discovering
that the Russian 76mm gun could shell them from any visible
range—and that at 1,000 yards it could penetrate their thickest
armour; simultaneously the Germans found that their tanks had
to close to 200 yards to make a kill. In boxing parlance they
were outreached by a weightier opponent.

How then did the Germans continue to destroy Russian armies
when the numerical and technical balance was in the latter's
favour? Of course there were as yet only a few KV and T34s
about, but the real answer could be found from the infinitely better
German leadership, their greatly improved training and vastly
superior, systematic co-ordination of effort. Time and again the
Russians would laboriously assemble a strong tank force only to
throw it hastily and ill-prepared against an awaiting German
defence. The Russians seemed to value mass before surprise

while the Germans had learnt that, while mass was important, it could fail without the benefit of a surprise appearance.

The Germans would have warning of an attack because their aircraft, flying in comparative safety with all the benefits of command of the air, provided a superb information service. Indeed, bombing support was the least useful service provided since, as von Mellenthin points out, 'the enormous fronts . . . and the relative weakness of the air forces engaged limited the effect of air power'. It is on record that some German generals would resist the removal of reconnaissance and transport aircraft from their command with greater vehemence than the removal of bombers.

The Russians frequently telegraphed their approach when sent to the relief of besieged forces, as at Rava Ruska when a Russian tank corps followed the most obvious course and ran headlong against the minefields, assault and anti-tank guns of a German infantry division safely dug in and ready. After a day and night's fighting the carefully linked German fire had knocked out 63 Russian armoured vehicles. No ground was relinquished. It was true that the German deployment and marksmanship had been important, but they might have shot less well if the Russians had distracted them with a feint and harried their guns with artillery fire instead of plunging with an unpremeditated charge. Entering battle behind armour certainly enhances courage and only by experience do crews discover its fallacy. Undoubtedly, however, the presence of powerful assault guns permanently in support stiffened the German infantry. This was their own 'tank': without it they could feel deserted if Panzer divisions were not close by.

Not only were the Russians strategically unbalanced and tactically inept from the outset, they were woefully deficient in individual training and competent leadership. Tank breakdowns became more frequent due to rough handling by ignorant crews; shooting was inaccurate despite pinpoint accuracy being mandatory in tank battles. Most disturbing of all were the querulous and panicky relationships between commanders: where confidence should have been supreme there reigned pernicious fear and uncertainty. If Zhukov, an excellent commander and a student under von Seeckt in 1921, could suffer from the bullying of Stalin at the highest level, the performance of a junior commander, upon receipt of the order 'Why is your regiment not in the initial attack position? Engage at once unless you want to lose your head,' could be ruinous. Pavlov, the Western Front commander, was shot, in July, for incompetence.

Russia is said to have begun the war with 20,000 tanks, the majority of them light and obsolete, but by the autumn most had been lost.* Thus, like Italy, she suffered from having made an early start with re-equipment and for delaying too long with modernization; even totalitarian States have their economic and industrial limits and are prone to think twice before scrapping existing weapons.

So too were the Germans suffering, but for different reasons. They had opened the campaign with 3,200 tanks. In a campaign which had overrun vast territories at electric speed (Guderian advanced 413 miles in 25 days from Brest Litovsk to Smolensk) their losses were 50 per cent higher than in previous campaigns though as yet nothing compared with losses in similar offensives of the First World War. Now, however, they arrived at the end of a gruelling ten weeks of battle and, for the first time in two years, were nowhere in sight of final victory. Even after only six weeks Guderian had begun to worry about replacement tanks and spares, though he was but confirming Rommel's experience in the desert. The central repair organization, far in rear, was ineffective and supplies had also run out at the front. After the war the Germans would explain that wheeled lorries were useless on poor Russian roads and that only tracked, cross-country vehicles could have satisfied their needs. Perhaps—but in actuality a German industry (now supplemented by French factories) which was already incapable of producing enough tanks and armoured half-tracked infantry carriers could hardly have also built tracked supply vehicles, whose higher rate of breakdown would have thrown a quite insupportable additional load on the already inadequate repair organization.

And so the campaign ground on into autumn and then into winter,

* Evidence as to Russian performance and statistics is never satisfactory even when confirmed from official sources. The only accurate data concerns those of their weapons which have been examined and compared by experts outside Russia. It seems likely, however, that by December 1941 they had lost well over 15,000 machines and a million men.

the advance reaching Leningrad and stalling, driving towards
Moscow and running savagely through the Ukraine, past Rostov
on the Don. With every mile run the Panzer divisions became
weaker while the infantry divisions, with their assault guns,
began to play a more important role than ever before. There
was no shift in emphasis of strategy and tactics—Germans and
Russians still depended upon tanks to create opportunities to
maintain mobility—but the load had to be spread more evenly
throughout both armies, and infantry formations had to learn
to hold firm, on their own, against tank formations.

Up to now only one element of the German Army—the tank
force—had been consistently engaged in heavy fighting since
1939. The strain had lain heavily on them and it was not until
the Russian invasion that the infantry force as a whole had to do
more than consolidate the tanks' gains. Conditions on the Russian
front, particularly after the autumn rains brought deep mud,
followed by snow and paralyzing cold, loaded terrible stress on
shaken men and machines. Whereas the German Army had
campaigned at speed in comparative comfort until June 1941, the
bleak steppes and forests, infested by hardy Russian armies and
guerrillas, allowed them to carry only absolute essentials in the
front line. Men wore the same underwear for weeks on end;
work on vehicles and weapons grew progressively more difficult
and so standards fell; older men began to crack. The victorious
generals of 1940 suddenly had to give way to younger men
with better health. Guderian was to have a heart attack, Rundstedt and other Army Group commanders had to be replaced not
only because they had lost confidence in Hitler's direction of the
war but because, in weariness, they automatically resisted orders
from above and wanted to pull back. The exhilarating pace slowed
down: rates of advance of 19 miles per day in 1940 had fallen
to 16½ per day in 1941. Worst of all, no end could be seen
when once there had always been hope.

To pull back from a conquest was quite foreign to Hitler. Like
his tank forces he believed in driving ahead—first to conquer the
Ukraine in September and then to return to the charge against
Moscow in October. As additional Russian formations were identified the Germans had to begin what amounted to a fresh campaign
with men and machines wearied by many months' continual
fighting. The initial diversions to the Balkans and then the digres-

sions at Leningrad and in the Ukraine had robbed the central tank forces of their principal psychological weapon, the ability to move irresistibly and swiftly towards the enemy political and administrative brain—in this case Moscow.

Even so, in the first week of October, an attack by three Panzer and two infantry armies rolled up the Russians in the same old way. Vast pockets were sealed off by Guderian's Second Panzer Army between Sevsk and Bryansk; another great encirclement was completed by Fourth and Second Panzer Armies at Vyazma. And then, in the same old way, things slowed down while the contents of each encirclement were digested—a time-consuming and costly business.

According to Zhukov, who had been sent to command the Reserve Front, 'by 7 October all roads to Moscow were open' and it would be several days before 14 divisions and 16 under-strength tank brigades could be assembled from the other fronts, which necessarily had closed down as the Germans stepped up their drive against Moscow. Though Zhukov talked liberally of re-establishing a continuous front, this in fact was a council of desperation to a man who understood tank mobility. All along he was asking for more tanks—usually in vain—and those he got were badly crewed and unreliable. Thousands of people might feverishly dig fortifications and anti-tank ditches, but these were no more likely to stop German tank forces in front of Moscow than they had anywhere else in Europe. Zhukov wanted a *corps d'élite*, like the Germans, not an inanimate mass.

Why then did not the Germans drive the remaining 150 miles to Moscow almost non-stop?

Torrential rain was partly the answer—rain which collapsed the roads. To quote General Philippi, 'It was weather, not the Russians, which stopped us', but this may only in part be true. On the Russian front in the First World War the German infantry had advanced vast distances with hardly a motor vehicle in sight. Were they now depending too much on tanks? In any event, Zhukov was given just sufficient time to bring in reinforcements, but depended most on his tanks which, alone, could make German tank leaders diverge from their settled aim. Guderian was upset by the loss of two infantry battalions to an attack by Russian tanks and reversed 9th Panzer Division to restore the situation. Near Kholn an attack by 100 Russian tanks delayed

6th Panzer Division from completing its task: each delay, however slight, could be felt with a shudder throughout an entire army in which operations were so closely knitted together. It was always indicative of Russian failings that, even as at Kholn when their tank attacks started off concentrated, they soon fell apart in close forest and were destroyed piecemeal. It also remained inescapable that their tanks, particularly the KVs and T34s, could never be despised.

From mid-October every German account is filled with woe—a tale of broken-down tanks floundering in mud or blinded by snow; of a fuel or spares famine, of weary troops led or coerced by tired and angry commanders—all getting at each other's throats; of mounting Russian resistance and swiftly falling momentum until, with the Kremlin in sight, no further progress could be made. Something fresh then begins to tinge the German commentary. At first they seemed to ridicule everything that was militarily Russian, with the exception of the T34 and KV tanks; now they had to respect Russian adaptability to the appalling weather as it played hideous tricks. German tanks, which had sunk to their bellies in mud, suddenly became immovably fixed by an unexpected freeze as Russian counter-attacks developed. The 6th Panzer Division lost all its vehicles from this cause and for some weeks fought only on foot. Once Guderian had written that Panzer divisions should provide a reserve. For the first time they were used up and could no longer do so.

Yet the Russians were hardly better off. Though their tanks, many of which performed well in soft going and cold weather, could outclass the Germans, there were not enough of them. The widespread German advance had put vital munitions factories out of action. Although there is conflicting evidence as to their tank strength in the defence of Moscow, it is probably true that when Zhukov asked Stalin for 200 tanks in December he was told there were none to be had: everything was at the front already. One tank division was down to 30 lights and another to only four carriers. When Zhukov wrote 'We opposed these [German] armoured blows with a defence in depth that was relatively well provided with anti-tank obstacles ... and that was where we concentrated our basic tank forces', he indicated not only his understanding of mobile defence within a static framework but also his enforced need to economize in tanks.

The German Army was baffled by weather and by a basically infantry defence which, without sufficient tanks of its own, it could not breach. The Russian counter-offensive, when it came, enjoyed success only when it moved through wide gaps and past thinly-held German positions. Short of tanks themselves, they could no more easily dislodge well-emplaced, tough infantry divisions than could the Germans. In this broken-back warfare of the winter 1941–42 the principal Russian advantage lay in their better preparation for combat in the cold. The Germans had made no prior preparations since they had reckoned on fighting only a short summer campaign; their vehicles were unwinterized, their clothing of summer weight. Engine blocks froze solid; men died from exposure.

Yet eventually the adaptable Germans also turned the effects of the cold to their advantage. By occupying towns and hamlets they possessed themselves of the best available shelter when on the defensive. The Russians, on the other hand, had to move into the open to attack and there, in conditions of hard freeze, the under-strength German tank columns, issuing swiftly from cover, could strike them, cause losses and hurriedly return to shelter. Usually it was only by imposing prolonged isolation of a German garrison that the Russians could enforce its subjugation leading to an overall readjustment of an entire front. So long as the Germans could maintain tank forces to move and fight to keep open communications to the beleaguered garrisons, a loosely knit frontage could be held.

Guderian was bitterly disappointed. He believed circumstances alone had brought defeat: 'I would never have believed that a really brilliant military position could be so balled up in two months.' Another German, Gunther Blumentritt, was later to remark that 'The principal effect of that winter offensive was in upsetting the German plans for 1942.' It is indubitably true that the acid test would appear only when the performance of both sides could be measured in the spring. By then, in fact, the Germans would have recovered strength and composure and be stopping each Russian onslaught, by vast forces, with practised ease. The policy of permitting penetrations and then countering them by swift tank and infantry strokes held good. The Germans learnt fast and forgot nothing. The Russians had lost so many veterans that they were forced to pour in untrained recruits:

that way they could never build a cadre of experts to make use of the most sophisticated techniques.

In that hideous winter, in fact, the pattern of all future battles on the Russian front was sealed. From now on the Russians would depend almost wholly upon lunges in mass with all arms to which the Germans would deftly riposte with smaller, more agile all-arms battlegroups. On those grand occasions when the Russians achieved a totally overwhelming breakthrough to disrupt the German fabric it came about mainly because a vast preponderance had been brought to bear against over-extended German positions that nothing on earth—not even superlative men and equipment—could have stopped. Regardless of the methods employed, both sides agreed that tank forces held the key—the means to cut a hole in a front, to counter penetrations, to bolster intolerably-pressed infantry and bring speedy assistance across country when no other method would suffice. And since so much depended upon tanks it was disquieting to the Germans that they were becoming technically outclassed in that department.

There were other disquieting diversions too. On 7 December the Japanese attacked the Americans at Pearl Harbour and began to wage war on the British and Dutch in the Far East. Germany too declared war on the USA. Now came a new dimension to the struggle. Even if Russian tank strengths could be kept low by repeated battlefield attrition and the destruction of their factories, the vast potential of American production must eventually flood into Europe—unless the Americans chose to concentrate on the Japanese and leave the Germans to complete their victory over the Russians—or unless, by some master-stroke, oil, the life-blood of internal combustion-engine forces, could be cut off from the Allies before the Axis themselves ran out.

Chapter 16

THE EXPANDING WAR

The Desert War remains a matter of strong British sentiment —a wholly understandable emotion when it is remembered that, for nearly three years, this represented their only prolonged point of contact on land with the German Army. The desert therefore became the proving ground of their manhood in modern war. Nevertheless it must be remembered that the long-awaited Operation 'Crusader', launched on 18 November 1941, employed but five divisions pitted against six from the Axis—fewer divisions than armies involved on the Russian front. Hence such importance as could be claimed for the Desert War itself was not related to the numbers involved.

Strategically, however, it was another matter. British Middle Eastern strategy was always controlled by the need to guard the Canal and the oilfields beyond. Even though Axis strategy failed at first to include them as objectives it was a self-interested British assumption that this must be so. Yet Rommel's resources were so curtailed that he could plan no further ahead than to capture Tobruk: an ensuing drive to the Canal belonged only to the realms of hopeful conjecture. But if he had been allowed sufficient resources the Canal and, perhaps, the oilfields would have come within his reach—a scintillating prospect ideally suited to tank forces both in its tactical feasibility and its stunning strategic possibilities. For with the Japanese overrunning the Far Eastern oilfields, the loss of their Middle Eastern counterparts would have made the Allies dependent almost entirely upon American oil production. Furthermore it was always conceivable that the shock imposed by the loss of the British Middle East possessions might induce a wholesale national collapse with ramifications beyond all imagination.

In November the British, with 756 tanks, attacked Rommel with 400—their object the relief of Tobruk just as, at that moment, Rommel was planning its capture. This was to be a tactical exercise lacking a grand strategic aim—a battle for the destruction of tank forces without an immediate major objective, for

British schemes for conquering the entire North African coast were as yet opportunist since they had not the strength to do it alone. At the start the British Eighth Army executed its accustomed outward desert wheel employing strong tank forces, lunging from the Egyptian frontier towards Tobruk, where their garrison stood ready to sortie. Taking his time, Rommel correctly gauged that the British were actually moving dispersed in five groups, each about 150 tanks strong. Picking his moment, and keeping Afrika Korps under close, concentrated control, he dealt successive blows against each British group until, in a wild melée near Sidi Rezegh, he had fought the British to the verge of defeat.

His victory was not simply a case of better tactical handling mesmerizing a less well generalled opponent—though faults in British leadership when tank commanders (many of them ex-cavalry) took to charging opposition in the cavalry manner born undoubtedly contributed to their discomfort. More to the point was the growth of a feeling among British crews that they were out-gunned and under-protected. Their 40mm tank gun, they had discovered, did not penetrate German armour at much above 800 yards, and since this gun could not fire high explosive it was quite useless against German anti-tank guns—the 88mm and the new, long 50mm—which penetrated their armour from a range of 1,000 yards or more. In open desert where it was almost impossible to make concealed or stealthy approaches, the British were reduced to the tactics of a boxer with a short reach —the quick rush into a clinch in the wild hope of striking a lucky blow—but there the metaphor broke down as the method became debased, for, as had once been remarked in the twenties, a good shot would always hit a fast-moving bird—and the Germans were quite good shots.

By inflicting heavy losses the Germans rectified their initial numerical inferiority within hours and Rommel had merely to clinch matters by eliminating the spent and scattered British in the relatively narrow confines of the Sidi Rezegh area, for it was there that what remained of the British tank force and, of almost equal importance, the carcasses of many damaged or broken down tanks from both sides lay strewn about. This the commander of Afrika Korps, General Cruewell, wished to do, but instead Rommel decided upon something more grandiose— grandiose to the eye if not to the senses. He repeated, in fact, the

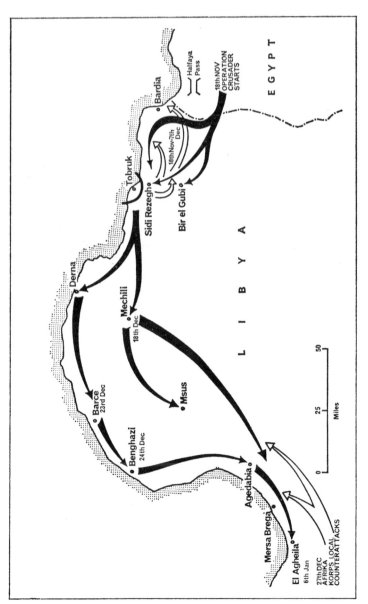

Map 13   The British Desert Offensive – Nov and Dec 1941
and early 1942

Halfaya
Pass

18th NOV
OPERATION
CRUSADER
STARTS

Bardia

E G Y P T

18th Nov–7th
Dec

Tobruk

Sidi Rezegh

Bir el Gubi

L I B Y A

Derna

Mechili

18th Dec

Msus

Barce
23rd Dec

Benghazi
24th Dec

Agedabia

Mersa Brega

El Agheila
6th Jan

27th DEC
AFRIKA
KORPS LOCAL
COUNTERATTACKS

0   25   50

Miles

blow which had decided the Battleaxe operation—a sweep to Halfaya Pass to link with the garrison there and cut off the entire British Army in one grand encirclement. But total encirclements depend upon adequate forces to seal off every enemy escape route, and forces such as these Rommel never possessed. So though he managed to inject momentary panic among the British, his vacating of the vital ground gave the British army near Sidi Rezegh a priceless opportunity to gather-in wrecked tanks to repair their own strength and, incidentally, to pass valuable time demolishing some of Rommel's cast-off tanks which might otherwise have been recovered by their previous owners. When Rommel at last returned to this critical area to redeem his victory he found a strengthened enemy in residence—one not only refurbished but sufficiently chastened to fight with greater circumspection.

Win successive tactical tank victories though he might, Rommel had irrevocably thrown away his first, hard-won advantage. Starved of petrol and replacement tanks he was impelled to withdraw to El Agheila in December and abandon to their fate his garrisons at Halfaya. This highly complex battle had been enthralling in its lightning changes in fortune. Men had imprinted their personalities on every engagement but the final outcome turned upon which side had armour and which had not. Brilliant though some of Rommel's tactical ploys may have been (though quite often the sagacity of General Cruewell had been more in evidence than Rommel's) he had overlooked one basic factor— the all-pervading tyranny of tanks.

Quite another kind of battle was in progress in the Far East as the Japanese moved down through the Philippines, Malaya and Indonesia and struck west into Burma. Neither they nor the Americans, British and Dutch deployed many tanks—the Japanese because their operations were mainly either amphibious or directed into close country where tanks could play only a limited role; their enemy because they had none available to speak of. It was the generally accepted view that tanks in jungle could achieve nothing of consequence. Thus a startling revelation appeared in the frequency with which tanks caused a total collapse even with the use of but a few lightly armoured machines. It was made easier for the Japanese, of course, because they were opposed by hardly any anti-tank guns, but often the mere appearance of their tanks was enough to start a débâcle.

In northern Malaya a potentially strong British position was tackled near Jitra by a weak Japanese reconnaissance battalion supported by ten medium tanks. Driving in the British outposts, the Japanese, moving through a heavy rainstorm, followed up so fast that they were amid the main position shooting up trucks in gay abandon before their presence was suspected. The weather played its part for, to their amazement, the Japanese saw 'ten [anti-tank] guns, their muzzles turned towards us, lined up on the road, but near them we could not find even one man of the crews. The enemy appeared to be sheltering from the rain under the rubber trees. . . .' It was not simply a case of negligence on the British part though this was plain enough—but the logical derivative of a doctrine which, for years, had discounted the value and pace of tanks in the most difficult country.

Proving that they, at least, were not overawed by tanks, the Japanese staunchly weathered an American tank counter-attack at Bataan on 7 April 1942—though it has to be remembered that the Americans were new to the game while the Japanese were old hands. Nevertheless, the American practice of using their light tanks in a direct assault in support of infantry was demonstrated in all its frailty: the attack broke down and fell into confusion as the Japanese turned their discomfiture to good use.

In Burma the British deployed two Stuart tank regiments crewed by men who had fought at Beda Fomm. But the Japanese were unlike the Italians: they declined to offer direct battle on a narrow front, but slipped infantry and a few tanks stealthily round the flanks through thick cover to build road blocks in the British rear. Compelled to fight in a series of bids to rescue the infantry and free their lines of communication, the British consistently had to give ground. Their tanks, boldly handled, frequently cut a way through but finally, when a bridge over the River Chindwin was prematurely destroyed to prevent its capture intact, only one tank had reached the home bank and the rest had to be destroyed.

Tanks, it had been repeatedly shown, could operate powerfully in jungle: their numbers and point of impact all depended upon the size of effort put into transporting them to the front. Once there, impact reacted in proportion to the conditions. For instance, a single tank in Burma moving aggressively along an unguarded track could break a front with the equivalent effect of an armoured regiment fighting its way through opposition on a plain five-miles wide in France.

Tanks would play their part in the Far East for the rest of the war, although the Japanese contribution would be small. With only a limited industrial capacity serving a predominantly maritime strategy, they had chosen differently from their land-biased German ally and concentrated on naval construction instead of on tanks; indeed, in many ways the position of the two was synonymous in that neither had nearly enough of his preferred articles. But their opponents, the British and Americans, could afford to build almost everything—strong fleets, great air forces and unlimited and diverse armies containing tanks which could swim ashore as part of an amphibious landing force and heavier tanks which could be made to straddle narrow tracks, break down trees and climb rugged terrain. In 1942, when the Axis were winning with technical superiority, quantity was less important; thereafter the mighty production lines in the West would turn the scales.

As the war became truly world-wide the impact of events in one theatre supervened in others. At rock bottom, repeatedly, lay obsession with the battle for oil—how to seize or protect the sources of the life-blood of mechanization. The Arcadia Conferences in Washington at the end of 1941 established the grand strategic Allied aim of dealing first with Germany and then with Japan, but this decision in no way obviated the need to reinforce the Far Eastern theatre of operations immediately, for there the Japanese were in the process of gobbling up every oilfield from Borneo to Burma. Soon only the American and Middle Eastern fields would be left to the Allies and the latter might also be in jeopardy if the Germans burst out southwards to absorb the Russian fields in the Caucasus and then extend their advance into Persia and Iraq. Already there had been dilutions of men and machines in the Middle East to help prop up the Far East and the repercussions were not yet spent. Now it had to be asked: how far and in what strength could the Axis reach out?

If Allied nightmares of Axis depredations gave them sleepless nights, how much worse was it for the Axis? As the war expanded,

Germany's natural and synthetic fuel supplies became progressively inadequate and stocks began to run down. The growing fear that the Allied bomber offensive would destroy the synthetic oil plants drove Hitler to project the seizure of the Caucasian oilfields: 'If I do not get the oil of Maikop and Grozny then I must end this war.' Thus Germany's grand strategic direction in 1942 became obsessively pointed in that direction, and was to stretch her Army to the limit, along many, widespread frontiers, where mobile warfare alone could keep her in business. Without petrol there could not be mobility or a militant Germany. Yet even Hitler could sometimes recognize the limitations of his tank forces and for him, at first, the Middle East fields lay too far over the horizon. But he underestimated Rommel.

Rommel's part in reshaping Axis strategy grew phoenix-like from sheer tank opportunism. The British Eighth Army, under General Ritchie, faced the Germans near Mersa Brega in early January 1942 and was busy rebuilding its strength and endeavouring to amass supplies at Benghazi. Only 150 tanks, belonging to the newly arrived 1st Armoured Division, were at the front, as was mostly known to von Mellenthin from sources of Axis higher intelligence and the overhearing of British radio conversations. He told Rommel that for three weeks the Axis ought to enjoy numerical superiority in tanks and Rommel deduced that a sudden local blow might prolong that period and give heart to the Italians who were considered incapable of sustaining further defensive fighting.

Moving secretly into assembly positions by night (and forbearing to tell the Italians his intentions) Rommel launched forth on 20 January rather as he had done the previous March. And rather as in the previous year the enemy was found wanting. Rommel pressed on, ambushed unwary British tank regiments, ran out of fuel, squeezed every drop he could from his lorries and from captured enemy stocks, lashed out again and, to the surprise of all, suddenly arrived in Benghazi with the wrecks of 1st Armoured Division strewing the desert behind him. The British, practising control by consultation instead of command by decision, had no option but to pull back to the defence of Tobruk, choosing to hold an artificially-created line near Gazala. Rommel's forces, quite exhausted and down to a handful of operationally fit tanks, could only follow at a respectful distance.

But Rommel was back in business in North Africa and, although he could not obtain approval for an all-out attack against Egypt, he could at least squeeze enough out of Berlin and Rome strikingly to improve both the numbers and, above all, the quality of his tank forces. More powerful tanks were being produced to counter the Russian threat—as will soon be told—and some would come Rommel's way. Might it not then be possible to go further than official Axis ambitions allowed and do more than capture Tobruk and the island of Malta? Could not the vital oil be seized through the backdoor? But which would come first —success by tanks drinking too much oil or collapse from an unslaked thirst for oil?

Chapter 17

MECHANICAL SYMPHONY

Historians agree that 1942 marked the watershed of the Second World War, the year in which the protagonists' fortunes changed place. So it is perhaps significant that the same period coincides with a watershed in tank warfare—when the swift escalation to bigger guns mounted in larger tanks with thicker armour thrust new and enormous loads on every nation's industry and, in due course, radically altered battlefield procedures.

The stimulants of this abrupt revolution were the Russian KV1 and T34 tanks whose battlefield appearance in relatively small numbers in 1941 had so shaken the Germans. In KV1 the Germans met a tank which was all but invulnerable; in T34 they recognized a paragon of mobility, hard-hitting power and adequate protection—something they envied and desired for themselves. The fact that the 76mm gun could fire high-velocity armour-piercing shot *and* a well aimed and good high-explosive shell made possible a formidable dual-purpose weapon system: in effect a combination of the contemporary tank with self-propelled artillery.

Panic and ignorance could be detected on the part of those German soldiers who demanded that their industry should at once slavishly copy T34. This asked for the ridiculous. To effectively copy a vehicle which was built on totally different lines from German practice would take many years and still further overstretch German industrial capacity. Plant for casting such a large turret could not immediately be found: nor could the manufacture of the special lightweight diesel engine be arranged in haste. T34, in fact, represented many years of careful Russian research and development—employing Italian basic expertise, as it did, perhaps—but still a unique Russian product. It presented the Germans with two basic problems to solve—in the short term for dealing in 1942 with T34/76, and in the long term, perhaps by 1943 and certainly by 1944, of advancing themselves technically to defeat the improved successor to T34 when it inevitably appeared. T34 as it existed in 1941 could not be copied by 1942, but by 1944 a copy would be out of date.

For the short term the Germans possessed three solutions almost ready-made. They could, and did, redouble the armour thickness on their Mark III and IV tanks; they could also rearm the Mark III with a long 50mm gun and the Mark IV with a long 75 since plans for these evolutions were in readiness. In addition they could mount their assault guns with bigger 75mm guns and step up production of these simpler machines more rapidly than with tanks. In the longer term they would—at last— urgently prosecute designs for both the medium and heavy tanks begun, respectively and tentatively, in 1937 and 1939. The Germans, guided by Guderian, had been cool in the thirties to bigger, costly machines, and to achieve mobility they had gone for agility and quantity without much regard for achieving the upper hand in armour protection and armament over their opponents. Then, too, tank leaders had resisted the introduction of assault guns, dismissing them as a poor substitute for that epitome of an out-right weapon of offence—the tank. Now the Russian technical lead—oft suspected but always well concealed—left no alternative but to engage at enormous cost in a furious gun-and-armour race regardless of type and shape of vehicle.

The heavy tank, the design of which was furthest advanced in 1941, would be hastened into production in 1942, armed with an 88mm gun and shielded by 110mm of armour: this would be the formidable Tiger I and nearest to Hitler's concept of the tank as a battleship. The eventual medium design, radically revised to incorporate the T34's best features (including its well sloped armour), would carry a new, long-barrelled 75mm gun; but it would not be ready for battle until 1943. This would be Panther —the tank soldier's first choice. Threatening though this delay in introducing the new tanks was, hope remained high in German hearts, for when grim defensive tactics encroached ever more on the older style of gay offensive abandon, the assault guns came more into their own—and in quantity.

Tactics had to keep step with technical changes. More powerful guns could engage armoured targets at longer range and there-fore individual vehicles could dominate wider expanses of country. Higher-velocity guns, while introducing a host of complex sighting problems, were nevertheless more accurate than their predecessors and so could register hits with great frequency and engage more targets in a specified time. Bigger guns introduced larger and heavier ammunition, however, and this could reduce a gun's rate of fire and aggravate the difficulties of production and supply. Bigger guns also caused increases in turret (and therefore tank) dimensions—and the heavier the tank the more complex the transport problem when, in particular, trying to cross water obstacles. Assault guns were usually lighter than their tank counterparts but, because their guns had only limited traverse, were forced in prudence to lie back in action, supporting the tanks while they manoeuvred freely in the forefront of the battle. Soon Germans and Russians, who also used assault guns in quantity, would mainly allocate tanks to the first wave of attack and restrict assault guns with infantry to the second.

Alongside the general escalation in size, the number and variety of specialized tanks went on the increase. Obsolete chassis, including those of light tanks, were converted into special reconnaissance, artillery or engineer vehicles. As more men went into battle under armour the power of light field artillery fell into a slow decline, though in 1942 there were still more than enough 'soft' targets on the battlefield to make the presence of these guns worth while. Field artillery and anti-tank guns found tanks a less dangerous foe when few tanks carried guns firing high-explosive shells, for then the gunners often enjoyed the advantage of opening fire outside the range of tank machine-guns. But once tanks could lie out of sight behind a ridge and deal with exposed guns on better than level terms it was not only no longer profitable for tanks to charge to close range but quite unnecessary to do so; they could stand off, manoeuvre for position and engage their opponents at long range from carefully selected concealed positions.

No tank had need to adopt these methods more than the American Medium M3—the Grant as the British called it. M3 was a child of necessity—a bastard offspring when the Americans, in 1940, perceived not only that future tanks would need a dual-purpose gun of not less than 75mm calibre but that they would be unable to manufacture a fully rotating turret to house such a gun before 1942—far too late. So M3 came into being in 1941, packed its 75 in a hull sponson and carried only a 37mm gun in its small, rotating turret. Thus to fire the 75 over direct line of sight forced the tank to expose most of its high sides to counter-action and hence the need to lie back and engage German anti-tank guns with indirect fire was dictated by the demands of sheer survival—the most impelling of all demands in war.

In 1942 the British had nothing so good as Grant. Its arrival in the Middle East was both a salvation and, for them, the beginning of a revolution in tank gunnery. Gradually they would wean crews from attempting crude, head-on charges and induce them to indulge in more skilful sparring for superior positions in long-range shooting. Caution would supervene—at a price in audacity.

During these cardinal months of change the industrial empires of almost all the combatant Powers were in downright confusion —if not in chaos. The sudden intensification of the war, linked with the impetus of heady new ideas, drove theoretical require-ments well ahead of practical manufacturing possibility. Lead time in the delivery at the front of some new key weapon, such as a new tank or gun, could as decisively tilt the scales in 1942 as it had at Cambrai in 1917. A redoubled load was imposed on teams of soldiers, designers and manufacturers who had to work faster yet in closer consultation than ever among themselves. To waste but a few weeks in the production of a new weapon system could lose battles and, perhaps, campaigns.

German industry, told by the military to increase production violently and, at the same time, introduce a whole new range of vehicles which had little in common with their predecessors, could justifiably complain that the demands were incompatible. High production was the associate of long runs on stabilized production lines; new designs took time to get started and absorbed much specialized effort before even a few models could be finished. Until the end of 1941 the Luftwaffe continued to receive first priority; always political factions, intriguing for power and cutting across the normal competition to be expected of indus-trialists vying for manpower and materials when in short supply, hampered progress.

In February 1942, when Albert Speer became Hitler's Minister for Armaments, there was no central control of production of tanks or anything else. In 1941 only 480 Mark IV and 450 Mark III tanks were made. Yet in 1942, after Speer had but tickled the problem, 904 Mark IVs and no fewer than 1,907 Mark IIIs were built, and so it is clear that, until then, men in the German factories had been under nothing like the same pressure as those in the Panzer divisions.

In Russia the loss or upheaval of factories incurred as a result of the German invasion brought debilitating tank shortages, but at least the Russians were in no doubt as to the dominant importance of the tank forces. To strengthen this side of production they spared no effort—as the Germans grimly noticed when they saw how thoroughly the Russian factories had been stripped of their heavy machinery to equip new factories being built in the east. Even though the production of T34s is estimated at only 5,000 in 1942 (it is said to have been 10,000 in 1943) this was still a mighty effort. Nevertheless the bulk of the 1942 production would not appear until the end of that year and so the Germans would still face only some 4,000 operational Russian machines in mid-1942 with 3,000 or more of their own.

As to the Russian equipment itself, it was rugged but serviceable. Only essential parts received a high standard of 'finish', but where 'finish' was needed it was good. This simplicity not only boosted production by cutting out time-consuming processes in the factories, it also suited the limited abilities of the Russian tank crews—men whose courage was resolute but whose mechanical background and aptitude left much to be desired. All soldiers are by nature rough with their equipment and the Russians were insensitive to theirs.

While there remained serious imbalances in the process of Russian recovery, this applied particularly to their administrative support. Due to a dire shortage of mechanical transport everything ran on a shoe-string. Thus the Russians were forced to rely quite frequently upon sustaining their advances with stocks of captured enemy fuel, while, later, the vast shipments of trucks which had been sent from the USA undoubtedly became the vital element in making possible the large-scale operation of the mass of tanks being built. British and American officers visiting the Russian armies were usually perplexed by the off-hand Russian approach to logistics, and the Germans were frankly baffled by the way Russian armies seemed to advance without visible support. Yet to Albert Speer, with a civilian technologist's knowledge of Russian tank superiority, it was inexplicable how the German Army in 1942 were able to withstand the Russians at all. Though the Russians as yet misunderstood tank warfare the Germans remained in ignorance of the latent prowess of their principal opponent.

British recovery in the tank field since the débâcle at Dunkirk in 1940 had been less spectacular than with the Russians after Moscow in 1942. Compelled to go on making obsolescent tanks armed only with 40mm guns (since to turn over to larger machines with the 57mm gun would have meant no tanks at all) the British were forced into battle in 1942 using tanks that were virtually powerless. Because production of the 57mm and its successor, the 76.2mm gun, had been deferred, these would not arrive at the front until, respectively, mid-1942 and early 1943. But it was not only a matter of production policy but too slow an evolution of fresh designs by the tank hierarchy who were compelled to allow British factories to go on churning out so many of the older tanks in 1942. There had then been incompetence to develop a battleworthy cruiser tank of the next generation armed with the 57mm gun, to meet the laid-down specifications, and obstruction as well as difficulties in mounting this bigger gun on the existing types.

Unlike the more foresighted Russians and Germans, the prewar British designers had failed to take into account the need for adapting one generation of tank to be fit to accept the next larger gun without a major re-design. The net result was further retrogression in the race for combat superiority against the Germans. But in defence of the prewar designers it must be stated that financial stringency had kept their number and quality below the level of inspiration while the directions they had received from a bickering and confused General Staff had been misguiding.

The Americans were probably in best condition of all, for their Grant would come into service in the nick of time to turn the scales in battle, while its successor, the greatly improved Sherman, would make use of many parts common to the Grant. In any case, American production was expanding at so colossal a rate that waste was acceptable: in the USA quality was good but quantity came before all else. Faced in 1942 with a proposal to reduce Sherman production in order to start manufacture of a new and much more powerful medium tank—the T20—they

Top left Colonel Ernest Swinton
Top right Colonel Estiénne
Left Colonel J. F. C. Fuller
Above Colonel A. R. Chaffee

A French Schneider advances with its infantry

British Mark Vs advance for the Battle of Amiens

British medium and light tanks at manoeuvres on Salisbury Plain in 1931
Bottom A German tank and infantry team advances during the Battle of France in 1940

Top German assault guns with accompanying infantry in the Russian winter, November 1942

Bottom British Matildas in the Western Desert in 1941

Top Russian T34s pass one of their victims – a knocked out German PzKpfw III

Bottom Russian T34s and infantry on the attack – Kursk, 1943

Top Specialized armour lands on the Normandy beach-heads on D-Day

Bottom Shermans pass a knocked-out German Tiger in the bocage

Opposite top An Israeli Centurion in action in Sinai, 1967

Opposite bottom Armoured personnel carriers – the modern light tank – of the United States Army in action in Vietnam

Top left General Heinz Guderian

Top right General von Manstein

Left General George Patton,
General Omar Bradley and
General Sir Bernard Montgomery

Above General G. K. Zhukov

opted to continue with improved versions of the Shermans—a decision which, in battle at a later date, was to cost both them and their allies much blood and concern against stronger German opponents.

Enfeebled weapons in quantity would compete with a force of diminishing quality as the tank-dependent armies in Europe and the desert lined up at the turning point of the war. In the final analysis, however, fuel would be the crucial factor and by 1942 it was the sources of oil production which had become the targets of grand strategy.

Chapter 18

THE OIL SEARCH

After Rommel had taken Benghazi and moved his light forces closer to the British at Gazala in February 1942, there came a pause in the Western Desert. There had to be: the British were spent and the Germans starved of petrol. In Russia, however, the fighting hardly ceased, for as their counter-offensive at Moscow died away the Russians attempted to recapture the industrially important Donets Basin in attacks from 18 January 1942 well into May. At peak periods the Russians threw in upward of a thousand tanks and yet the final result was invariably the same, for having committed practically every sin in the tank tactical manual they were ignominiously destroyed by the Germans.

To the south of Kharkov a conventional artillery and infantry attack had gained the Russians a broad salient along with the options to strike in any one of several directions towards the German rear. A prominent Russian historian, taking up the story, underlines Russian ineptitude in failing to integrate breaching operations with the succeeding exploitation: 'By the evening of May 14 the right conditions had been provided for introducing mobile forces into the battle in order to exploit the success... but for a number of reasons this profitable opportunity was not seized.' He goes on: 'false intelligence that the enemy was concentrating large Panzer force near Zmiyev... delayed the introduction of the [Russian] mobile formations. . . .'

Quite apparently the Russians still divided operations into separate compartments and were incapable of switching smoothly from one to another, but in addition they were hypnotized by the mere suggestion of a non-existent German tank threat as once the Germans had been mesmerized in 1918 by an Allied threat. But once the Russians had lost momentum the initiative passed to the Germans who, launching a quick double pincer across the base of the salient, within hours had encircled the Russian assault formations and within days eliminated them. Panzer divisions and corps were by now the masters in smoothly changing their posture from defence to attack and thus exposed to ridicule the inflexible Russians.

Published Russian statistics emphasize the German ability to concentrate at the vital point, for while the Russians claimed a two-to-one numerical advantage in tanks in the Baravenko sector they admitted to the Germans having achieved a four-to-one superiority at *their* point of impact. Strategic excuses are given in mitigation of the failure to deal with this surprise attack and it is true that troops who are poised for attack can find it difficult to switch to defence. But well-led tank forces possess the inherent ability to change strategic in addition to tactical direction if command and control are speedily exerted. The Russians' reaction at command level was slower than tank speed in spring 1942. Once off balance their recovery was always problematical.

The restoration of German tank strength depended upon the economic employment of machines behind a wall of infantry divisions. It was the infantry divisions, well supported by assault guns, which usually absorbed the shock of the Russian attacks while the Panzer divisions tried to stay uncommitted until the Russians showed obvious signs of weakening. By the middle of June much had been done to repair the ravages of the winter crisis and many of the modified tanks were in service. Between Voronezh and Rostov a mighty force was gathering for the prime strategic blow of the year. But already in the Western Desert the seeds of strategic dispersion had been sown.

Rommel swarmed round the southern desert extremity of the British line at Gazala on 26 May—making his approach by night and his tanks' entry into battle at first light. His aim was the swift capture of Tobruk and with it the destruction of the British army: thereafter he was to stand on the defensive while the Luftwaffe turned to spearhead an invasion of Malta and, once and for all, eliminate the threat to the Axis supply line to North Africa. Until that was done an advance into Egypt could be tactically risky if not logistically impossible.

In tanks Rommel was stronger than ever before—560 all told including 19 of the new Mark III Specials, but 228 of the old Italian types. Yet the British were stronger still with 849 tanks, including 167 Grants, and a great accumulation of guns of which the new 57mm anti-tank gun was an important addition. Dug in behind deep minefields they prepared their own attack though aware that the Germans were likely to strike first. Only in aircraft was Rommel greater in numbers—with 497 in service compared with 190 British. Air power would not decide the campaign, however, for both sides were by now inured to its terrors.

Surprise was what Rommel needed to offset his other disparities, and this was denied him for the British were forewarned and, though committing many of their old errors by making diluted tank forays instead of concentrating their attacks in time and space, struck back hard. General Ritchie, a wiser commander from successive drubbings at Rommel's hands, exhorted his tank leaders to work in close collaboration and to resist the temptation to launch hasty, unco-ordinated attacks. But in a fast-moving battle, when opportunities are fleeting, exhortation is no substitute for firm control and frequently this can be imposed only from the apex of command where the most up-to-date information is available—the only level from which fully co-ordinated instructions can be issued.

In this centralization lay a snag, however, for orders which were sent in clear by radio were open to the prying ears of enemy monitors while encoding took more time than was often to spare. Telephonic communication, though more secure, was extremely vulnerable to interruption not only by shellfire but also from the hundreds of vehicles cutting cables. Messengers were also slow and vulnerable to interception and this applied to commanders, too, when sometimes they endeavoured to rendezvous for a conference. Lacking a clear-cut understanding of armoured tactical doctrine and confused by muddled communications, the British commanders temporized. Moreover Ritchie himself leant heavily on Auchinleck as they indulged in protracted correspondence about the conduct of the battle. Firm decisions frequently seemed to wear an apologetic air; speed in their execution was at a premium.

In a haze of misunderstanding—and this was not confined to the British alone—the tank and gun crews, British, German and Italian, fought with steadfast determination. To Rommel the Grant tank came as a shock. 'Our heavy tank losses (more than a third by the 27th) were no good beginning to the battle.' Lieutenant Schmidt, one of his officers, met the Grant at close range: 'I saw some [of our 50mm] shells bounce harmlessly off . . .' and then: 'From out of the dip emerged rank after rank of the new tanks. . . . They came at us with every muzzle blazing.' Some Grants burst into flames, but Schmidt and his men were overrun, the high-explosive 75mm shells of the Grants ripping his guns to pieces. (One wonders, however, why the Grants took the risk of a charge since they had the capability of shelling the 50mm guns out of effective anti-tank range; but the ancient concept of getting blood on the tracks still held the British in thrall.)

On the British side, Lieutenant-Colonel 'Pip' Roberts of 3rd RTR detected a trend as worrying to him as were the Grants to Schmidt: '. . . 8th Hussars almost entirely incomplete. . . . Advanced Div HQ had been "put in the bag" including the Div Commander—things must have been very out of hand for that to have occurred. . . .' This was the confusion of a tank battle at its zenith—clouds of dust, whirling vehicles with flashing guns, utter confusion and hovering uncertainty, fear and bravery. Only night, when the gunners could no longer see to shoot, might give a breathless pause to regroup, replenish and restore a shaken composure.

By the 29th, having failed to defeat the British tanks in battle, Rommel found himself high and dry at the end of a supply line which had been intercepted by the British in the south. In desperation he was forced back against the British minefields, trying to clear a new, short-cut route through the mines to the west. Simultaneously, and with a suspicion of desperation in the position that his boldness had placed him, he tried to recuperate by recovering and repairing broken-down machines; for him there were few replacements while the British, he knew, had plenty and might soon throw an overwhelming tank force against him in his temporary, immobile haven known as the Cauldron.

With everything in their favour the British still lay victim to the habits and fears of past experience. The need to attack the Cauldron suggested, to them, an old-fashioned set-piece assault put in after long deliberation—even though every hour lost was one gained by Rommel to strengthen his resistance. Conference followed conference in a boundless debate from which incisive orders rarely emerged. Artillery units were not co-ordinated and serious obstruction was raised by infantry leaders who feared what might befall if they were left without armoured protection.

Evidence that Rommel was in no position to threaten anyone seems to have been overlooked but, of course, the British were unaware that on 30 May Rommel admitted that 'If we don't get a convoy through tonight I shall have to ask General Ritchie for terms', but they had no need to guess very hard to realize that he was in dire straits. As it happened a convoy did get through that night but even so the opportunity to strike an annihilating blow remained. A week later, however, on 5 June when at last the British blow fell, it was both too late and inept.

The British artillery barrage which was intended to engulf Rommel's dug-in guns fell harmlessly on empty desert and so their tanks and infantry crawled forward to the concentric lash of accurate German anti-tank shot. Once the initial British plan had broken down there was a hiatus. The British tanks, milling aimlessly at the mercy of what amounted to an ambush, merely presented unrivalled targets to unshaken German gunners while British artillery failed to concentrate its efforts.

There followed the epitome of tank opportunism as, seeing his chance, Rommel threw everything into a violent counter-attack. The British back-pedalled, stopped attacking, broke into fragments and in the days to follow were harried to destruction. The mere tally of tanks in action ceased to have meaning, not even if official computations allowed three of the older British tanks to be equal to one German tank with only the Grant considered at parity—a tenuous parity, in fact, when measured against the first few Mark IV Specials just beginning to arrive. British command and control collapsed ignominiously—the chorus of woe filling their radio links providing Mellenthin's monitors with a clear story of disruption and a word-picture of the British dispositions. Before the issue could be fully grasped the British tank and artillery force was all but destroyed, the survivors swept back into the Tobruk garrison or across the Egyptian frontier and Rommel was launching a tumultuous attack into Tobruk on the lines he had intended the previous November.

So sudden was it all that Axis thinking became as shaken as their opponents, for given the sight of the dream of conquering Egypt within a matter of days (for all the logistical risk) Hitler and Mussolini scrapped the plan to take Malta and seized the opportunist line of strategic approach. With less than 24 hours' consideration Hitler reacted to Rommel's request for an attack against Egypt as a tank commander at the front would react to the glimpse of a gap in a line of anti-tank guns. By 25 June the Axis tanks were on the outskirts of Mersa Matruh, having travelled 200 miles in four days.

Rommel's tank victory had overturned Axis strategy. On the eve of the German advance into the Caucasus he had now to justify by another tactical victory, against 150 British tanks, his claim to be leader of the southern prong of the offensive in search of oil. But his means were extremely limited for the tanks which had won him the chance were faltering at low strength. Moreover his opponent was beginning to take a grip, although British confusion was still rife.

Auchinleck sacked Ritchie as the Axis attack on Mersa Matruh was beginning. General Gott, commanding the XIII Corps, was a tired and dispirited man—one who had endured two hard years of intensive armoured battles and whose ideas were as exhausted as his physique. Fast-moving tank warfare multiplies strain and eats up the endurance of men: there is no place for despondency and every reason to give commanders as well as followers a periodic rest. At Mersa Matruh Rommel's errors (and he too was getting weary even if he did not show it) and British combatance brought the Germans to a halt on the very edge of defeat. Yet wrongly judging that the Axis had won through again and surrendering to the pervading atmosphere of defeatism, Gott prematurely pulled back his tank forces on the road to El Alamein. Pleasantly surprised, Rommel followed and on 30 June arrived at El Alamein, momentarily ahead of the 1st British Armoured Division since he had motored down the coast road while the British drove more slowly through the deeper desert sand.

There, at El Alamein on 1 July, Rommel experienced something new. Auchinleck, deprived of all but a small and shaken mobile reserve, was compelled to hold the 40-mile gap between the Mediterranean and the Qattara Depression with partially immobile infantry formations. But since there were too few infantry to hold a continuous line he had to depend on the one strong arm left to him—the strong arm of British artillery fire positioned as to bring down flexible concentrations of fire both in protection of the scattered infantry fortresses and to deluge the spaces in between. When Rommel tried to seize individual

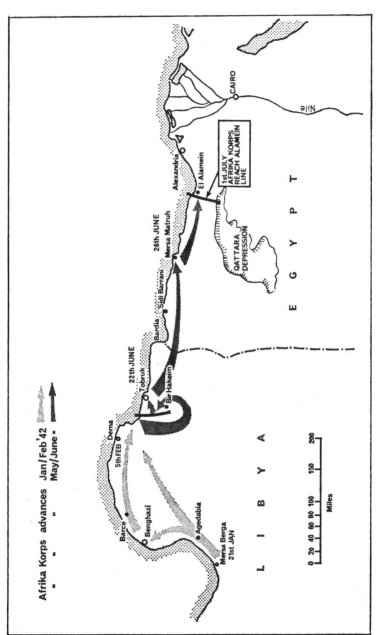

Map 14   The German advance to Alamein

fortresses by direct attack he found it too expensive: when he tried to by-pass them his tanks sometimes got through but the unarmoured infantry and artillery could not penetrate the barrage of shells. No longer could the British be bullied into retreat by a lonely tank threat. The Alamein position held out and Egypt was safe from invasion because there was no other approach for tanks. Indeed, on 4 July it might well have been the Axis who suffered a serious defeat since by then only 50 of their tanks were left and these might easily have been cut to pieces by 1st Armoured Division. But the British tank crews, disillusioned by repeated reverses, were stopped dead by the crack from just a few 88s.

For the rest of the month a seesaw struggle raged the length of the Alamein front. Lacking room for wide manoeuvre tanks and infantry hammered by guns became locked in a head-on grapple. The side on the defensive held all the trumps as artillery came to dictate the battle as once it had held sway in the First World War. Tanks, whose crews were more circumspect in action than ever, took inordinate care to avoid risks. Thousands of mines clogged the few open spaces between defended localities. The British, seeking the Axis areas of least resistance, picked on the weaker Italian infantry formations, hoping to overrun them at night and then to be ready at dawn with tanks and guns to check the enemy reflex action—the abrupt counter-attack by German tanks. If with care and a little luck the British tanks managed to wend their way through soft sand and minefields on to the vital ground, they stood the chance of catching their opponent at a disadvantage in the open. If they failed and became stuck in the open themselves, it would be their infantry who would be rounded up by German attack while they were shot to pieces at the standstill.

Both sides had to fight it out in a slogging match without recourse or space for subtlety or evasion. A tank driver wrote:

We were scrapping against some tanks and we were hit twice on the front. I saw the sparks fly from the first one just like welding and the next took the visor away. It is about a foot square and I lay flat.... Didn't it look a big hole though. The major shouted down 'was I alright' and to keep my head out of sight as he couldn't pull back just yet. I said I was doing fine thanks but not to make a night of it. Soon after they broke and ran for it.

In due course exhaustion had to set in to leave the Alamein line littered with tank carcasses. One new British brigade, in its first action, contributed more than a hundred of its 180 machines when they attempted a series of Balaclava-like charges across open ground. Two hundred men were lost too—not a high figure, perhaps, by the standards of an infantry battle, but expensive in terms of trained specialists. For the moment, however, the way to the Canal and the oil was blocked. But in the Caucasus the Germans appeared to be doing rather well.

As Rommel neared El Alamein, the German Army unleashed its Caucasus offensive on 28 June. Army Group A, including Eleventh and Seventeenth Armies and Kleist's First Panzer Army (four Panzer divisions) would cross the Don above Rostov and make for Baku via Maikop and Grozny, while Army Group B, with Paulus's Sixth Army and Hoth's Fourth Panzer Army (between them six Panzer divisions) would thrust out flank protection in the north along the Don and seize a protective bastion on the Volga at Stalingrad.

The Russians, after losing so many troops in the south already and having also located the bulk of their reserves north of Voronezh, were in no state to withstand the onrush of more than 3,000 tanks and assault guns. At times, on the Stalingrad sector, the ratio of German to Russian tanks would be two to one, and in the bend of the Don, where Kleist made the main effort, even higher. Of tank battles, however, there was only one of protracted importance and this took place against Fourth Panzer Army at Goroditnie in a battle of classic form. Recalling that Fourth Panzer Army was provided with direct command over its own air reconnaissance, von Mellenthin summarizes the German technique with words as terse as the action itself: '. . . the leading Russian tank formations ran head on into the anti-tank guns of the Panzer Corps and were then wiped out by German tanks attacking them in flank and rear. As our commanders were able to look in good time at "the other side of the hill" they could set traps for the approaching Russians and smash their counter-attack one after the other.'

A tank sergeant remarked of the Russians: 'They fire their guns like madmen, but they don't hurt us.' The tanks crashed through to the Don and from Hitler downwards people began to talk of the war in the East entering its final stage. But with tank success came the customary euphoria and tampering with strategy. To Hitler and the High Command it seemed that almost automatically Stalingrad would fall to the Sixth Army. Therefore since the Caucasus was the main objective Fourth Panzer Army could be safely diverted to assist First Panzer Army in the crossing of the Don.

But the defective German base organization had yet to be properly decentralized to cater for repairs in the field. Hence a deluge of tanks converging on the narrow confines of the Don bend in mid-July not only overloaded the entire German administrative system but stranded many tanks for lack of spares and service. In any case, Kleist did not need help. It took him just two days to construct bridges over the river where Russian resistance was so paltry that the men took time off to swim. Kleist's leading tanks crossed on 25 July—those of Hoth's Fourth Panzer Army not until the 29th—and Kleist could have gone much faster had not the traffic congestion, redoubled by the arrival of Hoth's mass of vehicles, clogged the roads and partially strangled fuel supplies.

Yet First Panzer Army, when once it got started, simply bounded ahead—75 miles in four days to Proletarskaya, 120 miles in seven days to Stavropol, 100 miles in four days to Maikop and then a long chase ever deeper into endless steppe towards Mozdok and Grozny. Always short of fuel and never seeming to capture sufficient from the Russians (who had all but vanished) Kleist gradually began to lose momentum. Tanks were wearing out and the men losing their enthusiasm. The increasing volume of worries besetting Kleist's sense of purpose came not so much from conditions at the front—which were peculiar enough—but from strategic changes taking place over his left shoulder. At the front the one-time vacuum in the Soviet defences had first of all been replaced by heavy air attacks— attacks which could put a brake but not a stop to the tank columns—and a gradual hardening of local resistance by indigenous troops in the most difficult hilly and wooded country. There was no such thing as a front—merely a string of moving

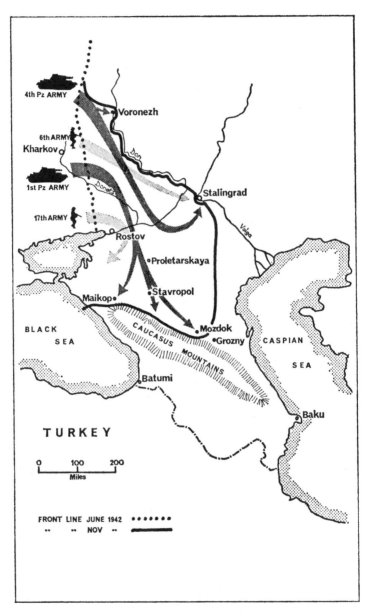

Map 15   Drive to the Caucasus and Stalingrad – 1942

tank pockets fighting a widespread guerrilla war against an opponent who set ambushes, hung on the flanks and made periodic raids on lengthening supply lines. And as German movement became sluggish the Russian attacks increased in efficiency and frequency.

At Stalingrad, however, the front was becoming all too well defined. Sixth Army had been slow making its way to the secondary German strategic objective and slower still as it met and found it could not overcome the stream of Russian reinforcements pouring down from the north. Hoth's Fourth Panzer Army soon found itself switched back to the original objective but, whereas this could have been snapped up easily in June, by mid-August the opposition was tough. And as it got tougher the secondary objective turned, in Hitler's mind, into the primary goal. Having changed a military objective in the desert into an economic and political one, he converted the economic objective in Russia into a military one in an effort to destroy the Russian Army once and for all. But in the relatively narrow space between the Don and the Volga and with only one objective clearly in view—Stalingrad—the Panzer army had no free options for strategic manoeuvre.

Inevitably when the tanks gradually became committed to close battle in the city's environs the lessons learnt in 1939 at Warsaw went overboard. At Stalingrad two Panzer corps commanders—Wittersheim and Schwedler—protested at the waste and were sacked by Paulus, the commander of the embattled Sixth Army. Down in the Caucasus Kleist protested when every vestige of air support (except for reconnaissance aircraft) was removed from him in order to reinforce the Stalingrad front. The Panzer armies were being immobilized in battle for the first time in their history.

It was much the same on the Russian side, too. The German presence at Stalingrad threatened the integrity of the entire front, for if the city fell the south would be isolated from the north. Prestige was also involved with Stalin constantly pressing Zhukov, the newly appointed Front Commander, into premature relief attacks. Short of ammunition and fuel, the Russian tanks and infantry were sacrificed between the Don and Volga as the German tanks were being sacrificed in the suburbs of Stalingrad. Once manoeuvre had been rejected in favour of head-on assaults the vicious circle tightened. Each tank was relegated to the status of just another weapon, shorn of its inherent omnipotence. But the Russians saw where this was leading whereas the Germans had become blinded by the smoke of battle.

Zhukov and Vasilevski, conferring with Stalin on 12 September, considered there must be some other way out than just unadulterated attrition. They decided, to quote Zhukov, 'first, to continue to wear down the enemy by an active defence; second to prepare a counter-offensive of such magnitude . . . as to shift the strategic situation in the south decidedly in our favour'. Yet, 'as for the Soviet troops . . . they were unable to defeat the enemy with existing forces. . . . But by November Supreme Headquarters would have at its disposal strong new mechanized and tank forces equipped with the world famous T34 tanks which would enable us to undertake more far-reaching tasks.'

The new wave of Russian tank production was flowing at last from the rejuvenated factories, and this must have been foremost in Zhukov's calculations at this moment. Meanwhile the flood from another spring was about to alter the strategic balance in Africa. The tide was on the turn.

Chapter 19

AT THE MOMENT OF CHANGE

So devastating were the sea and air attacks upon Rommel's lines of communication that, by 30 August 1942, he knew he had either to break through at once to the Nile Valley or forever admit defeat. Not only was he aware of the irreversible lowering of his own strength in contrast to that of his opponent, but he could sense the decline in the overall strength of the Axis in relation to the host of enemies gathered against it. At this crucial moment, moreover, he lacked the choice of direction which had always been the origin of his victories in the past—the options to move when he liked and where he wished without treading well-worn paths such as his enemy could predict.

He was compelled to execute a perceptible wheel round the southern flank of the British position at Alamein to burst through a gap between Deir el Munassib and Qaret el Himeimat, with the aim of getting astride the coastal road, after bypassing the enemy-occupied Alam Halfa Ridge. This merely repeated the Gazala gambit and gambled on the British falling into the panicky errors of the past. But in gambling Rommel put his money on a lame horse by tending to despise an enemy under a new commander — Lieutenant-General Montgomery—of unrecorded ability. Not only did Rommel ignore Montgomery, he also seems to have disregarded the importance of ground as a prime factor in tank warfare, though at the root of his miscalculations lay one imponderable—petrol supply.

Trapped during a night approach march amid unexpected minefields and soft sand, the Axis tanks were late turning north on the 31st. Moreover, they were forced to change their preordained direction, for the shortage of petrol enforced economies in running distance and diverted the axis of advance closer to the west and thus directly towards the Alam Halfa Ridge. And already there were signs that the British were reacting with unusual stability: they seemed under tighter control and disinclined to rush into a mêlée. Hardly ever could the long 75s on the new Mark IV Specials find an opportunity to come into action against exposed targets even at their extreme effective range of 1,200 metres.

Cautiously the Germans approached the Ridge, which looked ominously devoid of enemy, until suddenly, at a range of less than 1,000 yards, Grants appeared all over the crest and the scene was rent by the flash of tracer shot, the clouds of dust from gun discharge and track-blown sand and the crack of high-velocity shot. Unfortunately for the Germans they were unaware that certain posts protruding from the sands, and to which they often drove close, had been set out as markers so that the British tank and anti-tank gunners could tell the exact range at which to fire, thus increasing their chances of scoring a hit first time. Quite soon several of the leading German tanks lay silent or in flames as among them shouldered the Mark IVs, halting to let their gunners seek the range and then to begin a belated exchange with the Grants standing high on the slope ahead. Now it was the Grants' turn to burst into flames, their crews 'baling out' to run for cover; a gap opening up in the British line through which the Germans began to ease their way with sinister purpose. At a few hundred yards' range, however, two new factors affected play as concealed British anti-tank guns discarded their camouflage to open a deadly, short-range fusillade while yet more Grants and Crusaders drove on to the crest to close the gap. To the Gemans their losses became insupportable. With nothing more to offer in attack, they could but withdraw to 3,000 yards and hope the British would impetuously follow, as so often they had in the past, against a line of anti-tank guns lying in ambush. But again only bombing and shelling pursued them, and for hours on end, without relaxation, the tank phalanxes glowered—each waiting upon the other.

Rommel could not charge again and Montgomery declined to advance on ground of Rommel's choosing. And even when, later, Montgomery's tanks charged elsewhere, in an attempt to close the gap at El Munassib, an instant holocaust of burning Valentines lit the signal for a renewed standstill order. Only the bombers continued their non-stop pummelling to remind Rommel that he could no longer wait at the end of a disintegrating supply-line until, on 2 September, he took the hint and pulled back, the only alternative to being marooned. Indeed, by 6 September, 51 tanks the poorer, he had returned to the start point the wiser by a lesson he used to teach the British—that of the folly of throwing unsupported tanks upon an unshaken gun-line.

The arrest of Rommel at Alam Halfa, the slowing down of Kleist in the Caucasus and the frustration of Paulus and Hoth in the grapple at Stalingrad all imparted refreshed hope in Allied breasts. Not only in Russia might a turn of fortune be impending but the chances of grasping the entire North African shore became a real possibility. In the ports of the USA and in Britain convoys designated to land forces between Morocco and Tunisia were gathering. In Egypt preparations for an offensive were still further advanced, placing over a thousand tanks at Montgomery's disposal at El Alamein.

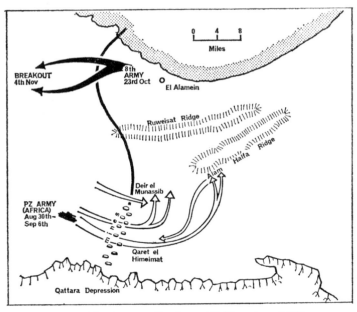

Map 16   Autumn Battles at El Alamein – 1942

Montgomery the infantryman, unlike the infantryman Rommel, would first attempt to destroy his opponent's unarmoured formations (virtually this meant the Italians) and would then shift his armour to places of vantage where they could continue the 'crumbling' of the Axis and, of vital importance, engage the Axis tanks as they were attracted to the rescue of their compatriots. Not only did Montgomery correctly surmise that the Axis tanks could 'not sit still and watch the gradual destruction of the infantry', but he revived and adapted the traditional British tactic of conducting a strategic offensive from a tactically defensive posture. His intention was to wage a battle of attrition fought by a combination of all arms—infantry, artillery, tanks and aircraft but with tanks relegated to a more subsidiary role than ever before in the desert.

Before Rommel had departed for Germany to take a cure for his failing health he had instigated a defensive system which, in its way, conformed to Montgomery's tactics. He had to restrict the movement of his tanks and therefore German and Italian armoured formations were integrated and layered behind and along the length of the infantry front, detailed to intervene in small groups in their immediate locality only if the British penetrated the infantry line. That this denied them the advantage of concentration was unavoidable: petrol shortage forbade high mobility and dictated minor tactics at a time when Hitler steadfastly refused permission for withdrawal to a safer place. But when Montgomery attacked on 23 October and Rommel (who had returned to the sound of the guns within 24 hours) discovered that the entire British effort was being channelled against one sector alone, the Axis plan collapsed. Piecemeal Rommel's tanks were drawn inexorably towards the vital point and there consumed. Ten days' pummelling, in which the Axis tanks fought almost invariably at a tactical disadvantage, so reduced Rommel's army as a whole that only a reversion of their natural mobile role, regardless of the consequences of fuel starvation, would suffice.

By then, it was true, the British themselves had also sustained heavy tank losses. But by that stage so large were their reserves that replacements almost kept pace with wastage and losses in machines to the British were of little account. One brigade, alone, when ordered to break out at all costs, lost 87 tanks—75 per cent of its original strength—in a few hours, and others suffered similarly. Yet when the time came to exploit the break-out, a mass of machines (including the powerful American-built Shermans in this their first battle) were ready to overwhelm only 40 surviving German tanks unaided by a single 88mm gun.

Although he had kept so tight a grip on the close fighting, Montgomery rather let the reins go slack when the time for ruthless exploitation arrived. Planning from a caravan and only occasionally driving to observation posts at the front or to his junior commanders' command posts, it was as if he assumed that tank units, like cavalry of old, could envelop the enemy by some divine process divorced from strong central direction. Certainly it had been impressed upon him by the tank leaders that the tank units were only too eager for fast runs, free of the slogging match, but when the time came they were neither poised for the chase nor administratively prepared. German tank generals, with greater experience, could have told Montgomery that a successful pursuit and encirclement operation requires closer control from the forefront of the battle than the infantry dog-fight. Frequently the Russians had failed because they, too, had relinquished close personal direction over mobile troops from the highest level: now Montgomery, somewhat remote from the battle, committed the same error and Rommel was allowed to escape on the run.

How far Rommel could run depended, however, upon what happened in French North-West Africa, for as his tanks shook Egypt's dust off their tracks, news came of the landing in Morocco and Algeria. Soon the Allied columns would be darting into Tunisia from the west and this to Rommel, racing back from the east, presaged 'the end in Africa'. To Hitler, meanwhile, they represented just another nail in the coffin of his bankrupt strategy.

In June 1942, at the end of a year's utter desolation in their prosecution of tank warfare, the Russian Chief of Armoured Forces published an official doctrine to bring senior field commanders up to date and into line. In several ways General Fedyunenko's intructions reiterated what the British tank leaders had said after a month's bitter experience in 1940 but, whereas the British had tried gentle persuasion in educating their commanders, the Russians were unequivocally dogmatic and spelled out the lessons. The armoured corps would be preserved for strategic missions, it was stated, and would not be split up to reinforce the infantry but used for deep penetrations to a depth of 25 to 30 miles for the purpose of encircling the enemy's main forces. Closer co-operation was demanded with air forces and with the artillery, infantry and engineers. When deep thrusts were made a second wave would follow swiftly through the gap to assist the tanks.

It was envisaged that these independent operations might be of 72 to 96 hours' uninterrupted duration, that they might be made in conjunction with partisans or airborne troops and that action should be against the enemy's front and rear—above all, by surprise and not frontally. In such detail was this order written that it even stipulated the rations to be carried by the tank crews—two to three tins of canned meats or sausage, soup concentrates, bread, sugar and tea, etc. The Russians thus admitted the paucity of previous fundamental organization when, so late in the day, they felt the need to record such minor detail in a major policy instruction. No doubts were permitted. From then on Russian tank skills showed startling signs of improvement along strictly governed lines.

The Russians claim that the plan for a counter-offensive at Stalingrad in November was worked out by the General Staff and was not a creation of genius by a single brain. Certainly Fedyunenko was involved in the planning, along with Zhukov, Vasilevski and others, and beyond doubt the rules laid down by Fedyunenko were rigidly applied. Yet to the vast 180-mile arena separating the two converging Russian thrusts, which were intended to envelop the Germans in the confines of Stalingrad, only 894 Russian tanks were committed to engage 675 German tanks at the outset—barely a few score more than the numbers at grips on the much narrower front of El Alamein. Concentration in space was not therefore the criterion against Germans who had been unwise enough to leave unguarded gaps along their extended flanks. Concentration in time was to be vital once the offensive had started—the time it took Hoth's armour to disengage from its close involvement near the city in order to assert its mobility against the Russian advance, and the time it would take the Russians to complete their encirclement and strengthen the arms of their embrace.

After the Russians had broken through, almost at will, on either side of Stalingrad on 19 November, it took them exactly the 96 hours prescribed by Fedyunenko to complete the encirclement with a junction of the two penetrating thrusts at Kalach on the 23rd. The speed of Russian execution had been unprecedented and deprived Hoth's tanks of sufficient time to concentrate for a

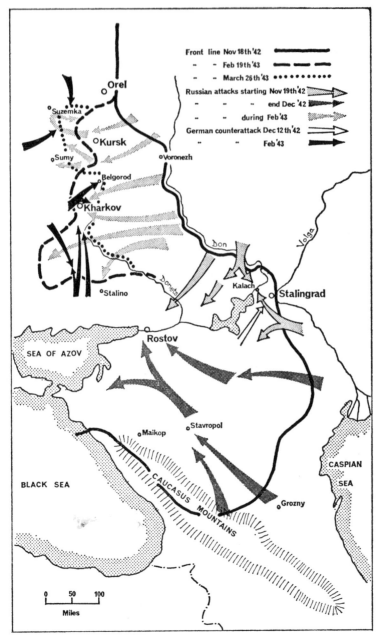

Map 17   Winter Campaign in Russia 1942/3

robust counterblow. Yet it was to be some days before the Russian embrace could be consolidated. Though off balance and attenuated, Fourth Panzer Army remained a deadly force if given freedom of action and, in any case, if Paulus had been allowed to withdraw from Stalingrad at once, as he wished, there would have been no stopping him. Numbers were about equal on either side and superior fighting quality by no means in the Russian favour.

But Hitler forbade such a move and insisted upon holding Stalingrad and launching a deliberate relief operation to open a permanent lane straight to the city's perimeter defences. Thus he surrendered a priceless asset—the power inherent in a resilient mobility free to take advantage of unlimited options for variable action. Thereby he sentenced his armies to a slogging match within the limits of a precisely defined and relatively small sector where any competent general could predict his opponents' reactions with practical certainty. Having flown in the face of propriety by sending tanks into Stalingrad in the first place, Hitler certified their doom by restricting the obvious course of relief to one easily computable direction.

There can be little doubt that the German predicament stemmed in part from the overweening confidence acquired after two years' success. Not only Hitler but also his General Staff had begun to accredit a handful of tanks with magical powers beyond the bounds of military reason. Even when danger was so obviously imminent, as it always had been at Stalingrad, they seemed to persuade themselves that a Panzer army's tank spearhead could wave a wand and cause the Russians to vanish as of old. No such thing happened for matters of fact and quality intervened. Chiefly the Russian machines were brand new T34s and KVs in excellent running order and as yet unharmed by their clumsy operators. Mostly the German tanks were old Mark IIIs and IVs with several thousands of miles, acquired in many a victorious drive, registered in their log-books and the scars of a hundred battles thick upon their armour. This mechanical disparity might have been bearable had a steady flow of new German tanks replaced their total losses. The issue, instead, of several French tanks of pre-war vintage was not simply an invitation to suicide but a sheer waste of the good human material sent to crew them. Numbers in warfare dominated by technology are not in themselves enough; nor is courage to be insulted.

Thus when, on 12 December, the German relief offensive began, directed by Manstein, it was executed by only four weakened Panzer divisions against an opponent of equal strength who was already holding strengthened positions in depth. The Russian tactics were simple, and founded upon their own harsh experience: 'To sever the German tanks from their motorized units and supply services, and then to destroy them separately along the Aksay river'. The forces they allocated to the task were predominantly infantry, while their tank corps were withdrawn in readiness for local counter-attacks and then for a renewed major offensive once the German relief blow had exhausted itself. Even so the ensuing battle turned into a close-run thing, for when the Germans reached the Aksay (within fifty miles of Stalingrad) the Russians were being forced to expend troops earmarked solely for the coming offensive. And at that moment a renewed German onrush of ten miles raised tension to breaking point. The corridor was actually opening up even though German tank strength was being strained to the limit in appalling weather conditions and at this moment of climax permission by Hitler for Paulus to break out westward might have done more than rescue Sixth Army: it could have crushed the Russian defenders and reversed German fortunes at a stroke. But Hitler desired Stalingrad and went on deluding himself that Manstein would cut a way through on his own.

It mattered not that Manstein's tanks fought to within 40 miles of Stalingrad on 18 December. By then the Russians had found ample time to establish strong blocking positions, the German tank crews were at their last gasp and all question of reinforcing them had been dropped. Kleist's First Panzer Army had already been milked dry for the benefit of the northern front and had now to withdraw in haste from the Caucasus in order to preserve its communications with the rear. For no sooner had Manstein's forces shown that they were spent than the Russians were at their throats again. On 23 December the Russians began their new offensive, pushing through three tank corps to recover in a few days everything which Manstein had taken and increase the distance between Stalingrad and the rest of the German Army to 125 miles. Not only did this seal the fate of Paulus and his men but it threatened to isolate the entire German southern front.

The shock to the German Army was immense, while for the
Russians the encouragement was intoxicating. For a spell the
Germans thought they had lost the war, on the spot, just as the
Russians believed they had won it. Yet as the next two years
were to demonstrate this was but the beginning of an ebb and
flow in which each turn of the tide would be governed by the tugs
and pulls of sheer exhaustion. As one side expended its tank
armies' energies in the struggle for some strategic objective the
other would strive to conserve its strength, to create the conditions
for an overwhelming counter-offensive and to cancel out the
other's gains before taking advantage of the confusion to extend
the conflict deeper into fresh territory. The ultimate, controlling
factor would be the tanks—applied not only by improvements in
their combat ability but in efforts to keep them continually on
the move.

If the war at the front was bitter, along the lines of communications it was ceaseless and exhausting. Yet as the war
progressed the energy behind momentum steadily atrophied and
the daily distance covered by mechanized forces was actually
getting less on average; Guderian's 19 miles a day over a prolonged period in 1940 was never exceeded, and in 1943 the
Russians were doing well to average eight miles a day. Defensive
measures had improved by then, of course, and air attacks on
lines of supply could be crippling, but it was the law of con-
tracting communications, as an army withdrew and renewed its
strength closer to its supply base, which ultimately dictated events.
By 1943 a tank army did well if it could maintain constant
momentum of more than 250 miles in a single bound.

Even so the increasing complexity and killing power of new
weapons had effects such as could tilt the local balance in a tank
fight, and it was this promise of new weapons early in 1943
which did so much to overcome German despondency. While
Manstein worked feverishly to reorganize and strengthen the
broken southern front in Russia, and Rommel tried to pull things
together in North Africa, prodigious efforts were made in
Germany to rebuild the tank arm as the key source of any
chance there was of holding the Russians at bay.

Although Albert Speer had increased German tank production
beyond all imagination in 1942, by the turn of the year a cross-

roads had been reached not unlike that met by the British after Dunkirk. On the one hand the establishments at the front had to be filled by new machines regardless of their vintage: on the other the brand new and as yet unreliable designs had to be rectified and got into large-scale production—twin demands which were beyond the scope of German industry in the span of a few months. Not that the new Tigers were surefire successes as yet; near Leningrad and in Tunisia a few had been given their baptism of fire and, for all their immense strength and hitting power, had done badly due to their unreliability; nevertheless Hitler ordered production to be raised from 13 to 25 per month.

Panther, meanwhile, was on the verge of entering production just as Mark III production was being closed down (in November 1942) in order to make only assault guns. This meant that, of the proven tanks, only the Mark IV remained in production just when disasters were at their height and when Panzer divisions' strength had fallen to an average of 27 tanks. As if that were not enough Hitler, at the request of the General Staff, ordered the cessation of Mark IV production in order to make only Tigers and Panthers!

At the peak of this desperate lunacy, however, Hitler was persuaded to take one logical decision—to recall Guderian to service to put the tank arm to rights. Yet even this was out of character for, having once sacked a man, Hitler was rarely prepared to have him back.

It must have been galling for Guderian to return and find the Panzer arm—the creature of his life's work—at death's door, yet nobody else in Germany possessed his knowledge of the problems involved in building a tank force. Now he would need all his skill to cut corners and win time. But he was suffering from a weak heart and therefore had need to protect himself from the erosion that a ceaseless war of intrigue in committee could bring. He agreed to Hitler's request, therefore, on the condition that he should be 'in a position to influence the development of our armoured equipment both with Army Ordnance and with the Armaments Ministry' (that is with Speer). It was axiomatic, of course, that 'I be subordinated neither to the Chief of the Army General Staff nor to the Commander of the Training Army but directly to Hitler'. In a totalitarian State only dictatorial methods made headway. No such licence had been allowed when Hobart had sought almost identical powers in Britain in 1940; democracies have to retain their outward and inward appearances even in moments of desperation. But in 1943 these decisions were crucial to the continuation of the war and Guderian, having done much to make it possible, now played a key part in prolonging it.

To all intents and purposes Guderian had his way, for although he made a great noise over the artillery arm intriguing to retain control of the assault guns, this did little harm to his cause in view of the fact that he struck up a close collaboration with Speer, and Speer could ensure that the production of assault guns and the like would not get out of proportion to the needs of the Panzer divisions. Rationalized control was indeed the criterion in putting right an industrial empire which had been allowed to run riot. Despite material shortages, labour difficulties and heavy destruction by aerial bombardment, Speer was to demonstrate that Germany's industrial resources had hardly been tapped. Wildcat schemes, such as the production of a 1,500-ton tank and the wholesale adoption of a hollow-charge shell for the artillery as the panacea anti-tank weapon, had to be pushed aside. A weapon like the hollow-charge shell might have a chance in the distant future when a means had been insured to get it on target, but in 1943 the need was for proven, conventional, high-velocity guns possessing the power to penetrate and kill hard targets and with the maximum chance of a first-time hit.

Guderian's vendetta with the artillery may at times have seemed petty, but he saw more clearly than them that the dominance of the tank, though threatened, was by no means finished. Tanks in the future merely had to overcome a stiffening challenge by superior tactics, employing more accurate high-velocity guns mounted in vehicles with enhanced protection. If the infantry could be given better self-propelled, armoured assault and anti-tank guns, so much the better since it freed his tanks for independent action. And if the infantry could be given the easily-made handheld, hollow-charge weapon of the bazooka type for short-range anti-tank work, that was acceptable too. His main task, however, was to restore the confidence of the tank soldiers in the General Staff and give them renewed belief in their destiny, for soon they would be taking on the world in armour.

Whatever came from Guderian by way of doctrine, tactical methods or equipment the crews would accept as good. What he could not win them was time—the whole of 1943 without committal to a major offensive—to rebuild their strength to the level necessary for an overwhelming counter-stroke in 1944. Guderian wished for everything to be under armour by then— infantry, and artillery too. He also demanded that the subsidiary theatres of war should be deprived of the best tanks—meaning Africa and the other occupied territories. This was pure idealism, of course. Guderian could neither hope that the politically orientated Hitler could allow a whole year to pass without mounting a prestige offensive to give confidence to wilting allies; nor could he have all the weapons he said were essential. But Guderian did manage to instil some of the old fervour in his men and to make them feel that not only were they the givers of victory but also the recipients of weapons consonant with their calling.

At the root of the psychology fostered by Guderian was the belief than an armoured vehicle consolidated courage in a team of men. A single man under fire is the prey to his own will—strong or frail as it might be. To an infantry commander the problem of persuading individuals, hugging the ground in some open field or hiding in a building or hedgerow, to get up and advance against fire is enormous since he can only communicate directly with those closest to him. To a tank commander it is easier. If his is the strongest spirit present his orders to the driver are direct and enforced by personality: they are difficult to disobey and so the driver who lets in his clutch and drives ahead takes with him not only a powerful weapon system, capable of overawing a shocked enemy, but those others in the crew who might, in other circumstances, boggle at the risk. Thus tanks reduce waste in action by cutting down erosions by personal failure. For psychological reasons alone it is easier to initiate a quick tank attack than an improvised infantry assault.

And from 1943 onwards Germany could neither afford wastage nor failure in any department. Faced by overwhelming odds—the combined manpower and production of Russia, the USA and Britain which gave them a superiority in tanks alone of at least ten to one—the Germans could not hope to hold linear defences even had they so desired. Guderian's original concept of Panzer divisions to hold Germany's frontier by mobile defence was soon to be an inescapable actuality, but he seems to have hoped for too much from his reorganized forces to achieve total victory, good as they were to be. No longer did the 1940 psychological pattern hold good: the victims had learned to be steadfast; the smaller battalions could no longer totally prevail; big nations were proof against being unresistingly slain by a few tanks.

Chapter 20

STUDY IN CRISIS

German tanks played David against the Allied Goliath in Tunisia for the last time in February 1943. Yet when first the Allies had landed and rapidly seized the whole of Morocco and Algeria it had looked as if the Axis would be hard put to hold Tunisia at all. If the Allied spearheads could have won the first race for possession of the port of Tunis Rommel's fate would have been sealed, but the advanced guard, composed wholly of British troops and mainly motorized infantry, possessed but a single regiment of outmoded Valentine and Crusader tanks to provide the armoured punch. It was not that the British had forsaken tanks but simply that shipping difficulties had prevented them from bringing in a higher proportion with the first sea convoys. Thus only a handful of German tanks was required to rebuff the British and those, belonging to the improvized Axis battle groups (including a few Tigers) brought in by sea from Italy, were just in time to clash with the Allies near Djedeida, on the outskirts of Tunis, on 27 November.

By then, however, the Allies had outrun their strength, though the opportune arrival of some American Stuart tanks, as part of the advanced party of 1st US Armored Division, nearly turned stalemate into a renewed crisis for the Germans. Commanded with a dash worthy of their great cavalry patronymic, they had penetrated a gap left inadvertently open by the Germans and abruptly charged across Djedeida airfield to wreck 20 Stuka dive-bombers of the force then busily engaged in non-stop attacks against the advancing Allies. Although nothing was available to follow up, this was the essence of Chaffee's dream while the emotional effect on the German land force commander—once Guderian's Chief of Staff—was classically stunning. 'Nehring rang me up in a state of understandable excitement and drew the blackest conclusions,' wrote Kesselring, the Axis C-in-C, though Kesselring's response was also in the classical mould. He curtly told General Nehring to gather all 40 of his tanks and attack. As a tank specialist Nehring had credited the Allied tank force

with the sort of power German tank forces possessed: as an air-
man Kesselring may have underestimated the power of tanks but
his judgment was better balanced.

In the Medjerda Valley a total of fewer than a hundred tanks
postponed the end of the African campaign by some months, for
this tank battle in miniature not only deprived the Allies of
taking at one bounce the ports of Tunis and Bizerta, it bundled
them back into the hills, there to be penned while the Germans
built strong infantry defences guarding their lodgement area.
Furthermore the Allies had been thoroughly outfought in individual tank encounters and had suffered heavy losses in a series
of ambushes. On one unhappy occasion, when Combat Command
B of 1st Armored Division had to abandon 18 American tanks
with 41 guns and 130 other vehicles in a bog at night, just
about the entire remaining Allied tank reserve had been lost
without a shot being fired.

When the battle receded from Tunis and the winter rains fell
to reduce fighting on the northern front to a squabble for hill-tops
above mud-drenched valleys, infantry and artillery took over from
tanks and mobility died. It was thus to the south, where the desert
led towards Tripolitania, that the American armoured force
turned to test is prowess in an arena well suited for tank jousting.
And this too was the obvious assembly area for all three Panzer
divisions present—10th from Europe and the remnants of 15th
and 21st as they reached the end of a 1,500-mile retreat under
Rommel from Egypt.

Intent on rebuilding his strength and standing in the old
French Mareth Line fortifications to block the approaches to
southern Tunisia, Rommel had at least secured his communications
with Europe and with Kesselring, and could look round for a
chance to exploit a temporary advantage in strength. The obvious
targets were either the indigenous French Army, fighting again in
the Allied fold, or the Americans; the former because their
equipment was antiquated and their techniques of 1940 vintage,
the latter because of a self-advertised brashness similar to that
exhibited by the British in pre-Alamein days.

Sparring took place throughout the first six weeks of the year
as both sides searched for openings among the rocky passes inter-
secting the Eastern and Western Tunisian dorsals. Each skirmish
confirmed the Germans in their appraisal of a brave enemy who

lacked comprehension of the modern realities of tank warfare. On 14 February they put their theory to the test with a simultaneous flurry of hooks and thrusts by tank battle groups from 10th and 21st Panzer Divisions, enveloping the American CCA at Sidi Bou Zid. In a matter of hours they had smashed more than 40 tanks and a host of other vehicles and put the survivors to flight. Instantly, it was the Western Desert all over again with the Americans reacting bravely, conventionally, and utterly suicidally as, next day, they hurled a solid phalanx of tanks, self-propelled guns and armoured infantry full tilt towards Sidi Bou Zid—intent on retaking what had been lost but forgetting to consider what the Germans might do. In isolation, from a nearby hilltop, American infantry watched CCC approaching and, fascinated, observed the German tanks sidle to the flanks, thus opening a sack for the Americans to enter, prior to lacing the plain with a lethal crossfire. The smooth jinking of German tanks and the wild struggles of Americans in a death agony contrasted hideously the practice of one side with the immaturity of the other. Those American crews who survived the débâcle had been shown the full meaning of scientifically-applied anti-tank gunnery.

Rommel came up from the south to join in the Axis pursuit to Kasserine Pass and there the columns divided, some making for Sbiba, others for Thala and a few more in the direction of Tebessa —but none in a strategically decisive direction or with the strength to achieve a total disruption of the Allied front in the north—as both Kesselring and Rommel had desired. A schism split those at Rome in Axis Supreme HQ who, from such a distance could not hope to gauge the situation at the front. But the key factor, as usual, was to be logistics. When British tanks came to stiffen the Americans there was a check, but when the Germans ran out of fuel upon first meeting a solid Allied defence, with American crews making an encouraging come-back, an Axis withdrawal became unavoidable with all hope of achieving a major success abandoned.

The fatal schism in the Axis High Command now reduced their tank policy in Tunisia to absurdity. While Rommel yearned to strike strategic blows, his opposite number in the north, General von Arnim, intrigued to execute local, spoiling attacks with tanks withheld from Rommel. But von Arnim had yet to construe

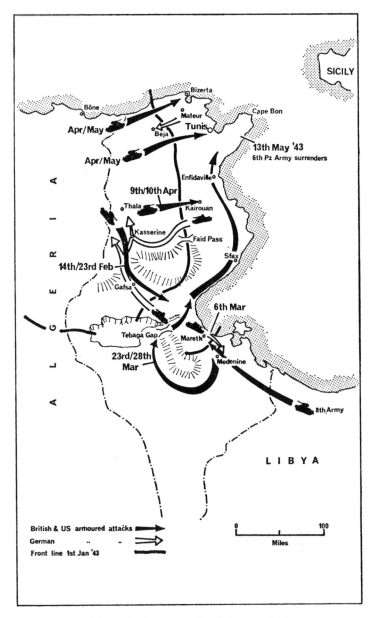

Map 18   Tunisian Battlefield — 1943

the true role for tanks among mountains and so his headlong attacks against the British down narrow valleys between frowning hills to the west of Tunis at the end of February cost nearly 50 tanks in a month when only 52 had reached Tunisia from Europe. This battle earned Lang, the Battle Group commander, the unenviable nickname of 'Tank Killer'—yet he did only as he was told. Rommel did no better on 6 March with a consolidated thrust by all three Panzer divisions against Montgomery at Medenine. Here he lost yet another 50 tanks for his trouble without destroying a single British tank in return, for the British defence had devolved almost entirely upon anti-tank guns and massed artillery, and the first appearance of their 76.2mm anti-tank gun, with its ability to reach out and kill at long range, had come as a shock. From now on not even the Tiger was entirely invulnerable.

From now on, too, in Tunisia, battles were dictated solely by superior Allied numbers. They were in a hurry to finish the campaign ready to launch a July invasion of Sicily, and so with little time to spare and more than 2,000 tanks at their disposal it became the style to execute direct assaults instead of apparently time-consuming manoeuvres. Montgomery's celebrated left hook at Mareth took prior place in his plans only when his direct assault on the Mareth Line had failed—and failed because tanks could not cross an anti-tank ditch in sufficient strength to forestall a German tank counter-attack.

Patton's abortive struggle to overcome the Axis flank guard where it held hill positions, and to project his II US Corps from Gafsa against the rear of the Akarit Line at the end of March, and Alexander's miscalculated attempt to thrust 6th British Armoured Division through the Fondouk gap and interpose it across the route of the Axis mobile force retiring on the Tunis bridgehead, were all indirect in intent though completely direct in tactical application. Because they were either too late in execution or clumsy in approach they fell victim to the rule which gives advantage to a force of equal prowess engaged in a strictly tactical defence of difficult terrain.

Overshadowing everything lay the stopping power of the latest high-velocity guns which could convert a massed tank assault into a pile of scrap iron with the same mechanical efficiency as a machine-gun firing against men. Only one type of tank refuted this trend—the Tiger, which could stand like a stone wall and take on a squadron or more of Shermans, Grants, Crusaders or Churchills without self-embarrassment.

In the final drives for Tunis and Bizerta tanks were omnipresent but in dire trouble whenever their opponents stood. Thus each Allied thrust depended at source upon an overbearing deluge of air and artillery power, to blanket the Axis defences, and a mass of infantry to secure difficult but vital ground where tanks could not climb. Yet the fact that the Churchill tank *could* climb where others often could not badly upset the Germans, since its unexpected appearance at the top of steep slopes, such as Long-stop Hill, which had been left almost unguarded against tanks, not only won tactical victories but posed every Axis defence of the future with the need to expend greater resources to block approaches which had once been assumed as tank-proof. Technical surprises of this sort rarely succeeded more than once before an antidote was found—the long-term effects merely put an additional tax on an enemy's ingenuity and redoubled his involvement by multiplying the need for precautions.

Inevitably a collapse ensued and the Axis surrendered in Africa. The haul in prisoners was rich, the booty in material enormous, but among the most serious losses to the Germans were tank crews of impeccable and irreplaceable merit. A rescue plan to evacuate them at the last moment came too late for implementation. Their disappearance, when added to those missing in Russia, amplified Guderian's task in rebuilding the Panzer arm, for the men of Africa would have been a priceless cadre for new divisions.

As the tide ran out in Africa it also changed direction in Russia. In February the Russian tank flood had swept the Germans out of the Caucasus and back to the start line of the previous June's venture. Against poorly equipped and only partially mobile Rumanian, Hungarian and Italian armies the Russian Tank Corps practically had it all their own way, encircling and crushing at will. But repeatedly Panzer divisions mysteriously eluded capture, battle groups seeming to appear only at crucial moments to strike hard blows and then vanish. Generally the Russians enjoyed a free run for weeks on end, but caution should have

prompted them to ask why, after the fall of Stalingrad on
31 January, they had captured so few German prisoners.

In fact the Russian leaders seem to have fallen into the trap
of crediting their propaganda's claim that the Germans were
finished, for having crossed the Donetz on a wide front between
Lisichansk and Belgorod, and become convinced by false evidence that the Germans continued in uncontrolled retreat, Marshal
Golikov drove hard for Kursk and Marshal Vatutin plunged deep
into the southern Ukraine. Both chased phantoms with armies
which had been reduced to ghosts of themselves. Supplies were
on the point of running out at the end of frail lines of communication and, in Vatutin's Group, only 53 tanks represented what, on
paper, were four tank corps and two tank brigades.

Manstein, closely observing Vatutin's approach, liked to use a
tennis simile to describe his methods. Thinking always within
the conception of a strategic defence (nothing else remained
to him) he preferred to allow his opponents 'to start an offensive
and then to hit them hard "on the backhand", or ... to attack
as early as possible ourselves and ... strike a limited blow "on
the forehand".' Hitler, seeking political prestige so as to impress
his allies, always preferred the forehand, but in February his
instincts were in disarray and, to Manstein's personal surprise, he
was permitted to practise his favourite shot—a strong backhand.
Secretly Manstein assembled three Panzer corps on Vatutin's
southern flank with a fourth to the north along with other
miscellaneous formations. Though the Germans might possess
hardly more than 350 tanks on this front these represented, in
fact, no less than three-quarters of their total tank force in the
entire theatre at that time. Of vital importance, they gave Manstein a seven-to-one superiority at the critical point. Such was
the condition of broken-back warfare then being practised by
the emaciated forces of both sides.

On 20 February, at the very moment when Manstein decided
to unleash his stroke, the leading Russian tanks were marooned by
shortage of fuel and, with others, caught napping and annihilated
in what rapidly deteriorated into a débâcle. Automatically extending his reach, Manstein now improvized a full-blooded offensive
copying, in principle, Wavell's desert spoiling offensive of 1940.
And, like the Italians in 1940, the Russians broke, for as Vatutin's
group fell apart, Golikov's had need to stop. Soon the entire line

had recoiled to the Donetz. Kharkov and Belgorod fell, Russian morale sank and, as a by-product, the reconquered territory yielded a great crop of abandoned tanks. But then came the thaw, turning roads into mud-baths, reducing the supply lines to ruins and halting the attenuated Panzer divisions. Ahead but unattainable lay a great Russian salient—100 miles across and 80 deep with Kursk at its centre—ripe for plucking but for the mud. Yet this salient could now be seen either as the launching place for a Russian offensive or the target for a Manstein fore-hand blow. Either way it held an immense fascination for both sides.

Time pressed the Germans harder than the Russians. Should the Germans decide to attack it would have to be done quickly—not a moment later than when the ground had dried sufficiently to make tank movement once more possible and, better still, before the Russians could recognize the impending place of impact and secure it with fresh forces. An early Manstein 'forehand', employing the first trickle of new-generation tanks from the Fatherland, would not be easy to mount. But every postponement, such as Hitler's insistence on waiting for the new, untested Panthers to arrive, reduced its chances, particularly since even those Panthers which would be got ready by June would be unreliable and, above all, almost impotent because optical troubles inhibited their shooting. Manstein's original intention, to pinch out the Kursk salient in May using the 1,500 older tanks then available, might have succeeded even though his force would mostly have been Mark IVs and assault guns plus only a few Tigers. He would have hit an enemy whose local tank strength was inferior and whose commanders had not fully divined German intentions.

By the end of May, however, to quote Zhukov, 'we knew virtually all the details of the enemy's plans to strike with the new Tiger tanks and Ferdinand self-propelled guns'. Reports from a spy network, systematically confirmed by aerial reconnaissance, gave ample opportunity for the Russians to devise a defensive system that, in depth, was virtually tank-proof. Zhukov was happy to play Manstein's 'forehand' from the baseline, to construct six defended belts composed of anti-tank posts each of three to five guns laid out over a depth of 110 miles—a zone infested by thick minefields and 3,500 miles of trenches dug by 300,000 civilian labourers: a work in fact of military engineering which surpassed the immensity of the great Hindenburg Line of 1917. Better than with the old Hindenburg Line, however, a revived tank corps waited in reserve should the Germans penetrate too far, but set aside, mainly, for a crushing offensive along the entire front once German exhaustion in attack became evident.

Operation 'Citadel', as Hitler's great politically-motivated armoured offensive was called, at last kicked off on 4 July, throwing into collision the greatest single assembly of armoured vehicles ever achieved—the assembly itself the very acme of staff work and traffic control along roads and tracks the broken state of which often defied description. No fewer than 2,700 German tanks and assault guns were opposed by 3,306 Russian machines and abetted by 10,000 German to 20,220 Russian guns, masses of infantry and, of aircraft, 2,500 German against 2,650 Russians.

The axes of the twin converging German pincers, projected symmetrically across the base of the salient, owed nothing to surprise and everything to the application of sheer brute force. Yet the great armoured strength of the Tigers and the Ferdinand assault guns was but a temporary guarantee of immunity against the hail of Russian shot, the debilitating effects of massed artillery fires and the crippling grasp of minefields. Moreover, by advancing in their long familiar wedge formation, with the Tigers at the front and the lighter tanks echeloned back in flank, the Germans contributed to their own discomfort since the older, more vulnerable, tanks would be stripped from the Tigers like the skin from a banana, and the formation would disintegrate into isolated elements—the strong, the weak and the dead.

Almost at once the Panthers failed—an ironic tragedy in the light of the delay imposed to incorporate this machine in the attack. Instead of the swift elbowing aside of Russians associated with Panzer divisions in the old style, the Germans found themselves inextricably entwined on both fronts with a tenacious Russian defence which, at first, made little use of tanks. Two days' slogging in the north yielded an advance of six miles at a cost of 200 tanks and 25,000 casualties: that could not last. To the south the price was cheaper and the gain ten miles. Indeed, for a while, the old magic, made easier by meticulous artillery and air support, seemed to be at work.

Yet it was not until 7 July that Mellenthin, himself the Chief of Staff to XLVIII Panzer Corps, saw a ray of hope. All of a sudden the Russian defence faltered as they fell back through Ssyrzew and 'the fleeing masses were caught by German artillery fire . . .; our tanks gained momentum and wheeled to the north-west'. Yet soon there came a check following a tank counter-attack but, 'on the right wing we seemed within reach of victory' when, in fact, a false raising of hopes had been caused by a misleading report from troops in the lead who had lost their way. On 8 July the Germans were still keenly at work to accomplish the major breakthrough that would link up with the stalled attack in the north. By the 10th, however, they were bogged down in a mire of local envelopments formed of individual battle groups fighting to eliminate the network of Russian strongpoints while simultaneously fending off the growing intervention by Russian tanks which frequently were happy to stand off and shoot the Germans at long range: '. . . the Russian tanks, which had a magnificent field of fire . . . seemed to be everywhere and singled out the spearhead . . . allowing it no rest.'

Grave anxiety permeated the Russian resolve and at one moment Vatutin was driven to demanding that 'the Germans must not break through etc'—the orders of a desperate man who had used up all his reserves. Zhukov has admitted that 'the average density of artillery and tanks had been calculated incorrectly'. Not only was this true but it summarized Russian philosophy—the application of bulk against skill to achieve victory at any price. To Vatutin, with his front at cracking point and his last reserves expended, this was of little consolation. The Germans had pushed a wedge 20 miles wide between 6th and 7th Guards Armies and it was to take the intervention of two fresh armies, pulled out of central reserve on 9 July, to put matters right. Moreover those two armies had been subtracted from the forces set aside for the main offensive due to exploit the German failure when it came. As Manstein put it on 13 July, when these fresh forces became fully identified, 'the battle was at its climax and the issue apparently at hand', but his comment was really only a plea to continue *after* Hitler had called off 'Citadel'. Thousands of miles away the Western Allies were landing in Sicily and the Italian front seemed in need of urgent reinforcements which could come only from Russia.

The issue at Kursk was certainly at hand, though Manstein

misread it, for although he persevered with local attacks on the
14th and 15th 'to smash the enemy's armoured reserves', he
flew in the face of events in the north where a Russian offensive,
which struck towards Orel on the 12th, was cutting across the
rear of the German tanks embedded in the Kursk salient. At that
moment, on the evidence of Mellenthin, 'our Panzer divisions . . .
had been bled white'.

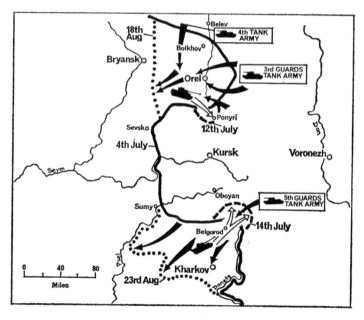

Map 19   Kursk and after – 1943

When the Russian tanks began to come into the open, carpeting
the open spaces between woods and villages with their massed
formations, a weapon which, until then, had hardly affected individual tanks made its debut. Russian anti-tank aircraft had
previously made ineffectual rocket attacks against the Germans in
1941 but these unstable missiles had even less chance than
bombs of scoring direct hits. Seeking the essential pinpoint
accuracy, the Germans began mounting two 37mm cannon in
some Stuka bombers and a 30mm cannon in Henschel Hs129 B
aircraft in 1943. These had their first big chance at Kursk. The

approved technique demanded attack only against the thinly armoured tops and sides of the Russian tanks since only there could such a light-weight shot penetrate. Firing a gun from such an unstable platform demanded that the pilots take undisturbed aim, pressing their attack directly at the small target without taking evasive action—tactics which stood only fair prospects of survival if enemy fighters had been swept from the sky and if local anti-aircraft fire was practically nil. At Kursk, as it happened, the optimum conditions were on the German side and several tanks were knocked out—though it seems unlikely that a profound effect was made on the balance of forces. The Russian tanks kept on coming and an indication that they were impressed was to be found only later in the gradual arming of their tanks with anti-aircraft weapons and improvements of their own aircraft's capability to destroy tanks up to the point when even the Germans had to admit that they were a menace.

Nobody can say with assurance that aircraft caused significant tank losses. A few pilots possessed a knack for this work and may have scored a high rate of kills. Undoubtedly others entered highly exaggerated claims, not necessarily out of self-glorification but simply because their misinterpretation of shot dramatically kicking up dirt near a tank seemed to indicate a positive kill when, in fact, only the nerves of the tank crews or a few less important pieces of external equipment had been damaged. Air power's most important contribution to the tank battle remained its indirect effects against the lines of communication by destroying bridges and supplies and disrupting the mobility of tanks.

Strategically, of course, the bombing of the German industrial base and the interruption of tank production *could* be of long-term importance but, in fact, all German weapon outputs actually rose throughout 1943 and 1944 when the aerial bombardment was rising to its crescendo. Again it was the erosion of an indirect source—oil supply—which was most debilitating and was to cause the Germans mounting difficulties as the war progressed. Not only would land vehicles become hamstrung but aircraft too would be hampered. Later it would be the Allied pilots who would find themselves able to take almost unhurried aim at tanks as the German pilots had done at Kursk.*

* In June 1942, in fact, the British had fitted two 40mm cannon to their Hurricane fighters in North Africa, but the results achieved were

Before the Germans desisted at Kursk the Russian flood was well on its way to Orel, though, at first, their counter-attacks in the south of the salient were designed only to retake ground recently lost. It was not until 3 August that 5th Tank Army, reorganized after its unintended involvement on Vatutin's behalf in the moment of crisis, could launch its major endeavour to recapture Kharkov, where it stood at the tip of a narrow German salient. Set a problem not unlike that faced by the Germans at Kursk, the Russians seem to have lost their heads and also to have rejected the rulings of the Fedyunenko order. They simply rolled machines, inadequately supported by any other arm, straight at the German defences, presenting row after row of tanks as targets for the gunners of three Panzer and six infantry divisions. In their own time, as they shifted deftly from cover to cover on the flanks and front of the Russian phalanx, the Germans picked off Russians.

It was Sidi Bou Zid all over again but on a much greater scale: one German account quotes 184 T34s knocked out by 32 Tigers, 96 Panthers and 25 heavy assault guns in a few hours' fighting. Even so the Russians went on battering away for a further 24 hours on a narrow front until finally, and quite clearly badgered by intemperate orders from above, they attempted something unusual for them—a tank attack at night. It was pandemonium. By the light of burning buildings and vehicles the gunners could see to aim only at about 100 metres. A contemporary account describes a moment when 'the German anti-tank guns could no longer fire properly since they could hardly distinguish friend from foe. German tanks had entered the fray, ramming Russian tanks in a counter thrust or piercing them . . . at gun-barrel range in order to block the breakthrough'.

For a few days longer the Germans held out, winning a backhand victory of the highest calibre. But they could not perform with such intensity at every threatened spot. The battle moved irresistibly westward. Never again would the Germans effectively play a forehand shot against the Russians.

---

more dramatic than accurate and at that time official British air doctrine tended to frown on aircraft becoming involved in the land battle at the front.

Chapter 21

A SORT OF STABILIZATION

Midway through the War a position of balance had been reached in tank combat and this, by definition, stabilized the art of war. No longer, except in the most extraordinary circumstances, could tanks ride rough-shod to create opportunities on their own and win strategic decisions as in 1940 and 1941. From 1942 onwards, although tank forces would continue to overshadow almost every encounter on land, they would have need to fight with increased ferocity against more enlightened opposition to create the fluid environment in which alone they could flourish—and they were even more dependent on other weapons to assist them. While these rules were largely applicable to the crucial battles in the boundless void of Russia, in southern Europe they were absolute where the terrain militated against a tank free-for-all.

For being ejected so cheaply from Europe in 1940 and 1941, the Allies had to pay a high price to return. Not only would they have to fight hard for each renewed lodgment but they would be hampered at first by the invariable need to spend time, at a loss to momentum, in building up the complex base systems essential to mechanized warfare. The initial problem of getting ashore was so daunting that it became obsessional. Too frequently, in the past, a landing on a hostile shore had proved both costly and abortive. If a reminder had been needed, there had been in 1942 the fiasco at Dieppe where a squadron of Canadian-crewed Churchills, finding it almost impossible to climb the esplanade after leaving their landing craft, had mostly been shot to pieces at the water's edge and prevented from helping the infantry who, once inland, had become pinned by machine-gun fire. There were few survivors.

Sighs of Allied relief had accompanied the successful landings against French opposition in North-West Africa in November 1942. There the US infantry had been in trouble until tanks had struggled ashore, solved one or two local technical breakdowns, such as being swamped by following seas, and then dominated proceedings. The depositing of tanks on a hostile shore from landing craft had augured well for the Americans and for the next amphibious operation, against defended beaches in Sicily on 10 July 1943, where the early presence ashore of Patton's anti-tank guns and tanks was vitally important in averting serious trouble when several Axis thrusts made for the vital central beaches at Gela, on the 11th. Indeed if the German tanks, Tigers among them, had pressed a little harder and a few hours sooner the overall picture of an Allied triumph might easily have been ruined. All future opposed landings would conform to this kind of race for superiority at the landing places. The Axis would be forced to position armour near the coast, ready to throw it in at once, since to move it effectively from a far-off central concentration area would become almost impossible in the face of massive harassment from the air.

But once the lodgments in Sicily and then in Italy had been made, warfare reverted to its archetypal form. After Patton's formations had cleared the practically undefended western segment of Sicily he had been compelled to join in a slogging match alongside the British to clear the Axis-held bridgehead funnelling in towards Messina. This was grim mountain fighting similar to the latter phases of the war in Tunisia and anticipating worse to come in Italy. The narrow Italian peninsula with its mountainous spine, flanked by small coastal plains heavily enclosed by plantations and villages, was among the last places in the world in which to practise high mobility. This was infantry and artillery land, a place where tanks wallowed in mud and had to be hauled to hilltops or, failing that, driven to taking post behind long ridges to lob their shells at an entrenched enemy —a useful but second-grade supplement to massed field artillery. When the pressure overcame them and the Germans were compelled to take a step backward, from one prepared position to another, the tanks might gallop ahead, as in the desert days, but they galloped on the curb and almost invariably were forced to halt when the enemy declared. For in a country where every feasible approach was known, every byway blocked by mines and demolitions and each river a tank obstacle, the defender could choose the strongest and shortest line from Adriatic to Tyrrhenian Sea and hold it long enough to prepare the next impregnable position to the north—a process that was prolonged for nearly two years.

There were no tank victories to be won in Italy. Only bitter memories for Allied crews who, too often, were flung into a charge to clear some narrow defile or cross some unfordable river in a suicidal attempt to mitigate the lot of infantry—the universal sufferers when tank mobility was at a premium.

To a certain extent, though in widely differing circumstances, similar considerations held sway on the northern and central Russian fronts. Throughout 1943 and 1944 the Russians were to push back the Germans, squeezing down constricted axes of advance between dense forests while the expansive battles of manoeuvre were decided on the steppes in the south. In the north rivers provided many natural stop-lines, but where rivers did not conform to strategic necessity deep, entrenched systems were constructed as shelter for the limited German forces conducting the withdrawal from Leningrad and Moscow. The German way of absorbing the Russian pressure towards Smolensk has been closely defined and is of particular interest when compared with the swift German drive through the same region in 1941 (see Chapter 15). By the end of September 1943 the Germans had retired, intact in organization if not in numbers, to a line running 40 miles to the west of Smolensk, after prosecuting a controlled retreat reminiscent of their withdrawal from France in 1918.

General Heinrici, the German Fourth Army commander, told Liddell Hart after the war how, without reserves, he managed with only ten divisions to keep a grip on a 90-mile front and to constrain anything up to four times his numbers of Russian divisions even when they concentrated against him on a 12-mile sector. 'The problem turns,' he said, 'on the ratio of space to force' —but he could have added that timely failure to detect the centre line of each thrust would have been disastrous. He economized in force by digging in his men along successive lines of defences held in place by knots of resistance—'hedgehogs' in which anti-tank guns covering minefields were the staple weapon, though sometimes dug-in tanks were kept immobile as well.

Always the Russians attacked to a set-piece timetable, sending in infantry helped by groups of upwards of fifty tanks rolling forward behind a crushing artillery barrage in attempts to knock holes in the German line. The Germans would retaliate with their own artillery storm, provided by a centralized artillery group of 380 guns, backed up by small teams of tanks and assault guns moving to and fro along well reconnoitred routes to blast each local enemy penetration as it occurred. Never was the line broken even though each German infantry division lost the equivalent of an infantry battalion a day. 'The Russians did not try any large armoured drive,' said Heinrici, 'because no considerable gap was made in the defences.' Neither, however, did the Russians delude themselves of the possibility nor deploy a specific tank army for that purpose, preferring to rely on the smaller tank element in their infantry mechanized corps to exploit whatever success the infantry element might achieve.

Heinrici's experience confirmed the opinion, once postulated by Liddell Hart, 'as to the superiority of defence over attack in the tactical field', but the German's opinions were founded on experience which held good in circumscribed conditions. To the south of his embattled trench line, where the rolling plains of the Ukraine precluded the creation of continuous lines of defence by a German army lacking the strength to fill them, everything depended on an audacious tactical offensive spirit, even when defence was the motivating factor. In the region of Kiev a drive by vast Russian tank forces, following the existing lines of communication where they led into Poland and Rumania, was resisted by German infantry formations holding the key communication centres as pivots while the Panzer corps undertook cut and thrust blows against the flanks and rear of the Russian columns.

In theory this was all very well, but in practice the leaving of large static forces to be encircled could later extract insupportable sacrifices if the timing of their relief or extraction was not carefully arranged. A moment would arrive when it was no longer economic to hold a locality after the Russians had achieved their aims elsewhere and by other means. If relief or retirement was not accomplished at that critical moment a new Stalingrad would recur, if only in miniature, and might cancel all the good achieved by the initial operation. If, on the other hand, a breakout operation could be exquisitely timed to catch the Russians between the relieving and the relieved forces, the resultant success might be out of all proportion to the effort. But since Hitler put a personal and stultifying veto on many important movements at the front and had to be argued out of holding every metre of ground, the inherent flexibility, so crucial to the German policy of instant mobility within a fixed framework, was crippled at source. The German tank force in the east might have resisted longer had it not been impelled to undertake extensive rescue operations to the exclusion of more resounding, Manstein-type backhands.

Mellenthin, whose cavalry background ideally suited him to the constantly changing fortunes and the variable tactics of the highly mobile encounters, fairly summarized the conflict between two schools of thought when discussing a proposal by his commander, General Balck (himself a cavalryman), to cut across the base of a deep Russian thrust as it debouched from Kiev in November 1943, 'hamstringing any further Russian advance to the west and perhaps trapping and destroying very considerable forces. Unfortunately,' goes on Mellenthin, '...the commander of Fourth Panzer Army regarded this plan as too ambitious.... Our idea of a lightning thrust, far into the rear of the Russian masses, was discarded in favour of an operation which was essentially orthodox in character ... to crush the huge Kiev bridgehead by pushing at it frontally from the west.' Mellenthin stresses how 'the history of armoured warfare—and of cavalry warfare before that—shows that the great prizes can be won by speed, daring and manoeuvre. The "play safe" school of generals was all very well on the Western Front in 1914–18 but is out of place in this age of the petrol engine and the aeroplane.'

Heinrici probably belonged to the 'play safe' school but both sides were right in context since the solution to Russian mass tactics rather depended upon where you were standing at any particular moment. General von Manteuffel, the commander of 'Gross Deutschland' Panzer Division, threw light on the negative side of deep raids when he described the vast horde following each Russian tank spearhead, largely mounted on horses: 'You can't stop them like an ordinary army, by cutting their communications, for you rarely find any supply column.' But he added, 'these penetrating raids proved very effective in spreading confusion'.

Manteuffel also described the guiding theme of tank-versus-tank combat in a nutshell as 1943 gave way to 1944 and the latest Russian tanks—the T34/85 and KV85, both armed with the

powerful 85mm gun, and the heavy JS (Josef Stalin) IB with its
122mm gun—began to appear. Near Jassy in May 1944.

> The Russians were repulsed and only 60 of their tanks got
> away.... I lost only 11 of mine. It was here that I first met
> the Stalin tanks. It was a shock to find that, although my
> Tigers began to hit them at a range of 2,200 yards, our shells
> did not penetrate them until we had closed to half that distance.
> But I was able to counter their technical superiority by
> manoeuvre and mobility in making the best use of ground....
> In a tank battle, if you stand still you are lost.

Manteuffel could have added that he owed his local mobility
not only to his own tactical insight and the ingrained skill of his
crews but also to the well-tuned German staff and communication techniques which were much more advanced than those of
the Russians. It was still noticeable that once a Russian
manoeuvre had progressed beyond its first planned phase it
began to lose cohesion whether in the use of tanks, artillery or
any other arm.

Now that the technique of defence could stand up to attack
with a good chance of survival the time-honoured equilibrium
of the battlefield had been restored. It was even possible to
reassert the fears of those early doubters who had postulated
the slaughter of tanks by anti-tank weapons as a matter of
course. The future could be blurred by interpretations of trends
which could be all things to all men. Liddell Hart's belief that
the defence would be superior to the attack in the tactical
sphere, contradicting his original concept of tank-expanding
torrents (in line with Fuller's idea of tank omnipotence), could
both be adjudged as right and wrong, practical and impractical.
Ground, numbers and the infinite host of conflicting battlefield
conditions, all adding up to or subtracting from the help that
could or could not be given to tanks, reasserted the classical
balance of power between the basic battlefield inhabitants. Even
Chauvineau's claim that infantry could hide like mice and strike
tanks from behind now looked feasible as the hand-held, short-
range bazooka-type weapons came into prolific use.

Yet that great hope of the 1920s—the light tank—had been
pushed far into the shades. Many still existed but had to stay in
hiding for fear of the heavier armoured beasts roaming at large;

they could carry out reconnaissance on sufferance but, lacking powerful armament, stood no chance of saturating the defence in open combat. Everything took second place to the tank contest —whether among the enclosed valleys of Italy, the dense forests of Burma, the open steppes of Russia or in some grim assault on a Pacific atoll such as Tarawa—but now it was becoming a battle of giants between heavily armoured machines armed with enormous guns, each equipment ponderous, frightfully weighty and terribly expensive.

Soon, however, a point of no further increase in size was bound to be reached. Already bridges, roads and railways were groaning under the weight of the 55-ton Tiger I; within a few months Tiger II at 68 tons would be tramping about and there were projects being built which weighed well over a hundred tons. Like prehistoric monsters these gigantic beasts would perish from their own enormity. Conversely the American policy of restricting the weight of their tanks to simplify the problems of shipping them from one theatre of war to another was injurious since it meant that their main battle tanks went into action too thinly armoured to compete with tougher, indigenous opponents in Europe. Compromise in tank design came out of necessity and main battle tanks the world over would settle at weights ranging between 40 and 50 tons, armed with guns in the 80 to 122mm calibre class to fire rounds of ammunition weighing 40 to 50 pounds each—for yet another limiting factor in size was the strength of the loader to push rounds into the gun and maintain a satisfactory rate of fire.

Once a condition of design stability had been reached—and on the Russian front this was almost the case in 1944—the art of war would revert to the optimum use of weapons governed by the traditional skills of generalship—the application of surprise, concentration in time and space, and so on. Technical surprise would be reserved, whenever possible, for the great occasions in the knowledge that once disclosed they might never be repeated with the same effect. Yet if a point of equilibrium had been reached in Russia, extraordinary to relate, this was not so in Europe as the Allies prepared to land in Normandy in June 1944. There, on both sides, the most diverse imbalance was about to warp the shape of battle in the most highly mechanized campaign ever to be conceived.

Chapter 22

STRUGGLE IN THE WEST

If all the words describing the Second World War were tabled by campaigns it is probable that the story of the invasion of Normandy, the fighting in the beachhead, the subsequent break-out and the pursuit would top the poll. Here, rather than refight the story, the basic considerations governing the tank battles will be examined against a background of fighting moulded by mechanical forces. Montgomery, brought back to Britain to command the invasion under the supreme command of Eisenhower, laid it down that his first aim was 'the establishment of a firm base from which to peg out claims forward'. Thereafter he demanded 'deep penetration with armour early'. From beginning to end this dictated the struggle.

The tools essential to Montgomery's method were ready for use. In March 1943, General Brooke, the British Chief of the General Staff, had instructed Hobart, the commander of the 79th Armoured Division, to develop and train certain specialized armoured forces suitable for leading the assault from the water's edge to crack even the toughest parts of Hitler's vaunted Atlantic Wall, to crack them, moreover, in one continuous action and with the minimum exposure of men to fire. Dieppe had provided essential evidence of the problems involved in moving armoured vehicles across a defended beach as a preliminary to tackling the inland defences, and since 1942 much work had gone into devising adapted tanks to overcome all known types of obstacle. It had been Hobart's task to adapt the adaptions—to remove the impracticalities from fanciful gadgets and turn tender mechanical devices into rugged weapons of war. In addition he had to teach the crews to convert and combine their individual and specialized activities so that, from their arrival on the hostile shore, they would methodically and without pause overcome every successive barrier.

On 6 June 1944, a detached observer of events in Normandy might have been astonished not only by the terrifying grandeur of an armada sailing towards the shore and the awesome sight of the bombardment, but by the more unusual events to be seen in detail upon the wider canvas. He would know that the German lines of communication leading to Normandy had been cut to ribbons by days of air attack and that Allied deception measures had fooled the Germans as to the time and place of the assault. Under cover of the final bombardment, saturating the concrete defence at the shore line, he would have seen what looked like a conventional flotilla, of tank and infantry assault craft making for the land. Then, at anything from 2,000 to 6,000 yards off-shore, he would have been surprised to see what looked like unusually small assault craft lurching through the doors of landing craft into the choppy water to thrust ahead as the first wave of the invasion. These, in fact, were the first of Hobart's 'Funnies', as they were sometimes known—ordinary Sherman tanks but kept afloat by a canvas screen and driven through the water by propellers powered by the tank engine. These were called DD (Duplex Drive) tanks and their real purpose could be understood as their tracks touched bottom to pull them out of the water, the screens were dropped and their gunners went to work shelling those German emplacements which had survived the bombardment, to quell resistance by direct fire before the next wave of attack arrived fast in their wake.

Next to come ashore would be tank-landing craft, weaving through the obstacles to deposit ashore still more unusual tanks —Flail Shermans with chains on rotating drums to beat the ground ahead and clear passages through the mine-fields up to the first obstacle—which was either a deep ditch or the esplanade itself. Then yet stranger looking tanks would disembark to follow the Flails and DD's—Churchills converted into so-called Armoured Vehicles Royal Engineer (AVRE), to transport sappers under armour to place or throw charges by a short-range mortar on concrete obstacles or pill-boxes. In addition, these AVREs could transport portable bridges to help other tanks climb the esplanade or cross wide ditches, or to drop fascines (just as at Cambrai) to fill the ditches.

The observer would see these special tanks working their way, by stages, deeper into the German lines, opening lanes and beating down the German defences as infantry assault craft beached to let their occupants wade ashore, almost unmolested, to join in a battle already almost won. The progress of the armoured siege train—for Hobart's 'Funnies' simply garbed the ancient function of breaching a fortress wall in modern dress with mechanical devices—moving inexorably inland was not, of course, without setbacks. Tanks of all sorts were destroyed by guns, or crippled by mines, bogged in sand or stranded on obstacles. But always a carefully worked-out battle drill provided replacements, from a reserve, or devised improvizations to make good the damage—improvizations made easier because as many of the special tanks as possible were armed with a normal gun. For instance, flails, when they were not flailing, could supplement the DDs' fire, and the sappers could dismount from AVREs to help clear those mines the flails had missed.

Only where specialized armour failed to land in the van or in strength did the infantry suffer badly. On one British sector a company took heavy casualties when, due to a series of accidents, they landed ahead of the tanks. On Omaha beach the toll almost caused complete failure since here specialized armour had either been excluded from the assault, because the Americans doubted its necessity, or because DDs had been sunk through being launched too far out to sea in rough water which had overcome their frail screens.

Mostly, however, special tanks overcame the concrete and steel facade of the Atlantic Wall with astonishing ease—and it was not as if the Germans had given up without a fight. They had simply been outclassed. Indeed, British reaction was just as at Flers in 1916 when the follow-up troops, so astonished to see tanks performing the unimaginable, hung about near the shore instead of, in a body, rushing off inland. Having for years been fascinated by the problem of getting ashore, many had a myopic inclination to remain on the beach instead of 'pegging out claims'. At all events the armoured struggle which was about to envelop the lush, Normandy agricultural land would be demanding of space if the Allies were to develop their full powers of mobility. To the Germans, however, mobility was something to be kept as confined as possible.

Both Montgomery and his opponents, Field-Marshals von Rundstedt and Rommel, were in accidental but mutual agreement that the final outcome would be decided by tanks, no matter how crowded with artillery or infantry the battlefield would become or how intense the intervention by aircraft. The Germans

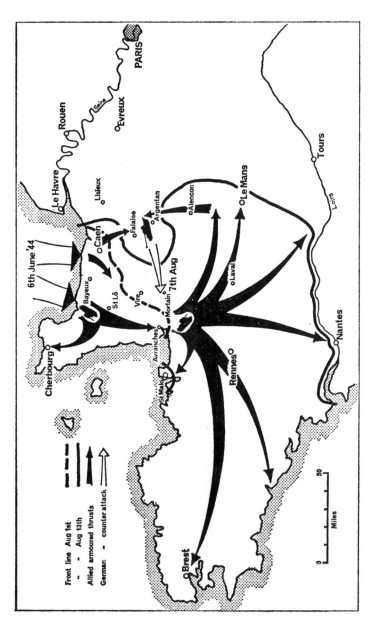

Map 20   Armoured breakout from Normandy – 1944

had gone to infinite pains in deciding the location of their Panzer divisions but in the end arrived at a poor compromise between two widely separate contentions. Rundstedt believed in a classic grouping of the armour in a central region prior to moving it for one irresistible blow against the main Allied effort when it had been identified—a process which might take several days to complete. Rommel, with recent and personal experience of the power of Allied aircraft to interdict lines of communication, and dreadfully aware of the strength of modern anti-tank defence, was convinced that, unless the Allies were attacked almost immediately after landing, the central reserve could never be fully deployed in time and, even if that were possible, might be ineffective against a consolidated enemy.

The fact that both German generals felt the main Allied blow would fall on the Pas de Calais and that it was there they positioned their strongest forces had nothing to do with what might have been possible in Normandy on the day of the invasion. For, half in support of Rundstedt and half as a sop to Rommel, three Panzer divisions lay close enough to the beachhead to have intervened, perhaps decisively, within a few hours. That they were withheld was said to be nobody's fault but Hitler's; it was his insistence upon vetting all decisions and his delay in releasing the tanks for action which fatally withheld the one threat the Allies most feared. Yet a good staff might have quietly set the tanks moving in the right direction had a clearly defined plan existed.

The topography of the Normandy beachhead presented its own peculiarities to affect tank operations. Close by and to the south of Caen lay an open plain ideally suited to the deployment of a tank phalanx: elsewhere to the west and east there stood the bocage—a close-knit patchwork of small fields bounded by thick hedges and intersected by narrow lanes. The bocage was no place for German tank movement against opposition—if for no better reason than that their tanks, whose best tactics were to stand and shoot from 1,000-yard range or more, would come face to face with Allied tanks at ranges of 200 to 400 yards where the Allied inferiority in armour and striking power was less noticeable. Logically the Germans positioned their armour close to the best tank country, near Caen, and resisted every temptation to bury it in the bocage.

This, as it happened, suited General Montgomery's original, and constantly maintained, strategic concept. He desired to draw the German reserves into battle against the British in the close proximity of Caen, on the eastern flank of the bridgehead, to 'write down' their armour while poising American armour for a surprise attack out of the bocage, on the western flank. By correctly playing on the German natural susceptibility to the threat of an orthodox attack taking the easiest and most obvious axes into central France, and later throwing the main tank punch through the poorest tank-worthy terrain, Montgomery demonstrated shrewd insight into the German military mind. Montgomery has been criticized for misunderstanding tanks, despite his justifiable claim to have won all his victories with them. In Normandy he showed that he remembered as much about tank warfare as the Germans had forgotten, for the latter, steeped in the law of war in 'ideal' tank country of Russian space, had overlooked the genius of their triumphs of the first two years of war when victory had been won by passing tanks through difficult country into the open spaces beyond.

The central struggle in Normandy revolved around the preservation by the Germans of a short and continuous line of resistance and in attempts by Montgomery to wear out the Germans on the eastern flank before debouching from the opposite end of the front. Rommel had convinced himself that, in the face of an overwhelming Allied air superiority, he could not afford to wage mobile war. In the event it took him all of 23 days (!) to assemble sufficient Panzer divisions to make a really formidable counter-offensive, only then to see his tanks stopped dead in their tracks by the British near Caen. It is known that Allied air attacks hampered the arrival of fresh troops, but it is also likely that Rommel was badly served by his staff—and Rommel without a good staff could be a tyro.

Montgomery's strategy worked well of its own accord, but once the Americans began extending their possessions close to St Lo early in July to make room for their main breakout, the Germans were compelled to the reality of fighting in the bocage with so few infantry divisions that Panzer divisions had to be drafted in to maintain a front. Nevertheless, despite increased British pressure and the fall of Caen on 9 July, Montgomery apprehended, as the month advanced, that the Americans could neither get ahead fast enough, nor could the German tanks be kept away from them unless the British made one more supreme effort to retain those Panzer divisions already in Normandy along with those arriving daily, bit by bit, close to Caen.

Montgomery's solution was a renewed assault southward from Caen—a direct blow, composed of a central punch by three armoured divisions down the only feasible corridor flanked by infantry divisions which were themselves heavily endowed with tanks—the whole monstrous affair preceded by an immense air bombardment. This was not intended as a knockout blow but simply an attempt to dominate a small area of ground which the Germans were constrained to defend with tanks. At this time, however, the British and American tank forces, mostly made up of Churchills, Shermans and Cromwells armed with 75mm guns, were hopelessly outgunned by the Tigers, Panthers and the latest German self-propelled guns. In these circumstances it would have been better, in theory, to occupy the area with a basically infantry force and draw the German tanks on to ready-positioned guns and tanks.

General O'Connor, the commander of VIII Corps, realized this and with characteristic ingenuity (not in the least blunted by more than two years spent in Italian captivity) asked for armoured personnel carriers (obsolete tanks with their turrets removed) to be put at his disposal to transport his infantry under armoured protection deep into the German lines in order to forestall the obvious German riposte. His request was refused. Montgomery was handicapped by a shortage of infantry due to their already heavy losses, but he was strong in the air, in artillery and tanks, and these he *must* now use in preponderance.

Operation 'Goodwood' probably brought about the greatest-ever concentration of tanks in a confined battle arena. On 18 July an estimated 1,350 British tanks came to blows with about 400 German armoured vehicles in an area only 8,000 yards square, and by the 21st no fewer than seven of the nine Panzer divisions had been attracted to the Caen sector. Yet Goodwood, though achieving its strategic aim and giving the Americans enormous scope for their breakout on the 24th, had been a tactical holocaust. Packed close in open terrain the leading British armour, practically deprived of infantry, was decimated by German tanks firing from hull-down positions at their optimum range. 'With

no time for retaliation,' wrote one British survivor, 'no time to do
anything but take one quick glance at the situation, almost in
one minute all of the tanks of the three troops and Squadron
HQ were hit, blazing and exploding. Everywhere wounded and
burning figures ran or struggled painfully for cover, while a remorseless rain of armour-piercing shot riddled the already helpless Shermans. All too clearly we were not going to break through.
It was going to be a matter of not how much we should advance
but whether we should be able to hold on to what we had gained.*

In fact this was only a German backhand. Indeed they had no
reason to adopt the forehand when, within 72 hours, they
destroyed something like 300 Allied tanks. And, in any case, on
25 July, the American breakout, gaining momentum after a
fiendishly tortuous beginning in the thick bocage, where one
Tiger was worth a company of Shermans at any time, was heaving
southward to Avranches in a seemingly endless flow—no fewer
than six armoured divisions soon to be joined by the British
and others. No longer could the Germans hope to refrain from
mobile warfare and so no longer could they escape defeat.

Least of all could they achieve much with a forehand stroke,
though their attempt to cut through the American swathe at
Mortain was really just that—and too late. The American defence
at Mortain is recorded as a triumph for their soldiers' staunch
behaviour. This it was. At the time, however, considerable credit
was given to Allied aircraft for knocking out a phenomenal
number of German tanks. This was not so. Without in any way
questioning the bravery or integrity of the pilots concerned,
they entered claims which were neither substantiated by
immediate post-battle examination of the area nor by German
reports. To take as an example, one such attack by RAF Typhoons
was plotted, rocket by rocket-hole in the turf, and not one was
found to have hit a tank in an action when many had been
claimed as destroyed. This is not surprising when it is remembered that each rocket had only a 0.5 per cent chance of killing
a Panther.

At first the German crews were seriously frightened by rocket

---

* It is worth mentioning that out of the crews of 41 tanks lost in one
regiment, only 17 were killed and 39 wounded — the rate of fewer than
two men per tank lost being a fairly representative ratio in all tank
actions.

attacks. They lost confidence and momentum even though few of their tanks were hit. Rapidly, however, once it was realized how inaccurate the attacks were against armoured targets, confidence was restored. But 'soft', lorried transport always suffered severely and it was the wholesale destruction of supply vehicles by near misses which starved the tanks to death. Many more captured German tanks were either shot up by ground anti-tank weapons, had run out of petrol or had broken down through a shortage of spare parts than ever fell victim to direct air attack.

Still the truculent German defence held firmly the terrain to the south of Caen, where a mere handful of German tanks and guns could easily pick off the slightest Anglo-Canadian advance by day. The morale of Allied crews sagged, obsessed as they were by fear of the Panthers and Tigers. So on the night of 7–8 August General Simonds, the commander of II Canadian Corps, tried a night assault—a drive by two columns composed of tanks and infantry, the latter carried in obsolete tanks with their turrets removed, driving down either side of the Caen to Falaise road. An advance of three miles through the German front line and beyond their second position was intended. Guidance was to be by compass direction, radio beacons and the marking of boundaries by tracer ammunition. Illumination would be by flares and, until moonrise, 'artificial moonlight' provided by searchlights shone above the battle zone.

None of the navigation aids proved fully effective and vision was seriously impaired by the dust kicked up by the artillery and air bombardment. Tanks from one column blundered into another; there were collisions and shunting. 'The column soon disintegrated into utter chaos,' wrote one British commander, yet individual initiative repeatedly kept momentum going until daybreak and although the German lines were not penetrated to the desired depth panic gripped their soldiers, who fled in disorder. Again it was a combination of vigorous action by one German leader, General Kurt Meyer, in rallying a mere 30 tanks and a few guns at dawn, allied to slow exploitation by the British and Canadians, which prevented a total disruption of the front. If, as at Kharkov in 1943, a night attack had again failed to gain all its objectives, it again showed that such attacks, given adequate preparation, technical backing and individual perseverance, were feasible.

The final breakout from Normandy could not be delayed indefinitely by self-sacrificing improvizations on the German part, but when at last it came it immediately presented Allied tank crews with yet another set of unfamiliar problems. Their last full-scale pursuit had been in Tunisia in April 1943 when the directions of their objectives had usually been canalized by topography. In France the pursuit became confused by a myriad of conflicting and unfamiliar factors. Open for exploitation were several axes of approach into Germany, any single one or combination of several could be tackled and each offered a strategic prize worth the taking and the most promising were those leading either into the industrial Ruhr or the North German Plain. But during a long pursuit to the extremity of diluted Allied lines of communication, the Allies would encounter the progressive, classical and remorseless aggregation of German armies as they backed into the existing Siegfried Line and gathered the reserves so easily assembled from the hinterland.

Moreover the Allied lines of communication ran through friendly countries, highly populated by hungry people who, while assisting the advance and hindering the German retreat, would also expect the Allies to feed them at a time of famine. The Allies also suffered from the frictions indigenous to an alliance—the impulsive motives of proud nationalities seeking to justify their presence and their labours—and exemplified, in this case, by Montgomery's desire to poke a relatively narrow thrust into the North German Plain as against General Eisenhower's insistence, as Supreme Commander, on advancing to the frontier on a broad front and giving everybody the opportunity to take credit.

Factions squabbling at the top transmitted negative pulses to the lower levels where strategic orders, to be of use, needed to be formulated a week or more in advance of their execution. Daily operations tended to become short-term, spasmodic, and slack in their essential smooth momentum. A high-level debate overlay every important alteration of direction in a rapidly changing mobile situation: the decision to split Patton's Third Army to send part into Brittany and the rest towards Paris; the scheme to create a small pocket at Falaise (when the Germans delayed

too long at Mortain) while the Americans swung in a short hook
north to link up with the Anglo-Canadians coming southward,
or the alternative—to concentrate on forming a single vast
encirclement by interposing Third Army as a barrier along
the line of the River Seine across the German rear; the selection of objectives for Montgomery's 21st Army Group, either to
allow it the kudos of the drive into the North German Plain, or
the vitally important task of clearing the Channel ports and,
above all, Antwerp, with first priority given to complete assurance
that adequate supplies would maintain an invulnerable invasion
of Germany.

History tells us that the Allies failed to knock Germany out of
the war in 1944 because their strategy fell between stools. When
the Germans conquered the West in 1940 with an inferior
numerical force, they had put all their tanks into one blow
backed by the entire resources of their homeland base. When
the Allies, in 1944, with a tank and air strength capable of
triplicating and more the original German effort, tried to achieve
similar results with a three-pronged advance backed by resources
with capabilities equal to supporting only one strong thrust, they
were doomed to failure. Many striking and dramatic advances
were made by the Allied tank formations.

Patton, the man who in the 1920s had foretold no future for
deep penetrations by mechanized formations, managed to advance
as much as 60 miles in a single day and some hundred miles
between 26 August and 1 September. Of this flamboyant commander, revered in America for all his inconsistencies, Grow,
who in 1944 was one of his divisional commanders, has written:
'He visited my division almost daily. I am glad to say that he
seldom found me as I was at the front where he frequently
chased me down. He insisted that his subordinate commanders
lead their troops when the occasion demanded. He was the kind
of leader that made you do things that you thought you couldn't
do.' The epitome of the audacious tank leader, in fact, yet no
more effective than those in other tank forces once the way was
open for supreme mobility. First US Army under General Hodges
covered 140 miles in seven days and in three quite startling days
the point of Montgomery's 21st Army Group went 200 miles from
the Seine to Antwerp and sealed off enormous German forces
along the Channel coast.

Yet none of these Allied thrusts struck to the heart of the German nation, and by the time they reached the Siegfried Line in September they were attenuated and approaching the end of their supply lines. It was significant that, when Montgomery projected the most imaginative strategic scheme of his career— the airborne carpet between Grave and Arnhem to pave the way for his armoured forces into Northern Germany—tactical failure became irreversible whenever his tanks failed to link up with the airborne divisions. Moreover it was stopped by two hastily reconstructed, understrength Panzer divisions, exploiting their protection, firepower and mobility, which could not fail to overrun airborne divisions tied immobile in a bridgehead—no matter how hard the airborne élite should fight. Without armour the infantry, held temporarily safe by massed artillery fires and made safer by a vast infusion of improved anti-tank guns, had no hope of achieving a permanent decision in European conditions. Armour without infantry did not fare so well either and, as German raids cut through the slim Allied corridor to Arnhem, the battle line came to a halt on Germany's frontier.

Once more, indeed, Germany had won breathing space—a pause made possible because both the Russian and Anglo-American forces had outrun their strength and because the Germans, compressed within their natural frontiers, could assemble a considerable armoured force, capable of achieving a decision of sorts.

But the German force was but one and their opponents many. Time was not on their side, the aerial bombardment of their nation must soon suffocate their economy and destroy all internal communications. The last great tank battles could not be long delayed.

Chapter 23

A DYING FALL

Hopping from island to island across the Pacific in the winter of 1944 amphibious forces, strong in naval and air power and led, inland, by tanks closed in on their ultimate objective—Japan. In the meantime, in Burma, an army carefully moulded of a preponderant proportion of infantry and artillery to tanks and liberally helped by air power, began the return journey to Rangoon via Mandalay. But while all this was going on the gaze of the Grand Strategists remained focused upon the enactment of the last rites in Germany—a country on the verge of collapse and the venue for the last great tank battles.

By extraordinary exertions, including the stripping from industry of surplus workers to renew the armed forces' manpower, and a more thorough mobilization of the nation, the Germans managed to stabilize their western frontier on the line of the prewar fortifications, stop the Russian surge in Poland and, simultaneously, recreate an uncommitted central reserve of nine Panzer divisions. In this reserve, for the last time, Hitler possessed an instrument of decision, but he could no longer indulge in a careful winter's debate with his generals to decide the course of action. Time was against him and there was mutual distrust within his entourage while innumerable physical difficulties hampered the issue of simple orders despatching the Panzer divisions, unchallenged, in any desired direction at a few days' notice.

For all the advantage Germany enjoyed by waging war from a central position on internal lines, those lines were crumbling under ceaseless air bombardment while the fuel to drive motorized forces under their own power flowed away, not to be replaced. In April 1944 the oil-fuel reserves had stood at about a million tons; at the end of August, as the Russians arrived on the outskirts of the vital Ploesti oilfields and with the home synthetic oil plants ravaged by air attack, barely 327,000 tons remained. In September the Wehrmacht had its allocation cut by half. From then onward all strategic moves of tanks, even of short duration, had to be rail-drawn by engines burning Germany's last remaining indigenous fuel—coal. And as the Allied air forces struck anywhere they chose the Fatherland's railways began to disintegrate and the military planners were forced to send everything by night in the interests of safety.

In these catastrophic circumstances, when to sue for terms was the only sane political course left open to Germany, Hitler searched for delay in some undefinable belief of victory by a miracle. One concrete fact was allowed to emerge, however, and that was the impracticability of deferring the commitment of his central reserve until after the enemy had declared *their* offensives. He could neither afford to give up territory nor guarantee to concentrate his forces in time and space at some critical point of rupture. Now, in fact, a forehand stroke alone was left to his discretion and if it were not launched before the New Year it was unlikely to get started at all.

Hitler's choice of a blow at the Anglo-Americans rather than the Russians possessed an underlying grain of good sense. Germany's strategic objectives, in the West, such as the port complex of Antwerp and the securing of launching pads for rocket attacks against Britain, were closer to hand. Moreover, Hitler reasoned, a healthy military victory stood more chance of fatally discouraging the democracies rather than the communists whose totalitarian structure inured them to setbacks and losses. The idea of an attack through the Ardennes was also sound, invited as it was by the paucity of the American defences there and recollections of the lessons of 1940 which might have been forgotten by the Allies. The synchronization of poor flying weather with the start time of the offensive was not a matter of coincidence either but an essential part of the plan to ensure that the German forces could assemble undetected and move freely in the opening stages.

As history tells us, Hitler's last fling in the Ardennes was a gamble which failed in its strategic purpose after winning a dramatic if indecisive run of initial tactical successes by surprise. The immunity from air attack of the German supply lines in the early days and, above all, the freedom to move unseen and inviolate from the air into the heart of the defended zone, were of immeasurable importance. But the angry temper of the combat in that closely wooded piece of Belgium was not to be compared with the mild brawl of 1940, despite early indications of

American dismay and unmistakable evidence of panic by their tenuously placed infantry divisions holding the line. Resistance was spasmodic at first but there was no unbroken chain-reaction collapse with the Americans as there had been with the French.

Whereas the French, in the warm May sunshine, had supinely allowed the Germans to infiltrate such readily defensible country to the open plain beyond, the Americans, in freezing winter over-cast, fought hard for the defiles and topographical features that mattered, seeing in small communication centres like Bastogne, Houffalize, St Vith and Stavelot the keys locking the door to mechanized forces in that confined territory. Unlike the French, moreover, the Americans avoided wasting tanks in static defence. From far and wide, flank and rear of the dangerous salient bulg-ing into their front, the American armoured divisions converged upon the vital centres in compact teams of all arms, and then so disposed themselves that the essential virtue of mobility was preserved.

Typical was the dash of the American 7th Armored Division —a formation which, but a few weeks previously, had been seriously shaken by German attacks in Holland. This division left its concentration area in the Maastricht Appendix on the night of the 16th, intending to motor about 70 miles on its tracks to help defend Bastogne on the 17th. Delayed in its start, it had not gone far before it was told to alter course and defend St Vith instead. Their journey was inauspicious and long before the division got there the men in the leading elements were con-fronted by a chilling sight: '... a constant stream of traffic hurtling to the rear and nothing going to the front. We realized that this was not a convoy moving to the rear; it was a case of "every dog for himself"; it was a retreat, a rout.'

The men of 7th Armored Division, disturbed as they must have been, resisted panic and shoved and bullied their way to their objective by forcing the rabble (senior officers included) off the road, arriving at the eastern perimeter of the town only a few hours before the leading German divisions appeared. As American units squeezed their way out of the traffic jam they were flung into the line, not to become a string of immobile pill-boxes but to hold vital ground for a defence based upon free manoeuvre. Thus when the first German column was seen approaching by an American tank leader he charged to meet the enemy head on: 'The fight was short and at point blank range. We destroyed the three enemy tanks. . . .' Later their own tank crews dismounted and were used as infantry.

Slowly 7th Armored Division spread itself around and retaining the shape and composition of its individual combat commands, if not its cohesion as a division, fell back through St Vith under fierce pressure. Not until the night of the 21st, however, was it finally expelled and by then it had thrown its opponents schedule out of gear, causing traffic jams in the German rear and the troops at the front to be starved of fuel and ammunition. Everywhere else, too, armoured knots such as these were holding the vital intersections. In effect they were buying time for other troops to prepare fresh defences in rear.

When the clouds lifted and all stood revealed to the Allied airmen, every German truck trying to replenish the tank spearheads was liable to destruction. At that the momentum of the German offensive died. Outclassed though the Allies were in quality of tanks, they could deploy such numbers in the German path that, destroy as many Shermans as the Panthers and Tigers might, a time had to come when the exhaustion of their crews overrode everything else. Without reserves of supplies and men, machines ran down and in December 1944 the Germans' central reserve was incapable of re-energizing the front-line units with men who were physically fresh. From the start, in any case, the Germans had chased a phantom hope, for the opponent of 1944 was not to be overawed like the enemy of 1940. At rock bottom lay the undeniable truth that, while tanks retained an important place in the order of battle, their prestige as the universal bully had been deflated.

Rebuffed in Belgium and then heavily assailed on 12 January in Poland by the Russians, what remained of the German tank force had to be sent to the eastern front leaving only small local reserves in the West. The last great tank battles in the Second World War were to have a 'dying fall' and no grand climax. By April, when the Russians were surrounding Berlin, the British approaching the Baltic and the Americans on the Elbe and entering Czechoslovakia with uncountable hordes of tanks at their beck and call, there were virtually no German tanks to oppose them. The last phase in Germany may have been occupa-

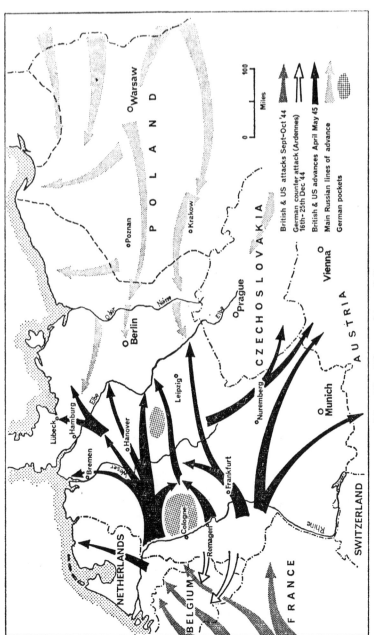

Map 21   The crushing of Germany

tion by force but the grand cadence of massed tank battles was
absent.

In the Far East the atrophy of the Japanese kept pace with
German emaciation, though only in Burma against the British and
Indian Fourteenth Army was tank warfare waged with anything
approaching the immensity of the encounters in Europe. For only
in Burma was there space to deploy large mechanized formations.
In the fearsome struggles for the gateway to India at Kohima
and Imphal, through March and May 1944, one British officer
likened Kohima to 'a dirty corner of the Somme, and was worse'.
There infantry were supreme and in costly contention while
artillery did its unavailing best to dominate and tanks
strictly played second fiddle. Since the few passable tracks could
be closely watched, a single Japanese soldier crouched in a hole
clutching a large bomb, fuse exposed, and a hammer, could with
certainty wait the arrival of a tank above him with a measure
of certainty before blowing them all to their own particular
choice of heaven. For all the difficulties of movement and
survival a few tanks, however, were perpetually needed at the
front to blast bunkers from close range and give the sort of
intimate support in trench warfare which had necessitated their
invention in the First World War.

It was not until the Japanese cracked and began their involuntary retreat to Mandalay, in December 1944, that high mobility
returned to Burma, but once General Slim's Fourteenth Army
entered the plains to the north and west of the famous city,
new horizons quite literally appeared. At last range of vision
widened from a few feet to several hundred yards and the tanks
could roll with unparalleled freedom. Their objective would be
Meiktilla, 75 miles south of Mandalay, where lay the main
Japanese supply depots and a complex of airfields grouped about
the communication centre—a classical target for an armoured raid.
Yet in such undeveloped country the secret 300-mile switch of
the complete IV Corps, comprising two infantry divisions and a
brigade of Shermans and Grants, across the rear of another corps
matched the daring of anything accomplished in the simpler
conditions of Europe. To quote a contemporary account, the
move 'by the narrow dirt roads was an outstanding feat of
logistics, the more so since Slim had lately lost the services of so

much air transport. To supplement his tenuous road supply, already 400 miles distant from railhead at Dimapur, the Fourteenth Army Commander turned to the resources at hand'—and by these he meant the River Chindwin navigated by improvized timber boats as his main supply route.

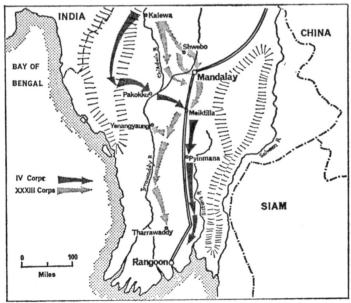

Map 22   The thrust to Rangoon

The insertion of this force, deep in the Japanese rear, was in the finest tradition of any German tank leader, comprising as it did a deception plan to delude the Japanese into thinking IV Corps was to the north of Mandalay when it was already to the west; the sudden eruption of the tank brigade outward from a bridgehead over the river Irrawaddy, near Pakokku, and the 85-mile race to Meiktilla in 85 hours; the cut and thrust of the tanks in seizing the supply base and, reinforced by infantry flown into the newly captured airfields, the disruption of each Japanese counter-stroke before it could be assembled and launched. Here, and in the subsequent pursuit to Rangoon, tank fought tank as never before in Burma, and the neglected Japanese tank forces were utterly outmatched by British and

Indian crews manning tanks of types which, in Europe, were outclassed. The defeat of the Japanese tank force was not a turning point in the struggle for Burma (credit for that goes to infantry aided by engineers, artillery and air power) but it was symbolic of Japanese decay in a mechanized war. Slim's army entered Rangoon on 2 May. On 5 August the first nuclear bomb fell at Hiroshima and the Japanese could end the war without loss of face.

Two days later the Russians invaded Manchuria, their entry into the war against Japan more political than military, the task before them more demanding of logistics than of fighting. Throughout 1945 they had been transferring veteran troops from the Western Theatre of operations, through Siberia, to man the 5,500 tanks and 26,000 guns which had been accumulated along the Manchurian frontiers. The Russian Far Eastern Front was under the command of Vasilevski and included the Sixth Guards Tank Army. Its basic plan was to rush the mountain passes and pour through an armada of tanks from three different directions at once, converging upon the centre of the country and then making for the south, for Port Arthur and North Korea. To withstand them waited the ghost of the once mighty Kwantung Army, allegedly 1,000 inferior tanks strong, stripped of its best men (who had been sent to reinforce other parts of the Far East), divided in command, undernourished in all types of equipment and thoroughly lowered in morale. The Soviet armoured juggernaut had only to organize momentum to advance over distances of three to four hundred miles in ten days. The techniques acquired by four years' bitter experience against the Germans were too much for the weakened Japanese whose defences collapsed with the familiar rapidity of an outmoded army confronted by a well organized, highly mobile armoured mass. On 18 August the local Japanese signed an instrument of surrender.

Throughout the world thousands of tank crews switched off their engines. But while citizen soldiers paid their last farewells to arms the professionals began to ask themselves what sort of future there was for armour once the atomic revolution got into its stride. The Second World War ended in 1945 leaving as many technical and tactical problems unsolved as had its predecessor in 1918.

Chapter 24

THE BYWAYS OF PEACE

Despite the tanks' triumphant march at the head of Allied columns through Axis territory in 1945, their part in the pursuit was neither without setbacks nor free from moments of dull suspicion that the future of armoured vehicles might lie in jeopardy. Though the Germans' principal anti-tank force—their tanks and self-propelled guns—had been ruined, Allied tanks suffered nagging losses to the bitter end, mines claiming a significant proportion of those damaged while the mass-produced inefficient short-range, hollow-charge infantry weapons, in the hands of determined men, scored many kills. Inhibited by the realization that a long war was nearly over and that life was sweet, circumspect tank crewmen imbibed exaggerated caution and demanded close escort by infantry whenever they advanced. But the infantry, who more frequently rode in armoured vehicles themselves, were likewise loath to go it alone on foot without close tank attendance. Fastidious arrangements had to be made for close co-operation between all arms at all times, a process so time-consuming as to cause a reduction in the tempo of operations and, possibly, higher losses than might have been incurred with a quick rush. Any weapon in the hands of cautious men is at a discount and in this respect tanks suffer more than most.

At different times, in changing circumstances and with varying degrees of success tanks had either fulfilled or failed to achieve the promise of the inter-war years. There was still no clear-cut valuation. At the call of harrowing memories and in the absence of extensive scientific studies, the tank might be emotionally categorized as the essential core to an anti-tank defence, a useful supplement to artillery, a close escort for infantry or the arbiter in independent operations. It was easy to forget that in widely different circumstances tanks had been readily adapted as maids of all work. A prolonged postwar debate between scientists and soldiers began, though it was some time before they reached a really close understanding. But in 1945 research and development at least took precedence—unlike 1919 when little more than lip service was paid to it. The war had shown not only that machines dominated but that they had to be persistently improved if the survival of fighting men was to be assured.

The revelation of German research and development in particular gave strong impetus to renewed investigations. Infra-red devices which made it possible to see and shoot in the dark were discovered; bigger mines, constructed to be much more destructive and difficult to detect and neutralize, were found. Most dramatic of all was the unearthing of an embryonic rocket-propelled, guided weapon, sent to its target by signals transmitted down a trailing wire. Overall a number of sophisticated anti-tank weapons came to light and seemed to raise defensive power still further above that of offence.

Evidence of these threats to the tank's survival promoted intuitive counter-measures. Defence against air attack (even after it became known that the threat was less severe than once thought), aids to obstacle crossing, means to improve protection against all novel forms of attack and to increase the tank's fighting capacity not only raised the cost and weight of tanks but prompted their critics to ask if so great an outlay was worth the trouble when, perhaps, the dominance of the tank had passed its zenith. As in 1919, the military establishments of 1946 were under pressure to make reductions while vested interests strove hard at self-protection. The argument might run that, however good it might feel to have sophisticated tanks at one's side in battle, the proposition failed if some cheap, new weapon made the tank impotent. Though valid in debate, such suggestions held good only when firmly related to a fixed point in time, and in 1946 the advent of these revolutionary weapons in reliable form could not be stated while the impossibility of a man being able to cross fire-swept ground without armour protection was incontrovertible.

Of course the need for close examination of the demand for large and expensive machines was undeniable. While a single main battletank had cost about £20,000 in 1939, by 1945 the price had more than doubled. Experience had shown the advantages of incorporating as many virtues as possible in one type of tank. If one machine could incorporate the power to destroy every known class of enemy tank, beyond the range at which the blow could be returned, and given the ability to help infantry in all conditions with an improved mobility so that not only deep obstacles but unfirm ground could be crossed with the least need for outside assistance, then the tank's life might be prolonged. If all these things could be made possible by day *and* night so much the better. A capital tank such as the Sherman, the Panther, the T34/85 and the Comet was required, but like the capital ship at sea it was bound to acquire a bigger gun and thicker armour in response to the various demands put upon it. It could easily turn into a clumsy, vulnerable white elephant.

Over all loomed the threat of the nuclear weapon with its potential for infinite destruction, not only by fire and blast but also by radiation. Faced with such threats men had either to wrap themselves behind an even thicker protective mass or take nimbler evasive action. This meant that those who survived an explosion (and those in a tank had a high chance of survival) would have to drive off rapidly, dig so deep or become so heavily armoured as to be almost immobile. Although the concept of immobile protection enjoyed a short-lived vogue in the 1950s the common-sense solution to survival on the battlefield could only be one of compromise. Digging there would be, but the tank, with the relatively high ratio of protection inherent in its balanced mass and mobility, convincingly showed by calculation and in trials that, no matter how deadly the threat, it still offered the optimum chance of survival *and* striking power if nuclear war broke out. Hence the tank became an adjunct to nuclear weapons and therefore an integral part of the Great Deterrent—seeking to prevent war by the presentation of a deadly counter-threat.

Against a background of international tension, broken at frequent intervals by outbursts of local fighting, tank research and development went on. The Korean War, beginning in June 1950, was at first fought between T34/85 tanks on the North Korean side and US tanks of similar vintage on the United Nations' side. But shortly the US forces were committing their latest M46 and M47 (Patton) tanks, armed with a 90mm gun, and the British their newest Centurions with its 83.4mm gun and sloped armour of anything between 115 and 152mm at the thickest part. In response the Russians, while stocking the armies of their allies with the outmoded tanks of 1945 vintage, would develop their T44 and its successors T54 and T55, to keep pace with what further improvements they knew the British and Americans must be concocting. And the British and Americans, believing the Russians would not stand still, went on designing even bigger tanks armed with guns up to 120mm and up-gunning their Centurions and M48s with the British 105mm gun. And yet even the Russians had their doubters and General Rotmistov had to fight a hard diplomatic battle for tanks against his political chief Khrushchev, who had come to look on tanks as 'useless'.

Without the firing of many shots in anger the whirligig of the gun armour race soared upwards and had not the smaller nations, who gradually acquired the cast-off models of the major powers, indulged in limited wars, the technological competition might not have been put to the test. But the post-Second-War period has had its 'Spanish incidents' to provide the testing ground for new weapons. The open combat phase of the Korean war was mainly fought in mountain and padi by tanks of Second World War vintage before the latest American Pattons and British Centurions arrived to find themselves virtually imprisoned in a war which had reverted to an entrenched stalemate. Nevertheless the employment of napalm bombs by the Americans against T34 tanks showed how a missile, which could destroy without achieving absolute pinpoint accuracy, might induce greater caution than ever upon tanks trying to manoeuvre in the open. Nor did the Sinai Campaign of 1956 (dealt with in more detail later) do much to change the art since, once more, outmoded machines and old-fashioned tactics were employed. But the fighting in 1965 between Pakistan, equipped with a number of US M47s and India, equipped mainly with British Centurions and French light AMX13s, gave the experts a unique opportunity to compare the qualities of one type of Western tank against another. And then in 1967 there came the first large scale stand-up battle between Western and Soviet tanks of modern design in the celebrated Six Day War; but since the armoured struggle in Sinai threw controversy into the melting pot it is a story which, within the context of this book, merits a chapter to itself.

To return to the short-lived engagements in the Indian sub-continent it is tempting to dismiss the war of 1965, largely because of the negative strategic and tactical verve of the two sides, and to concentrate on the ironic twist which put American-built against British-built tanks. With wide expanses of firm terrain providing ample space for rapid manoeuvre it was to be expected that the contenders might indulge in imaginative strategic moves, particularly since several politically important cities lay close to the frontier battle zone. Nothing of the sort seems to have occurred even though attempts at deep penetration were made. The build-up of effort was slow and then projected along lines of assured expectation into the other's territory.

Tank battles tended to revert to head-on encounters, productive only of corresponding losses on either side, and it is difficult to assess the true value of one side over the other. Suggestions that the gun and armour of the Pakistani M47s were inferior to those of the Indian Centurions, of similar vintage, may be valid, just as it may be possible that the simpler Centurion gunnery ranging and sighting equipment was more easily manageable in the hands of Indian crews than the complex optical ranging devices built into the M47s. At all events, after only a few days of stolid armoured battering had followed a bout of small-scale raiding, both sides reached a state of mutual exhaustion and were only too pleased to cease fire.

Significantly it was the wholesale breakdown of supply, both at the front and farther back, and the threat of mutual national economic collapses which, more than the fighting, forced a conclusion. Less well endowed nations discover, sooner than the great, that war with modern weapons is an exhausting pastime. Paradoxically, only the men at the front seem to have drawn any satisfaction from the encounter and Christmas cards published by Indian units depicting Pattons knocked out by Centurions had a self-satisfied look.

The stalemate on the Indo-Pakistan frontier laid emphasis not only upon the neutralizing effect of comparably advanced weapon systems but on the need, as seen by all the students of war since the 1940s, to quicken movement. In essence, and as expressed by Liddell Hart in 1942, this meant 'developing new means of communication and transmission of orders' and while experimenting with new technologies to simplify 'the system of control in particular, by shortening the chain of command'. Liddell Hart, in accord with others, felt that fewer headquarters should command more men and units up to their full capacity to think and then execute their thoughts. Chiefly throughout the 1950s every progressive army experimented with a plethora of new organizations in attempts to improve the flexibility of functions—to enable leaders and staffs to react more speedily and to readjust the balance of their formations to rapidly changing circumstances.

In the outcome, by the mid-1960s, this simply produced a series of different blends within the existing compound of formal or informal all-arms battlegroups and combat teams—reflecting, in fact, what Fuller had prophesied in his book *Lectures on FSR III*, published in 1932. If the Americans with their Pentomic Division in particular devised so flexible an organization that it defeated its own purpose in all its complexity, it was at least progressive. It explored every conceivable permutation of tanks working with the other arms in order to tackle any situation that was likely to occur in future battles of almost unimaginable complexity. But in war it is simplicity which succeeds when stress and strain undermine cool thought.

The fighting groups themselves, having enhanced their firepower, could dominate far wider expanses of ground than ever foreseen by Fuller. Not only had armament increased in range and accuracy to enable fewer troops to hold a specified frontage, but the nuclear threat made it a cardinal sin to concentrate for long in space; fast movement, alone, could give the vital concentration, but mainly in time. Once again the key to move swiftly in actual battle techniques was to be found in improved radio communications. The introduction of more powerful and reliable very-high-frequency radio sets enabled radio speech at all levels to acquire something approaching the fluency of a telephone conversation with a minimum of outside interference. Though still liable to interference and eavesdropping, radio became more potent than ever before and thus communications, by dominating events, acquired an even greater facility to multiply gun power. Therefore radio war—the struggle to speak without being heard and to hear without the enemy understanding—became, more than ever, an integral part of the war at the front.

Further twists to the mounting spiral of complexity and cost were added by the desire to operate in all types of terrain in all weathers and by day or night. Improvements to special devices that enabled tanks (like the DDs) to swim across rivers or to wade beneath the surface using a breathing tube advanced in conjunction with investigations aimed at helping tanks of their own accord to cross difficult gaps. Experiments with searchlights incorporating infra-red filters led to the introduction of greatly improved night-fighting devices on many armoured vehicles and the gradual supercession of General Grow's earlier, reasonable and typical practice: 'I preferred confining armour operations to day with smoke cover except for very limited objective attacks by a swing to a policy of action by night and hide and seek by day.'

As the great power blocs of NATO, the Warsaw Pact and others became aligned in delicate balance the cost and complexity of tanks rose astronomically. Ancillary devices, such as night-viewing equipment and radar—considered necessary as an assurance to the tank's survival on the battlefield—added a significant sum to the price of the basic vehicle which existed, in the minds of many, as a servant or adjunct to the dominating nuclear deterrent. But when it came to participation in the cold-war confrontations themselves, these expensive machines were as likely to cause escalation as prevent it.

Civil policing at its most sophisticated is the effective application of minimum force. Where police and troops have restrained themselves in a host of tumultuous internal control operations, violence has been kept to a minimum and long-lasting hatred averted. When aggression is applied by the forces of law to subjugate crowd violence the chances of achieving a lasting settlement recede. Tanks represent the pinnacle of aggression and are anomalous to crowd control—their use by the British against Egyptians, by the Russians against East Berliners, Hungarians and Czechs, and by the Americans against their own countrymen, may have restored a veneer of order, but no more; the appearance of tanks in the streets as counter to revolution or insurrection is but a sign of transient dictatorship on the march. Infantry stand a better chance of controlling a mob because they can get closest to the affected people and do not become isolated from the mood of the crowd by a wall of steel. It may be, too, that wheeled armoured vehicles cause less provocation than the tracked variety—possibly because they are quieter and in their silence generate less fear of outright violence.

Tanks, though often a deterrent, remain a symbol and, perhaps also, an incentive to war. Old-fashioned violence in the shape of a full-blooded tank battle will always be on the cards if a plethora of armoured vehicles finds its way into the hands of nations which are unconstrained by the nuclear deterrent. The Indo-Pakistan War was one such instance and the various Israeli wars are the latest supreme example, even if the Israelis are more conscious of the threatening loom of great-Power involvement.

Chapter 25

REFLECTION

On 16 October 1948 the first and only tank battalion then possessed by Israel set out to fight its first action—an attack against Egyptians holding Lod Airport. But of the ten 1935-vintage H35 French light tanks all broke down or fell into anti-tank ditches before getting into range, and while the solitary Sherman available to the battalion was not engaged, two Cromwells, purloined from the departed British Mandatory Power, entered the enemy's lines promptly to be knocked out.

If this inauspicious christening of the Israeli Armoured Corps* carried a faint echo from the first tank battle it need hardly evoke surprise. Both in September 1916 and October 1948 inexperienced men governed by infantry-biased tactical doctrine had driven unreliable fighting machines into what, for them, was virtually the unknown. In the days of 'tank discovery' the engagements by both the British and the Israelis had been preludes to programmes of a vast mechanical expansion in the art of war, but with the Israelis the struggle for survival, which stimulated their nation in a manner unknown to the British, was to mark indelibly their nascent army. While maintaining a tenuous clutch on the frontiers of their tightly compressed nation, the Israeli military doctrine included a mating of guerrilla aggression with a parsimonious determination to cling to every inch of ground as they worked for time to gain strength for what they foresaw as a long struggle against the Arabs.

It was desirable, if possible, that all battles should be fought in the waste lands *beyond* the more fertile, populated Israeli frontiers—a policy which called for an aggressive army necessarily based on mechanization. Yet this same demand equated neither with an enforced financial stringency nor with the basic infantry orientation of the founding formations. In fact, precisely

* Much of what is described in this chapter is based upon *The Tanks of Tammuz* by Shabtai Teveth, which has an authentic ring like no other description of the Israeli Armoured Corps.

the same restrictions as had hampered every tank force the world over since 1918 held back the Israeli tank men.

Within the Army the Armoured Corps chafed at what it regarded as the unrealistic and dangerous restrictions curbing its expansion. The progressives in the Armoured Corps—men such as Uri Ben-Ari—became restless bedfellows among the traditional arms. In exercises in 1952 the 7th Brigade, under Ben-Ari, ruined Army manoeuvres by driving contrarily to the controllers' schemes deep into the 'enemy's' rear. This so seriously embarrassed the umpires that they were forced to make an arbitrary ruling: 'A circle was drawn on the map...and the brigade was not allowed to emerge from it until further notice.' Unrepentant, the brigade repeated the salutary lesson in mobility in 1953—so effectively this time that the opposing infantry actually took to their heels in fright. In many ways this military experience with tanks was not so very different from that undergone by the British Army in 1927 and 1934. But with the Israelis in 1953 a political decision cut short the debate, not so much because of military enlightenment as because the Prime Minister, Ben Gurion, actually witnessed the infantry débâcle in person and, like Hitler, recognized in the tank the weapon his army must have. From that moment onward the Armoured Corps took precedence in the allocation of funds for expansion—regardless of what the infantry might fear.

The Israelis never accurately state the size of their forces, nor are they in the habit of giving information which might be of assistance to their many enemies: on the contrary it is much more likely that, by discreet misstatements, they seek to mislead rather than inform. Therefore although much has been written about the wars of 1956 and 1967 there can be no guarantee as to its accuracy.

It is plain, however, that the campaign which began in the Sinai on 29 October 1956 was not wholly intended by the Israelis to be dominated by mechanized forces. The proportion of tank to infantry battalions in their Army was in the ratio of only five to twenty-two and the tanks themselves were out of date—a mixture of French AMX13s and up-gunned Shermans. The secret of Israeli success was a vibrant dash in action, but their tactics were founded upon pre-Second World War British doctrine, featuring a formal infantry breaching operation against the

Egyptians at Kusseima to be followed up by an advance by the armoured brigade through the gap. This General Dayan, the Israeli Chief of Staff, intended, but in war as in peace the armoured brigade commander decided otherwise. By flagrant disobedience of orders he inserted the tank brigade prematurely into Egyptian territory but so close to Kusseima that it came up against solid resistance instead of moving into an open space. Thus it was reduced to making an abortive head-on assault against unshaken opposition—a familiar experience, one recalls, in the history of tank warfare.

Dayan admits that he was angry, but this did not discourage him from seizing a new initiative. Extricating the tanks from the stalemate, and leaving the infantry to clean up the remaining opposition at Kusseima, he flung the armoured brigade in a long chase through a wide gap to within sight of the Suez Canal. Here was the old tank magic at its best—an unimpeded phalanx roaring unchecked past bewildered opposition to totally undermine the enemy's resistance by the abruptness of its bold appearance in the most unexpected places. The Egyptian rout was complete and the haul of booty included 125 tanks—and all for a mere 150 killed on the Israeli side in a campaign lasting but eight days.

Much about the 1956 Israeli armoured force was impoverished and, in terms of equipment, a decade out of date. The fight for survival generated a superb spirit and bred a fierce individuality comparable with the irresistible cavalry dash of old. But with war machines growing ever more complicated and demanding meticulous handling, dash was insufficient if it ignored technical factors. The unsophisticated Sherman tanks were easy to operate, particularly from the point of view of gunnery. Poor crew maintenance and inaccurate gunnery passed almost unnoticed. But when, throughout the 1960s, an influx of sophisticated American Pattons and British Centurions (the latter mounting the highly accurate 105mm gun) were acquired, a vast expansion of the Armoured Corps went side by side with unavoidable demand for increased mechanical knowledge on the part of crews, most of whom were only part-time soldiers. These factors seemed at first incompatible and yet their resolution was vital to Israel's survival. In 1965 Israel possessed just over 1,000 tanks while the Egyptians had 1,300 and the other neighbouring Arab nations something like 750. Against these odds the Israelis had to compensate by far greater proficiency, as the Germans had done all along. Above all they had to improve their gunnery techniques and take full advantage of the more powerful guns they were buying. Yet it was not until 1964 that this seems to have been understood.

Skirmishes along the Syrian border in 1964, when Israeli Centurions fought duels with outmoded but dug-in German Mark IV tanks, at last revealed the inadequacy of the Israeli crews' training. A single hit on a Mark IV by a 105mm shot would be totally disruptive, but hits were all too rarely obtained, not because the gun was inaccurate but because it was rarely perfectly in alignment (zeroed) with the sighting equipment, and because the crews' gun drills were haphazard.

It was General Israel Tal's privilege as commander of the Armoured Corps to enjoy the powers of a Guderian and to have imbibed, through careful study, Guderian's zest for tank warfare. It was he who approved the purchase of the Pattons and Centurions, who laid down tank policy and who insisted upon a standardized training system which seemed, to some, to offend the traditions of crew individuality.

When Tal took charge in 1964 he had to reorientate the thinking of his men, overriding their objections that the Centurion was too complicated by insisting that they should master rather than be beaten by the tank. Yet demanding the tanks won by simplified and standardized training. All the emphasis was placed on disciplined gunnery techniques. No longer was the vital zeroing of the guns left to the crews; all guns were to be uniformly aligned to their sights by experts, making it possible for even an inexpert gunner to set his sights on a target up to 1,200 metres and be almost sure of a first-round hit. Proof of the validity of Tal's methods was acquired in limited actions along the Syrian frontier when, using a strict fire discipline, the Centurions picked off like clay pigeons the old Mark IVs and a few tractors. From then on crews pandered to their tanks.

When, by a series of diplomatic miscalculations, the Arab States impelled the Israelis to make a pre-emptive attack in the Sinai on 5 June 1967 the stage had already been set for a contest between the classic Soviet-type defensive system and an updated version of German 'blitzkrieg'. The Egyptians, tutored by

Russian advisers and largely equipped with Russian tanks, occupied a complex of infantry positions designed for all-round defence of the frontier—and placed their older heavy JS3 and T34s therein. Farther back, in reserve, waited the armoured divisions with some 450 modern T54s and T55s.

The Israelis attacked by surprise in three armoured columns with an all-out attempt by their air force to obliterate the Egyptian air forces on their airfields. Their hearty disrespect for Egyptian moral fibre was reflected in a determination to shock their opponents into immediate flight and then keep them on the run to exhaustion. 'They are only Arabs' went the cry and the tank attacks were ruthlessly pushed through layer after layer of defences regardless of what happened upon the flanks and what stayed behind. Also they fought regardless of the losses accruing from mines, anti-tank guns and tanks, for the Egyptians by no means gave up without shooting back—at first. This, for the Egyptian command, was the rub: their men habitually gave way after making a mere gesture. Had they held fast to key positions the outcome might have more nearly resembled the stalemate at Kursk in 1943 when the Russians had stuck it out. As it was, Tal's division in the north, having advanced 60 miles and made a series of break-throughs, found itself the poorer by more than 30 commanders (though fewer tanks) in the first day against the strongest opposition. General Yaffa's division, on the other hand, striking deep and almost unnoticed into the enemy centre, soon found itself clear and in a position to help Tal in the north by completing a pincer move of which Manstein would have been proud. Sharon's division, in the south, had a tough struggle for Abu Agheila, winning clear only on the second day after a night assault through minefields. Fight or run, the Egyptians were irrevocably defeated in the first 24 hours.

Taken by surprise and overborne by tanks, Egyptian infantry gave way in 1967 as the French had given way in 1940 and in the vital opening gambits of the tank-versus-tank battle when first impressions decided the future, the undoubted superior prowess of the Israeli tank gunners settled the issue. Old T34s and JS3s caught fast in their infantry-bound positions were defeated in detail and could be of little help when, at last, the armoured divisions with their powerful T54s and 55s arrived from reserve. Then, in the crucial encounters between the major

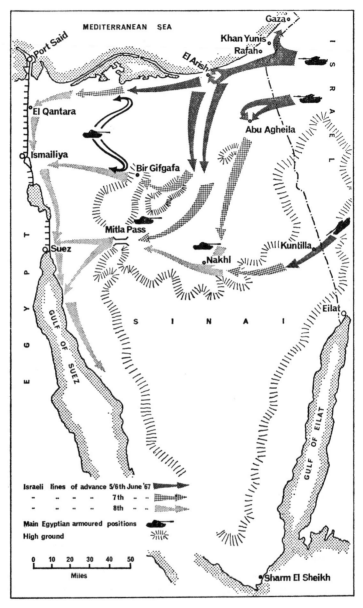

Map 23   Sinai in 1967

tank formations, the Egyptians seemed to become mesmerized. On the Ismailiya road, on 8 June, the Israelis outflanked a large Egyptian tank force by moving wide and unnoticed through soft sand such as the Egyptians considered impassable. Fascinated by Israeli tanks demonstrating to their front, the Egyptians suddenly found themselves under deliberate fire from the unguarded side and suffered the destruction of 70 tanks without recompense from only a few hours of coolly directed gunfire.

But as usual the administrative factor played its levelling part as so often in the great mechanized campaigns of the past. The Israeli supply columns were at best an amateurish crowd—a sluggish traffic jam of civil-impressed lorries driven by middle-aged gentlemen with a convoy discipline learnt in the streets of Tel-Aviv. Frequently lorries had to be forcibly pushed off the road to make way for reserves moving to the front; more perilous were the occasions when these same lorries failed to reach the front in time to replenish the tanks. At the Mitla Pass, in a vital engagement, tanks with few drops of fuel left towed others, bone-dry, into fire positions to block the Egyptian retreat.

For the Egyptians, of course, supply at the front was rarely a problem since so swift was their collapse that the need to replenish hardly arose except when their armoured divisions began tentative manoeuvres against the Israelis between El Arish and the Canal. The administrative factor came into play only as Egyptian fuel consumption rose in relation to the mobile phase just as Israeli air attacks took unhindered toll of so many lorries.

While the Egyptian Air Force never had an opportunity to affect the land battle, and was compelled to leave the Israeli supply columns to their self-inflicted strangulation, the Israeli Army also made do without air power until the second day. Then, however, with air superiority assured, more aircraft could be spared—though to what effect is hard to assess since post-war accounts are conflicting. As usual the apostles of air power have produced some impressive guesses of the number of tanks knocked out by aircraft. Accounts of the ground battle by men on the ground seem to belie this, taking most of the credit to fire for tanks, guns and mines. Indeed, it seems unlikely that air intervention in the land battle, even given the use of napalm, was much more effective in 1967 than it had been in 1945. It undoubtedly helped isolate the battlefield in favour of the victor and gave his lines of communication cover while providing an invaluable information service of enemy movements. It did not, on its own, decide the land battle or seriously threaten tanks themselves.

What strikes one most forcibly about the Six Day War is its crushing speed of execution. In four days in Sinai every sequence of a classical tank offensive was practised with rhythmic momentum—and at minimal cost. Eight hundred and fifty Egyptian tanks were captured after defeat by a force of which only about 600 had probably been committed. The Egyptian Army was routed so economically that the Israelis could swiftly turn about and defeat, in detail, the armies of Jordan and Syria. It cannot all be explained away by ribald disparagement of Arab courage, although it is likely that the underlying reason for their failure was a low standard of education leading to poor training and inept leadership. Try as hard as they might, the Russian instructors had been no more successful in teaching basically untutored men the complexities and subtleties of sophisticated modern equipment than the British before them. If the latest Russian tanks seemed like putty when pummelled by the Israeli's British, American and French built tanks, that was not to say that those same tanks in Russian hands would not have exacted a stiffer penalty. A tank force, after all, is viable only in the hands of a technologically inclined army. The Arabs have yet to acquire that status.

The Sinai campaign established Israel on the pinnacle of military prestige and the nations of the world looked hard for new lessons to learn from the victory. The pundits had a field day. But when it came down to brass tacks hardly anything new was attempted or achieved. This tank war was like those of the previous three decades. Was it possible then that Sinai in 1967, like Spain in 1937, gave a false impression for the future?

Chapter 26

THE FUTURE

From the tank point of view the Six Day War, for all its decisiveness, was remarkable not because the Israelis won by demonstrating the most ultra-modern weapons and methods but for their repetition of an original theme employing standard and, in part, obsolescent equipments. Against opponents armed with the latest guided weapons, communication devices, radar and the like, the Israelis conquered by employing well-tried, audacious strategic and tactical ideas combined with an imaginative and rational use of relatively unsophisticated weapons.

In South-East Asia there is corroboration of the theory that simplicity wins. In Vietnam, where the Americans strive unavailingly to bludgeon a guerrilla opponent into submission, using the entire paraphernalia of a modern technological army with the exception, so far, of nuclear explosives, they cannot reach a decision. There the basic methods of an infantry-preponderant, indigenous Viet Cong force prevail with short-range ambushes and hit-and-run tactics in which anti-tank defence is based on mines and simple, light hollow-charge anti-tank weapons. At first, it is true, the Americans themselves gave pride of place to infantry believing that armour could not operate with sufficient freedom and that only men on their feet, backed up by air power and, above all, a vast fleet of helicopters, would get to grips with an elusive foe. That has changed and now, by an enormous expenditure of effort, medium tanks as well as armoured personnel carriers are being driven into and through the most forbidding terrain.

Outwardly the demand for this laborious use of armour has been engineered by the traditional, instinctive desire to protect men against fire and thereby reinforce their courage. But another and perhaps even more compelling motive was internal pressure brought by those members of the American Armored Branch who saw in dominance by their own infantry of a major theatre of war a threat to their own occupation. If infantry took a major share of the fighting they would automatically receive the lion's portion of the financial benefits. Eventually a position might be reached in which the development of improved tanks for future use in those theatres of operation where tanks were king might fall into decay. In neglect the tank force would lie at the bottom of the list for research and development, production and man-power.

That the increased employment of armour in Vietnam seems to have left a political decision as far removed as ever is neither a fluke nor a condemnation of the men and machines. It simply underlines the ineffectiveness of a ponderous armed force when fighting opponents deny their enemies a sensitive political and strategic target. No matter how quickly air and land forces seem to re-deploy, the Viet Cong manage to slip away, and in extreme difficulties retire to some haven in an adjoining country such as Cambodia. The nerve centres are rarely exposed. There can hardly be a more potent antidote to tank forces than that sort of evasion.

The employment of strong armoured forces by the Americans in Vietnam has thus created sharp contrasts in basic philosophy and method—a duel between the world's greatest industrial nation fighting for an indistinct aim and an impoverished army kept in the field by sheer dedication, linked to a relatively minute supply of arms adjusted to a sound tactical scheme. Fuller would have approved the American desire to save lives and muscle-power by the use of machines, but he would also have applauded the Viet Cong's response. And so, in the grasslands and sometimes deep into the jungle, tanks press noisily ahead, crudely searching for a foe whose infantry tactics of hit and run inflict a niggling attrition of American strength but, more impor-tant, a sapping of will-power. Overhead the armed helicopters swarm, drawing and returning fire, taking their losses in the act of achieving a closer co-operation with tanks than the Luftwaffe ever achieved with the Panzer divisions. Nearby, to lend intimate support to the tanks, are the armoured personnel carriers, bristl-ing with machine-guns which rake the undergrowth to flush out enemy snipers. Inside crouch the infantry, ready to leap out yet anxious to enjoy the protection of armour plate until the last possible moment.

Fuller might have recognized in the modern armoured personnel carrier the true heir and successor to the light tanks whose virtues he had mistakenly espoused in the 1920s. For light tanks, having once been the technical offspring of the small machine-gun carriers and been found wanting in battle, have reverted to type, even though the modern version carries a much greater thickness of armour, can fire a far more formidable fusillade, and is so designed that it can often cross padifields without becoming stuck in the yielding ground. Yet virtually none of the armoured vehicles working with the Americans and South Vietnamese was designed for guerrilla warfare and so it is a sign of the adaptability of modern combat vehicles that they have been so easily converted to satisfy special local conditions. The proliferation of short-range weapons which festoon vehicles in Vietnam are mostly the products of improvization and made at the urgent demand of the local fighting troops. Sometimes the original machine is hardly recognizable.

The vast majority of American vehicles fighting in the Far East were first designed for the grand tactical exposition of war on a nuclear battlefield in Europe or the Middle East. Lessons taught in Vietnam, however, can be as misleading as those once learned in Spain and Korea when analyzed for conversion to European usage. Because a weapon performs well or badly in Vietnam it is no proof that it will do as well elsewhere and particularly on the fringes or in the heart of a nuclear battlefield even supposing that anything in such an event has the stamina to perform at all. The constricted, narrow-fronted engagements of Vietnam demand a different set of reflexes and techniques from those which would be mandatory in a wide-open war of sweeping manoeuvre in Europe or the Middle East. Against limited anti-tank forces in Vietnam the tanks usually prevail. The outcome might be different were they to be pitted against the full panoply of modern anti-tank weapons in the hands of a sophisticated and determined foe.

So long as tanks are rated the dominant weapon the full resources of armies will be devoted to devising antidotes. The tank antidotes of the 1970s are formidable—improved ways for detecting and shooting at targets by day and night; slicker communications to direct tank killers swiftly to the best tactical positions; more accurate guns to destroy, at one shot, even the toughest opponent at the longest possible range; an increased use of guided weapons either from special vehicles or helicopters;

a vast multiplication of the number of mines which can be laid mechanically at great speed; the projection of toxic chemicals— these and a host of other, lesser devices combine to reduce the tank's effectiveness either by its total destruction or by hampering its movements.

In response the tank designers have been forced to adopt additional passive measures such as mounting thicker armour and cluttering the machine with a collection of detection devices. Simultaneously the tacticians have been forced to merge the tank's activities even more closely within all-arms battlegroups. So far the tank of traditional shape has survived, but in its present highly complex and expensive state it attracts stiffer critical examination on grounds of economic effectiveness with every addition to the anti-tank armoury and whenever the need for a new generation comes up for consideration. The naval analogy is again appropriate if one equates the main battletank of the 1970s with the battleship after 1914—highly complex, ever bigger and more heavily protected, increasingly difficult to build and unthinkable to lose until in time so vast an escort effort has to be expended whenever it ventures forth that its existence becomes insupportable. Can it be that the 40- to 50-ton main battletank is entering that same category, to become the centrepiece of the battlegroup, but primarily the core of a fleet-in-being—a core which has to be preserved at all costs because its replacement is so difficult? Instead of the hunter of old, is the 50-ton tank on the verge of being the hunted—the bewildered prey of slings and arrows from lighter, more mobile and expendable creatures?

One thing is certain. With nerveless weapons of mass destruction becoming ever more potent and plentiful, the need for men to cross the battlefield under armoured protection is greater now than ever it was in 1914. So the mind turns to consider the introduction of smaller (though still well-armoured), simpler, less costly vehicles, yet probably more specialized tanks. One sees them co-operating as teams to achieve by combined action the same effect as the existing main capital tank, but spreading the risks through the multiplicity of numbers. It is ironic that technology, having solved the problems in 1970 of merging in a single vehicle the ability to do what was technically impossible in the 1930s, the sheer power and multiplicity of anti-tank forces demands a rejection of the all-purpose machine. Thus new tactical innovations may have to be devised to co-ordinate the functions of a team of vehicles—one 'tank' to carry a special anti-tank weapon, a second an anti-aircraft weapon, a third an artillery weapon and a fourth a squad of infantry armed with machine-guns.

Even so it is most unlikely that rationalizations in vehicle functions will simplify the operation of the individual vehicles and thereby rationalize crew training. Already it is clear that complex combat vehicles can only rarely be fully exploited by part time soldiers or those on short engagements. At least two years' training is needed to produce a fully proficient tank crewman and longer still to evolve a sound crew commander. In the 1920s the prophets dreamed of élite mechanized forces manned by a select few. The ideal was rarely achieved in peace and hardly at all in war. In the 1970s it will be enforced by the mechanical demands of the machines. Perhaps more powerful weapons served by an array of surveillance and communication devices require fewer men to serve them, but the 'few' must be of superior education and technically well trained besides possessing the soldierly virtues of strict discipline allied to a tough moral fibre. Proficiency and discipline are already in knife-edged balance, weighted one way by the independent tugs of intellectual power and the other by the demand for automatic reaction as the member of a team. Often there occurs an emotional contradiction to logical reason, while the preservation of personal initiative and enthusiasm remain of the highest desirable importance. Yet all have to be subordinated to a task of destruction.

The same complex escalation as afflicts weapon improvements also bedevils the difficulties of command and control. Yet the intricacies of future tank battles would be even more daunting were not staffs served by a formidable collection of devices, computers and displays (manned by more experts) to help them discover, synthesize and present battlefield data ready for conversion by their commander into speedy decisions for instant transmission to his executives. Let us see the system at work in an imaginary situation as a battlegroup enters action in the twilight period of war in a European setting before nuclear weapons have been used.

Reports have come in of an Aggressor Force advancing at full flood towards the communication centre at Arheim. The 57th

Combat Command, with its complement of reconnaissance and strike helicopters—the former carrying television cameras, the latter armed with long-range guided missiles—and its teams of special-purpose tanks and weapon carriers have been ordered to intercept. Information about the terrain—medium density country with villages and woods dotting rolling farmland and intersected by a single main and several secondary roads—and the location of friendly and hostile elements is presented to the commander from far and wide. If he feels this is insufficient he will, no doubt, reconnoitre the ground in person from his own helicopter.

Soon a coherent picture of enemy intentions begins to appear on maps, computer displays and TV screens, as the light forces, probing forward and outwards from both sides, see each other at closer range, feed back information, and come to grips in sporadic skirmishes ahead of the main forces. Fifty-seventh Combat Command knows from the start that it will be outnumbered by perhaps as much as five to one and therefore will have to compensate by exacting a heavy toll of the Aggressor from long-range engagements, ambushes and raids against the enemy's less well protected flank and rear. Therefore swift, prior knowledge of the enemy's weak and strong spots is vital. The Aggressor commander, set a goal to be captured within a short time, decides to roll forward in mass and trust to this momentum to barge a way through. For him sufficient information, at worst, is the crunch of combat.

Fighting intensifies. Armed helicopters, picking out those tanks on the move, fly carefully making efforts to remain at long range in order to make best use of their guided weapons as they endeavour to avoid stationary and partially hidden enemy weapons, shooting from shorter range. As night falls the two sides are becoming close locked and already one of 57th's combat teams has taken on some Aggressor medium tanks at a range of 3,000 metres and, by fire from guided weapons in concealed positions followed, as the Aggressors come closer, by high-velocity guns, have shot the enemy to pieces before they could close to 1,000 metres.

In the dark there is no respite and no sleep for the men. The Aggressors, moving in strength through unfamiliar country seeing their way with the help of infra-red and image-intensifying viewing devices, are first detected by 57th's short-range doppler radar and then fired on by gunners aiming either by the light of flares and searchlights or using their own night vision sights, Screened by the obscuration caused by the dust of movement and the smoke of fires, few engagements take place much above 800 metres and soon the Aggressors are not only among the 57th but themselves beginning to pick out their tormentors and to score avenging hits and kills. The identification of friend from foe, always difficult by day at the longer ranges, is by night unnerving and inhibiting to commanders and gunners. It is better for the defenders to hold fast, and then anything moving can be assumed as hostile and shot. But to stay still is an invitation to being cut off and then swamped by the flowing Aggressor torrent. Moreover, as 57th finds its zone of defence being steadily penetrated and eroded, its reserves have to be switched to block the newly threatened areas.

By dawn somewhat more than half of 57th is committed and entangled with the Aggressors and, having mostly got forward only two miles, the Aggressors have one success to their credit—a breakout, just before first light, of a strong, tank-preponderant combat team which is motoring flat out across country for Arheim.

The commander of 57th, sitting in his command vehicle, surrounded by a small staff and banks of maps and display panels, is almost instantly informed of the worsening situation and given every facility to simplify rapidly-formed decisions. Already he has sent his remaining, uncommitted reserve (consisting of three combat teams composed of complementary combat vehicles) racing towards the threatened sector to intercept and strike the break-through in flank. But there is a danger that they will be too late if Aggressor aircraft find and attack them. Setting aside the casualties which might be caused by napalm and by cascade bombs showering clutches of small anti-armour bomblets on to the thin upper decks of his tanks, it is realized that the mere threat of such an attack will drive the tanks into temporary cover and delay their movement. So the Aggressors must also be forced to delay. The 57th's commander calls on his entire force of armed helicopters, reinforced by any which can be made available from nearby battlegroups, to fly intensive missions and, by striking at the head of the enemy column, compel it to slow down or take cover to avoid casualties.

In relays the helicopters launch their attacks, firing a missile, breaking away out of range and retiring for a renewed delivery. In reply the Aggressor tanks take what cover they can find and halt—the 57th's object has thus been achieved—and bring up anti-aircraft vehicles whose supersonic guided missiles attempt to reach out to destroy the helicopters. In return other friendly helicopters, closely watching the scene, direct 57th's long-range medium artillery fire against the anti-aircraft vehicles in order to permit the armed helicopters to continue their work.

The fresh combat teams of 57th arrive, guided into position by reports from helicopters and reconnaissance vehicles. The battle becomes general. Aggressor tanks emerge out of cover to engage the approaching tanks of 57th. Again they present themselves as clear targets to the helicopters. Some of the Aggressors have been prematurely lured into sight to fire at bait—a few armoured personnel carriers trailing their coats while covered by gun and missile tanks lying in wait behind a nearby crest. The range of engagement which opened at 4,000 metres rapidly closes to 1,000 as visibility deteriorates amid the dust and smoke of battle. Aggressor aircraft, arriving to intervene at the critical point, find the identification of friend and foe difficult, despite minute directions from their ground controllers, and they themselves become the targets for 57th's guided missiles.

The battle sways to and fro—the lighter, more vulnerable vehicles moving aside to let the heavier ones fight to a finish. And when one side or the other give best it is the light machines which again take up the running while their guardians retire to replenish, to give rest to their crews and reserve themselves for the next crucial moment in a wild mêlée of ebb and flow.

If a time comes when one side or the other feels it can no longer hold the ring with conventional tanks and forces then, in the absence of a political solution, the nuclear fires will be called down and, in the ensuing escalation of destruction, a holocaust created which would outdo in violence the aggregate of every tank battle from 1916 to the present day. Then, even though the occupants of armoured vehicles might survive a little longer than other battlefield mortals, their contribution to strategic decision would be of only pygmy dimensions in the broken-back war to come.

In 50 years tanks—give them whatever name, form or shape you will—have raised their status in the minds of populations from Cinderella of the battlefield to that of a still more deadly and dominant weapon than the all-powerful but less tangible atomic explosive device. War is a beastly business, but so at times is life, and war being a part of life, and clearly to remain one of its central features in our era, cannot be ignored. If wars there are to be then it rests upon the combatants to limit their cost both in human life and material outlay. The early tank, by giving direct protection to its crews and indirect safety to infantry, economized in the expenditure of life by winning battles with much reduced casualties—casualties which, in the long run, were lessened on both sides since even the vanquished were per-suaded to surrender rather than fight it out in the face of an indefatigable weapon. When in the succeeding stage of its evolution the tank was to go forth and multiply the size of the combat area and demand greater material, as well as human resources than ever before, this demonstrated what could happen when a revolutionary system expanded too fast for human digestion—a warning that in modern war, once the checks and balances of ultimate deterrents are suddenly removed, there is insufficient time to comprehend the scope of a new weapon and devise an antidote before affairs run riot. Eventually the check to the tank was bound to come more from the exhaustion of national basic economies than from the weapons invented for its destruction. Thus we reach today's position when only the most powerful nations dare consider a prolonged, all-out contest and it is they—in reality a very few people—who control tomorrow's destiny.

It is claimed that a nation with a strong defence force, which includes a dominant tank arm, might cause any prospective aggressor second thoughts before launching a lightning, pre-emptive attack—and second thoughts could well be a persuasive element in preventing the fatal escalation leading to total nuclear war. Thus in the early 1970s the tank's future viability as a weapon system remains secure despite a persistent challenge to its existence from an increasing host of threatening armour-defeating weapons. The balance between tank effectiveness and an acceptable cost to national budgets still falls in favour of the tank.

Tanks, whose entire life-span has been spent as part of an environment of enormous change in warfare and in a period of terrible violence of which they have been among the principal perpetrators, may one day be compelled to suffer a violent change themselves. Yet when economic effectiveness shifts against tanks with such familiar characteristics and shape as the latest British Chieftain, German Leopard, Russian T62 and French AMX30, some other weapon system will take their place, though when that moment comes it can be assumed that man will either have discovered a more economical way to shift himself and his weapons in comparative safety from one part of the battlefield to another or he will be waging war by remote control. That such things can be done is far from beyond possibility, but until then there can be no movement without armour. A 'tank' in some shape or form will remain the dominant weapon on land.

APPENDIX

ESSENTIAL DATA OF IMPORTANT TANKS

Year	Nation	Type	Crew	Armament	Armour (Max)mm	Power hp	Wt tons	Speed mph	Remarks
1916	Britain	Mark I (Male)	8	2 × 57mm 4 mg	10	105	28	4	First tank in action. Female version sacrificed 57mm guns in favour of two additional mg. Mark IV version, used in 1917 at Cambrai, had shorter guns and 12mm armour.
1917	France	Renault FT	2	1 × 37mm or 1mg	22	39	6	5	Used in large numbers by French, adapted by Americans and many other nations. Still in use in 1940s.
1918	Britain	Medium C	4	4 mg	12	150	20	8	Basis of Fuller Plan but never used in action.
1923	Britain	Vickers Medium I	5	1 × 47mm 4 mg	6	90	12	16	Key to British armoured force experiments in 1920s and 1930s. Unbattleworthy yet a design trend-setter. Never in action other than as a pill-box.
1931	USA	Christie T3	3	1 × 37mm 1 mg	16	338	10	27	Progenitor of numerous Russian and British tanks which were the first genuine fast tanks to enter production.
1931	Britain	Vickers-Armstrong 6 ton B type	3	1 × 47mm 1 mg	14	87	8	22	Progenitor of many USA, Russian, Czech, Polish and other nations' tanks seen in action during Second World War. Not used by British. Outclassed by Germans in all encounters.

Year	Nation	Type	Crew	Armament	Armour (Max)mm	Power hp	Wt tons	Speed mph	Remarks
1936	Germany	PzKpfw IVA	5	1 × 75mm (Short) 2 mg	20	250	18	23	The key German tank until 1943 and saw service throughout Second World War. Was continuously developed up to 25 tons with a long 75mm gun and 80mm armour.
1939	Britain	Matilda II	4	1 × 40mm 1 mg	78	174	26	15	Queen of the Battlefield in 1940 and 1941. Incapable of being up-armoured and up-gunned and thus obsolete against better German tanks in 1942.
1940	Italy	M13/40	4	1 × 47mm 3 mg	42	105	14	20	Along with improved models this was the principal Italian tank in Second World War. Outmoded from the start, its paucity severely hampered Italian tank crews.
1940	Russia	KV1	5	1 × 76mm 3 mg	106	550	46	25	A tank to which the Germans had no answer in 1941, it dominated many a battle and set the foundations of many heavy Russian tank types to come.
1941	Russia	T34/76	4	1 × 76mm 2 mg	60	500	28	32	The excellent balance of armour, gunpower and speed enabled this tank to dominate German armour qualitatively from 1941. Produced in great numbers and steadily improved, this derivation of the Christie design sees service to the present day. Its successor is T62 now in front-line service.

1942	USA	Sherman I M 4	5	1 × 75mm 2 mg	76	353	30	25	A genuine all-purpose tank which gave the Allies a tactical advantage in 1942. Numerous improvements and a vast production hardly competed, however, with German qualitative advances. Yet, in modified form, Sherman sees service to this day.
1942	Germany	Tiger I	4	1 × 88mm 2 mg	110	700	56	24	This clumsy but powerful tank dominated the battlefield from its inception, yet was best used in a defensive role rather than for exploitation.
1943	Germany	Panther D	5	1 × 75mm 2 mg	120	650	43	27	Germany's reply to T34. A well-balanced design with a potential for marked improvement had it been desired.
1945	Britain	Centurion I	4	1 × 76mm 1 × 20mm 1 mg	121	600	42	24	Too late to take part in the Second World War, this tank (up-gunned) first saw action in Korea and since, after numerous improvements, with many armies including the Indian and Israeli. Its present-day successor is Chieftain.
1947	USA	M47(Patton)	5	1 × 90mm 3 mg	115	810	44	37	This, the main US tank development after the Second World War, has been supplied to many countries and has seen action in Korea, India, Israel and Vietnam among other places. Its present day successor is M60.

BIBLIOGRAPHY

The total bibliography connected with tanks and tank warfare is immense and I would no more claim to have read a fraction than I would state that the sources mentioned in my Preface or below are all I have consulted or that personal experience has been excluded. Those works mentioned here, however, have been my principal sources and, in all but a few cases, are the ones generally available to the public. I would merely add the many Official Histories—British, American, German, Russian, French and Italian—dealing with both World Wars which, where applicable, form the spine of my knowledge of campaigns, battles and technical development.

BARKER, A. J. *The Civilizing Mission.* Dial, 1968

BEAUFRE, A. *1940, The Fall of France.* Knopf, 1967

BIDWELL, S. *Gunners at War.* Arms and Armour, 1970

DE LA GORCE, A. *The French Army.* Braziller

ERICKSON, J. *The Soviet High Command.* St. Martin, 1962

FOLEY, J. *The Boilerplate War.* Walker, 1964

FULLER, J. F. C. *Memoirs of an Unconventional Soldier.* Nicolson & Watson, 1936

—— *Lectures on FSR II.* Sefton Praed, 1931

—— *Lectures on FSR III.* Sefton Praed, 1932

—— *Machine Warfare.* Hutchinson, 1942

GAULLE, CHARLES DE. *Vers l'Armée de Métier.* Berger-Levrault, Paris, 1934

GILLIE, M. *Forging the Thunderbolt.* MSPC, Washington, 1947

GUDERIAN, H. *Panzer Leader.* Ballantine, 1967

—— *Achtung Panzer.* UDV, Stuttgart, 1937

LIDDELL HART, B. H. Many books and articles but particularly *The Tanks* (1959) and *The Other Side of the Hill* (1951). Cassell

MACKINTOSH, M. *Juggernaut.* Macmillan, 1966

MACKSEY, K. *Armoured Crusader.* Hutchinson, 1967

—— (with BATCHELOR, J.). *Tank—A History of AFVs.* Macdonald, 1970

MARTEL, G. LE Q. *In the Wake of the Tank.* Sefton Praed, 1935

—— *An Outspoken Soldier.* Sefton Praed, 1949

MANSTEIN, E. VON. *Lost Victories.* Regnery, 1958

MELLENTHIN, F. VON. *Panzer Battles.* Univ. of Oklahoma, 1956

NEHRING, W. *Die Geschichte der deutschen Panzerwaffe 1916 bis 1945.* Propyläen, Berlin, 1969

NENNINGER, T. *The Development of American Armour 1917–1940.* (Unpublished)

OGORKIEWICZ, R. *Armour.* Praeger, 1960

PURNELL'S (ed. PITT, B.). *History of the Second World War.* Purnell, 1967

ROMMEL, E. *Papers* (ed. Liddell Hart, B. H.). Harcourt Brace Jovanovich, 1953

SENFF, H. *Die Entwicklung der Panzerwaffe im deutschen Heer zwischen den beiden Weltkriegen.* Verlag Mittler, 1969

SWINTON, E. *Eyewitness.* Hodder & Stoughton, 1932

TEVETH, S. *Tanks of Tammuz.* Weidenfeld and Nicholson, 1969

THOMAS, H. *The Spanish Civil War.* Harper & Row, 1961

ZHUKOV, G. K. (ed. SALISBURY, H.). *Greatest Battles.* Macdonald, 1969

INDEX